A Terrible Secret

ALSO BY CATHY GLASS

THE MILLION COPY BESTSELLING AUTHOR

CATHY GLASS

A Terrible Secret

**Scared for her safety,
Tilly places herself into care.
A shocking true story.**

HARPER
element

Certain details in this story, including names, places and dates,
have been changed to protect the family's privacy.

HarperElement
An imprint of HarperCollins*Publishers*
1 London Bridge Street
London SE1 9GF

www.harpercollins.co.uk

First published by HarperElement 2020

13 5 7 9 10 8 6 4 2

A catalogue record of this book is
available from the British Library

ISBN 978-0-00-839874-3

Printed and bound in Great Britain by
CPI Group (UK) Ltd, Croydon

MIX
Paper from
responsible sources
FSC™ C007454
FSC
www.fsc.org

This book is produced from independently certified FSC™ paper
to ensure responsible forest management.

For more information visit: www.harpercollins.co.uk/green

ACKNOWLEDGEMENTS

A big thank you to my family; my editors, Kelly and Holly; my literary agent, Andrew; my UK publishers HarperCollins, and my overseas publishers who are now too numerous to list by name. Last, but definitely not least, a big thank you to my readers for your unfailing support and kind words. They are much appreciated.

CHAPTER ONE

ANGRY AND UPSET

Lucy was pregnant. It was all I could think about.

As an experienced foster carer, I am used to dealing with other people's problems. Indeed, I pride myself on being rather good at it. However, now faced with a problem of my own, I found I was not as good as I thought. Lucy, my twenty-four-year-old daughter, had arrived home unexpectedly on 14 December, when she should have been at work, and announced she was pregnant. Two weeks later she and her boyfriend still hadn't decided what they were going to do about it, and I was worried sick.

In addition to this worry, I was now waiting for Tilly Watkins to arrive with her social worker. Tilly, aged fourteen, was upset and angry. Before Christmas she'd gone to the social services' offices and asked to be taken into foster care, claiming that her parents' continuous fighting was making her depressed and she couldn't stand it any longer. I had been told to expect her, but then she'd changed her mind and had decided to stay at home over Christmas, feeling that the festive season might help sort out their differences.

It didn't.

Far from helping, it had caused the situation to quickly deteriorate, and this morning – 28 December – her neighbours had called the police after hearing an hour of shouting, china smashing, and Tilly and her mother crying. When the police arrived, Tilly had a graze on her cheek and had demanded she be taken into foster care. Her social worker, Isa Neave, had telephoned me half an hour ago to say they were now on their way, so Tilly would be living with me for the foreseeable future.

My son Adrian, twenty-six, was at work, as was Lucy. Adrian worked for a firm of accountants and Lucy in a nursery. My youngest daughter, Paula, twenty-two, attended a local college but the new term didn't resume until the following week. She was out shopping at the sales with a friend, so there was just our cat, Sammy, and me at home. I was divorced, my ex having run off with a work colleague many years before – painful at the time, but history now. Sammy and I were in the living room, which is at the rear of my house. I was sitting on the sofa, gazing though the patio windows to the garden beyond, bare in the heart of winter. Sammy was in his usual spot curled up asleep by the radiator and blissfully unaware of the turmoil I was going through. How lovely to be a cat! I thought.

Even though I'm a very experienced foster carer, I still get anxious when I'm waiting for a new child or young person to arrive, hoping they will take to me and settle, and wondering how best I can help them. Now my thoughts and worries remained with Lucy, as indeed they were every waking moment, and often during the night. No one else in my family knew Lucy was pregnant apart from me. She'd didn't want anyone to know while she made the difficult decision – to terminate the pregnancy or keep the baby. She'd already discounted the other option of having the baby and putting it up for adoption. 'I couldn't bear to go through all that and give it up,' she'd said tearfully.

I'd nodded understandingly and listened.

The father of her baby, Darren, was aware of the situation and apparently also thinking what to do for the best. He was the same age as Lucy and a colleague of hers at the nursery where she worked. I'd met him briefly a couple of times and he seemed nice enough, but they'd only been dating a few months. Lucy told me nothing had been further from their minds than starting a family. They both had careers and she'd admitted to me she didn't think she was mature enough to parent a child yet, and in some ways I agreed. Although as most parents know, you mature very quickly once you're responsible for a baby. Lucy and I had had a few long conversations before Christmas and I'd said I'd support her whatever she and Darren decided, but it had to be their decision.

How we managed to get through Christmas I'm not sure, but we did and had a nice time. 'I'm not going to ruin everyone's Christmas,' Lucy told me. 'I'll make the decision in the New Year, on the first of January.' Which seemed a bit dramatic, but then Lucy can be dramatic sometimes. She knew she couldn't leave the decision any longer, for she would be ten weeks pregnant by then and if she was going to have a termination, it needed to be done as soon as possible.

Lucy hadn't had the best start in life. She'd come to me as a foster child, unsettled, unloved, with an eating disorder, and nowhere to call home. She'd done incredibly well to move on from her past and I'd adopted her, so she was a permanent member of my family. I loved her as much as I did my birth children – Adrian and Paula – and she loved us. She was usually lively, vibrant and outgoing, and could sometimes be impulsive and hot-headed, but that's just who she is. I tell Lucy's story in *Will You Love Me?*

Still gazing through the patio windows, I was suddenly jolted from my thoughts by the sound of the doorbell ringing. Sammy's ears pricked up. I immediately stood. It would be Tilly with her social worker, and they deserved my full attention.

Putting aside my own worries, I went along the hall and raised a smile as I opened the front door. 'Hello, love, nice to meet you. Come in,' I welcomed. 'I'm Cathy.'

The first thing I noticed about Tilly was the red graze on her cheek, the second was how scared she looked. I guessed that now she was here reality had set in as she realized she'd left home and put herself in care. She stepped quietly into the hall.

'I'm Isa Neave,' Tilly's social worker said, following her in, and shook my hand.

I took their coats and hung them on the hall stand. Tilly was slender, delicate-looking, about five feet six inches tall, with shoulder-length dark hair and a sallow complexion.

'I haven't got any of my things with me,' she said, clearly worried.

'I'll collect what you need later today. Once I've got you settled here,' Isa said to her, then to me, 'The police brought Tilly straight to the social services' offices so I'll need to speak to her mother and arrange to collect some of her belongings.'

I smiled reassuringly at Tilly and then led the way back down the hall to the living room where I offered them both a drink. Neither of them wanted one.

'Nice house,' Isa said, glancing around the living room as she sat on the sofa.

'Thank you.' Isa had short-cropped hair and wore a bright blue jumper over black leggings. I guessed she was in her mid to late twenties so was probably a newly qualified social worker. She had the alacrity and zeal of a young social worker just embarking on their career, before they became exhausted from dealing with child abuse day after day.

Tilly sat beside Isa on the sofa and I took an easy chair opposite them.

'I think Tilly is going to fit in well here,' Isa said positively. 'It will be nice for her to have the company of other young people.' So I guessed she'd read the form containing my details, which would have been sent to her.

'Yes, good,' I agreed.

'Tilly's the only child living at home, so it can be a bit intense.'

I nodded and smiled at Tilly, who was looking self-conscious.

'As I mentioned on the phone,' Isa continued, 'the situation at home with Tilly's parents has become very difficult.'

'He's not my parent,' Tilly said forcefully.

'Sorry, stepfather,' Isa corrected. Then to me, 'Tilly lives with her mother and stepfather. She has an older stepbrother and stepsister, but they don't live at home.'

'And neither will *I*, ever again!' Tilly replied, looking at me. 'My mother has chosen him over me. If she wants to ruin her life that's up to her, but he's not going to ruin mine.'

'I think everyone needs a cooling-off period,' Isa said. Taking a form from her briefcase-style bag, she handed it to me. 'The placement forms.'

'Thank you.' I put them to one side to read later. These forms would contain the basic information I needed for looking after Tilly – her full name, date of birth, address, parents, religion, school, any special needs, dietary requirements and allergies, etc.

I saw Tilly gingerly touch her sore cheek. 'Is that hurting you?' I asked.

'It's a little sore,' she admitted.

'Nothing appears to be broken,' Isa said. 'But if it doesn't heal or gets worse in the next few days please take her to a doctor.'

'I will. When did it happen?' I asked.

'Last night,' Isa replied.

'Dave threw a plate at my mother,' Tilly said. 'It hit me instead.'

'And Dave is your stepfather?' I asked.

'Was. They're always arguing.' Which I knew from Isa. 'Mum won't stand up to him and he treats her like dirt. I can't bear to watch it any more.' Her face clouded and she looked close to tears.

Domestic violence often plays a significant part in many child-care cases. Even if the child themselves hasn't been abused, for them to have to watch one parent repeatedly assault, threaten, humiliate and control the other is deeply damaging for the child. Also, there is the possibility that the abuser could turn their anger on them.

'How long has it been like that at home?' I asked Tilly.

'Years, although it's got worse recently.'

'It must be very distressing for you,' I said gently.

Tilly nodded sadly. 'I gave them one last chance over Christmas but nothing has changed, and Mum won't leave him. I don't want to be in foster care, but I've got nowhere else to go.' Her eyes filled.

'You've done the right thing,' Isa said, touching her arm reassuringly.

'Yes,' I agreed. 'I know it's difficult coming into a stranger's house, but I'll look after you, and my family and I will help you settle in. Try not to worry.'

'Thank you,' she said with a little sniff. 'You're so kind.'

I passed her the box of tissues. My heart went out to her. Like so many children and young people I'd fostered, all she wanted was a safe place to call home.

Isa went through some formalities, including the placement agreement form, which I had to sign. She checked I knew how much pocket money to give Tilly, asked about the bus she would need to catch to school, where she could do her homework and what time she would have to be in if she went out in the evening. Coming-home times can be an issue with teenagers. Although Tilly didn't appear to be in the mood for partying now, once she'd settled in and was happier, she might be, so it was worth setting the ground rules from the start.

'You have your phone with you?' Isa checked with Tilly.

'Yes, it's in my coat pocket. But it's on Dave's contract. He pays for it, so he's bound to cancel it.'

'If he stops paying then let Cathy know and she'll sort out a new contract,' Isa told her. This was usual and there was an amount included in the fostering allowance that carers receive to cover expenses like this. I would also be saving a set amount each week for Tilly, which she would take with her when she left. If she didn't leave I'd give it to her when she became an adult at eighteen.

'I need my laptop for schoolwork,' Tilly said. 'We've got an assignment to do for next term.'

'I'll collect it with your other things this afternoon,' Isa replied. 'Can you make a list of everything you need so I can ask your mother to pack them?'

'She won't know where anything is in my room,' Tilly said. 'It's better if I phone her.'

'All right. If you're happy to do that.'

Tilly nodded.

'What's happening about contact?' I asked. When young children come into care, contact with their parents is usually arranged by the social worker and is often supervised, but it can be different for older children.

'Tilly wants to see her mother, but not her stepfather,' Isa told me.

'I can go home when he is at work,' Tilly said.

Isa looked unsure. 'As long as you're not placing yourself in danger.'

'I'll leave before he gets home,' Tilly said.

'How often will you go?' I asked.

'Not sure,' Tilly shrugged.

'Tell Cathy when you are planning to go,' Isa said. 'And if you go there after school, make sure Cathy knows, otherwise she will expect you to come straight home.'

I would have preferred some firmer contact arrangements, but it was Isa's decision.

'I'll give you my mobile and landline numbers to put in your phone,' I told Tilly. 'And I'll put your number in my phone so you can let me know if you're going to be late back.'

'OK,' Tilly said amicably.

Isa then asked to look around the house before she left, which is usual when a child is placed. We stood and I led the way into our kitchen-diner and then to the front room and upstairs. Tilly didn't say much and I knew she was finding it difficult. Even though her house hadn't been a happy one, it was still her home. 'Your room will look much better once you have your belongings in it,' I said as we went in.

'It's nice and bright and looks out over the garden,' Isa said encouragingly, looking through the window. Tilly nodded and I continued to show them the rest of the upstairs.

Once we'd finished and were downstairs again, Tilly took her phone from her coat pocket and went into the living room to call her mother to tell her where her belongings were while I saw Isa out. My first impression of Tilly was that she wasn't the angry young person I'd been told to expect. However, that changed the moment her phone connected and she began talking to her mother.

CHAPTER TWO

NO GOING BACK

'I'm not coming home! I've told you!' Tilly shouted into her phone. 'I need my things, so just stop thinking about yourself for once and do as I ask! The social worker is going to collect them.' There was a pause as Tilly listened to what her mother was saying. I remained in the hall. 'You're as bad as him!' Tilly cried. 'It's your fault, not mine.' Another pause and then she burst into tears. I went in.

She was sitting on the sofa, phone to her ear, tears rolling down her cheeks. She looked up at me helplessly, a child in need of help. 'Let me speak to her,' I said. I held out my hand for the phone and she passed it to me.

Her mother was still talking, believing Tilly was listening, and clearly emotional. 'What's your mother's name?' I asked Tilly quietly.

'Heather.'

I nodded.

'Heather,' I said into the phone, 'it's Cathy Glass, Tilly's foster carer.' The talking stopped.

'Who? What did you say?' she asked.

'Cathy Glass, I'm Tilly's foster carer. She is very upset.'

'So am I.'

'I know it's difficult for you both, but Tilly needs some of her belongings. She was going to tell you where her things are so her social worker, Isa, can collect them later. If I put Tilly back on could you make a list?'

There was a pause, then, 'I'm not sure I can,' she said timidly.

'Sorry, why is that?'

'Her father wouldn't like it. He thinks she should stop all this nonsense and come home.'

'Is that her stepfather, Dave?' I checked.

'Yes.'

'Going home isn't really an option for Tilly at present,' I said as gently as I could. 'She is in care. I think Isa will have explained the situation to you.' Tilly was in care voluntarily so in theory she could return home at any time, but if she did and the social services felt she was in danger they could apply for a court order to bring her back into care.

Heather had gone quiet. 'Will it be OK if Tilly tells you what she needs so you can have it ready for when Isa arrives?' I asked her. 'She only has what she is wearing.'

'She has her phone with her,' Heather said tersely. 'I bet she didn't tell you her father pays for that. He's good to her. I don't know why she's trying to break up our family.'

'The social worker thinks a cooling-off period may be helpful,' I said diplomatically.

'Tilly and her father are both hotheads. I get caught in the middle,' Heather said, as if she bore no responsibility. I didn't point out that as a parent she had a duty to protect her four-teen-year-old daughter.

'If I put Tilly on, can she tell you what she needs and where to find it?' I said, trying to advance the conversation.

'I suppose so, but don't tell her father.'

'Thank you. Do you have a pen and paper handy or shall I ask Tilly to text the list to you?' Which I thought might be preferable, as they were both emotional right now.

'I don't have a mobile phone,' Heather said. 'Wait a minute and I'll get a pen and some paper.'

The line went quiet. 'It's all right,' I told Tilly, who was watching me. 'Your mother is going to write a list. She is upset too.'

'I know, but what can I do? She won't help herself.'

I nodded. Heather came back on the phone. 'Go ahead, put her on,' she said.

I returned Tilly's phone to her and sat in one of the armchairs, on hand to help if needed. Although Tilly was fourteen, she was very vulnerable at present and part of my role as a foster carer was to protect her from further upset. She began telling her mother what she needed and where the items were in a quiet, dispassionate voice. The list wasn't as long as it might have been for a young woman who had arrived with nothing – school uniform, some casual clothes and toiletries. I could guess why. Apart from any objection Dave might have, packing one's belongings is a defining moment for a child or young person going into care. It's a landmark, an acknowledgement that their life so far has failed miserably and that they are having to leave home, possibly for good. Often belongings are moved from home piecemeal, a few at a time, as it's less painful.

Once Tilly had finished, she said a sombre, 'Goodbye, Mum, I'll see you soon.' Her mother must have asked when, for Tilly replied, 'I don't know, in a day or so.' As she ended the call she looked close to tears. I went over and sat beside her on the sofa.

'I know it's difficult, love, but it will get easier. I promise.'

'Mum's upset and it's my fault. Perhaps I should just go home like she says.'

'Do you really think that's the right decision?' I asked. 'It didn't work out last time.'

'But I feel sorry for Mum. Who's going to protect her now?'

'Tilly, I know you love your mother, but it's not your job to protect her from your stepfather. She is an adult. Isa will advise her where help is available for victims of domestic abuse.'

'Is that what she is?'

'It sounds like it to me.' I paused. 'Why does Dave pay for your mobile phone when your mother hasn't even got one?' I asked. It was bothering me.

'He says she doesn't need one. She doesn't go out to work so she can use the landline.'

'What about a computer? Does she have access to email, social media and so on?'

'No. She doesn't use the Internet. I don't think she knows how to.'

'Does she have friends she keeps in contact with?'

'Not as far as I know. She doesn't really go out alone; he's always with her.' Which was classic for a victim being coercively controlled by their abuser.

'Do you have other relatives?' I asked.

'Only my gran.'

'That's your mother's mother?'

'Yes. Mum and I talk to her on the phone sometimes, but I haven't seen her in ages.'

'Why?' I could almost guess the answer.

'Dave doesn't get on with her. He says she's manipulative. Mum doesn't drive and relies on him to take her, and he doesn't.'

No surprise there, I thought, although the only one who was likely to be manipulative was Dave, isolating Heather further by keeping her from her mother. I'd been a volunteer in a refuge some years before and knew the signs of coercive control.

'Try not to worry,' I told Tilly. 'Have you got something you can do while I start some dinner?' It was 4.30 and Lucy, Adrian and Paula would be home later.

'I'll phone my friends – they keep texting to find out how I am – unless you want some help?'

'No, that's fine. Thank you, but you call your friends. I'll be in the kitchen if you need me. I was going to make spaghetti bolognaise. Do you eat meat?'

'Yes, although –' she stopped.

'What's the matter? I can soon make you something else.'

'No, it's not that.' A small, reflective smile crossed her face. It was the first time I had seen any sign of a smile since she'd arrived. 'I was going to say Dave doesn't like it, but I don't have to worry about that any more.'

'No, you don't, love.'

'He gets very angry if Mum makes him something he doesn't like to eat.'

'Have you told your social worker things like this?'

'Some, but not all – not about the food.'

'Mention it next time you talk to her. Call your friends now.'

I would make a note of this and any other disclosures Tilly made about her home life in my log and update her social worker. It might seem a small point now, but it could form part of a bigger picture. All foster carers in the UK are required to keep a daily record of the child or young person they are looking after. This includes appointments, the child's health and wellbeing, education, significant events and any disclosures. As well as charting the child's progress, it can act as an aide-mémoire and also be used as evidence in court. When the child leaves this record is placed on file at the social services.

I left Tilly in the living room about to call her friends while I went into the kitchen. Before I began cooking, I messaged my family's WhatsApp group to let Paula, Lucy and Adrian know Tilly had arrived, so they didn't just walk in and find her here. Then I set about making the bolognaise sauce for later.

As I worked, I could hear the rise and fall of Tilly's voice through the open door of the living room as she talked to her friends. She said pretty much the same thing to all of them, recounting the horror of another fight between her mother and Dave, the police arriving, her mother refusing to press charges and defending Dave, being taken to the social services' offices and then coming to me. One friend must have asked about me, for I heard her say, 'Yes, she seems OK, and the house is nice. But I worry about Mum.'

I hoped Tilly would find the strength to stay with me for the time being at least, for if she returned home I felt the situation was likely to deteriorate, and there was no guarantee the social services would apply for a court order to remove her. Their resources are stretched to the limit, and with over 70,000 children in care, and more coming in each day, a baby or young child whose life was in danger would probably have priority over a fourteen-year-old who had removed herself from care.

I heard the front door open and Paula return home. I left what I was doing to go into the hall to greet her. 'So you had some success at the sales then,' I said, pleased. She was carrying a number of store bags.

'I've spent a fortune!' she sighed.

I knew she wouldn't have done. Paula was careful with her money and only bought what she needed after much deliberation. I knew whatever she'd purchased would be a good buy. We went into the living room and I introduced her to Tilly. Tilly finished on the phone and the two girls said a shy hello. It would be some time before we all relaxed around each other.

'I'm going to get a drink,' Paula said to Tilly. 'Would you like one?'

'Yes, please. I'll come with you.' She stood.

I left the two girls to go to the kitchen and I heard cupboard doors opening and closing as Paula showed Tilly where the juice and squashes were and told her to help herself. I've found before that the child or young person we foster often bonds with one of my children before they do with me. Presently both girls appeared carrying a glass of juice. 'I'm going to my room,' Paula told me.

'Is it OK if I go to my room?' Tilly asked.

'Yes, of course, love. You do as you wish, make yourself at home.'

'Thank you.' She followed Paula upstairs and I heard them talking on the landing for a few moments and then go into their own rooms.

Ten minutes later Lucy arrived home, earlier than usual because the staff at the nursery were working shorter shifts in the week between Christmas and the New Year, as they didn't have many children in. Most companies had closed for the whole week, but the nursery was open with reduced hours.

'How are you?' I asked Lucy, as I did every time I saw her. It was a question laden with hidden meaning now, given her condition.

'OK. I feel fine.'

'Good.' She looked it. She hadn't had any morning sickness so far; indeed, she seemed to be blossoming. 'I'm going to get a drink of water,' she said. I followed her into the kitchen.

'How's Darren?' I asked as she ran a glass of water.

'He wasn't in work today. There were only three of us, as there are so few children in this week.'

'But you spoke to him?'

'He texted. We're fine, Mum, don't worry. Where's Tilly?'

'In her room.'

'How is she?'

'Finding it a bit difficult at present. I'm sure a few words from you would help.'

'I'll talk to her.'

'Thank you, love, I'd appreciate that.'

Lucy went upstairs. Having been a foster child herself, she knew what it felt like to arrive in a stranger's home and could usually say something to help. I tried not to think of the new life growing within her while she made the difficult decision of whether to go ahead with the pregnancy or not. Abortion is a highly contentious and emotional subject, but for me it has to be the couple's right to choose. If Lucy decided to have the baby then I would start to think of it as her unborn child. If she didn't then it would remain a foetus, not a viable life, harsh though that may sound. I love children and have dedicated my life to looking after them, but unwanted pregnancies ruin lives, and an unwanted child faces the ultimate rejection. Until there is a 100-per-cent effective means of contraception, safe and affordable to all, and available to men and women, then I believe termination has to be kept as an option. Also, it would be inhumane and barbaric to force a woman who'd been raped to go through an unwanted pregnancy and to give birth if they didn't want to. That's how I feel, at least, although I appreciate others feel differently.

Adrian returned home just before six o'clock and I introduced him to Tilly. I cooked the spaghetti and called everyone to dinner. We'd just sat down when the doorbell rang.

'I'll go,' I said.

Leaving everyone eating, I went to answer the front door. It was Isa, with four large bin liners stuffed full. 'There's more in my car,' she said.

'Really? I didn't think Tilly had asked for that much.'

'She didn't. Her stepfather was there and had packed the lot. He's a nasty piece of work, and angry she's gone.'

'He sounds very controlling,' I said, lowering my voice. 'Tilly has been telling me things.'

'Yes, she's told me a few things too. Where is she now?'

'Having some dinner.'

'Leave her to eat until we've finished unloading, then I'll have a chat with her. She's better off away from him. Her mother was in tears, but don't tell Tilly that.'

I took my coat from the hall stand, then went out into the cold dark night to Isa's car. We began unloading the bin liners and stacking them in the hall and front room. Her car was full. Once we'd finished, I counted thirteen in all, each one filled to bursting. I guessed this was most, if not all, of Tilly's belongings. Her stepfather was giving her a clear message: *You're gone for good. There is no coming back. You're not welcome here any more.*

As I shut the front door Tilly came into the hall and stared at all the bags. 'Are they all mine?' she asked, clearly shocked.

'Yes,' Isa said. 'I need to have a chat with you. Is there somewhere private we can go?'

'In the living room,' I said. 'Where you were this afternoon.'

'Thank you.'

Tilly and Isa went down the hall into the living room and Isa closed the door behind them. As a foster carer you have to accept that sometimes you are excluded from meetings in your own home. Isa had a right to talk to Tilly in private and she should tell me what I needed to know when they'd finished.

I returned to the kitchen-diner where Adrian, Lucy and Paula had finished eating but were still at the table talking.

'What's the matter?' Lucy asked, worried, aware that Isa hadn't simply dropped off Tilly's belongings and the two of them were now in the living room.

'Her stepfather is being quite nasty,' I said. 'Isa's having a chat with Tilly.'

'Tilly hates him,' Lucy said vehemently.

'Did she tell you that?' Paula asked.

'Yes, and she's angry with her mother for putting up with him and choosing him over her.'

'I know,' I said. 'He's sent most of her belongings. It's all in the hall and front room. Could someone help me take the bags upstairs? We'll stack them along the landing so Tilly and I can sort them out slowly in her own time.'

'Sure,' Adrian said, and they all stood ready to help.

'Not you, Lucy, you're excused,' I said.

'Mum, I have to lift toddlers at work who are heavier than a bag of clothes.'

'Have you pulled a muscle?' Adrian innocently asked.

'No, I'm fine,' Lucy said, while Paula looked at me questioningly.

I avoided her gaze. I hated having secrets in our family – I encourage openness and discussion – but I respected Lucy's wish not to say anything at present, difficult though it was.

CHAPTER THREE

A CALL FOR HELP

Adrian, Paula and Lucy helped me carry all the bin liners containing Tilly's belongings upstairs and stack them along one side of the landing out of the way, then they went into their rooms for some me time. I returned downstairs to the front room where I took my fostering folder from the drawer. While Tilly was with her social worker and I had the chance, I would read the essential information contained in the placement forms Isa had given to me earlier.

I sat in a chair in the front room and flipped through the half-dozen printed pages. As well as the child's full name, address and date of birth, it gave a few details of the parents. I saw that Tilly's mother was forty-nine and her stepfather fifty-two. Tilly was Heather's only child, but Dave had two other children – Tilly's stepbrother and stepsister, although she didn't see them. Neither did she see her natural father, and there were no details about him. Her ethnicity was given as British and her first language English. The box on the form for religion showed none, and her legal status showed she was in care voluntarily under a Section 20, which I knew. She had no special dietary requirements or known allergies. In the section on challenging behaviour it stated that Tilly could become angry sometimes. The name and address of her school came next, and the box for special educational needs was empty. The box for contact arrangements stated that Tilly could visit her mother at home by prior arrangement. I heard the door to the living room open and, setting aside the folder, I went into the hall. It was nearly seven o'clock.

'Tilly wants to visit her mother tomorrow,' Isa said. Tilly was standing just behind her social worker. 'I've told her I think she should meet her away from the family home for the time being, in case her stepfather returns.' This was slightly different from the contact information on the placement form and I assumed it was because of what had happened today. 'Tilly is concerned that her mother won't be able to leave the house to meet her because Dave won't let her,' Isa continued. 'But I'll speak to Heather tomorrow and see what can be arranged.'

'So we'll wait until you've spoken to her mother before Tilly sees her?' I clarified.

'Yes, please. I'll call you tomorrow.' And saying goodbye to us both, she left.

I turned to Tilly, who was looking anxious and over-whelmed. I wasn't surprised, given everything that had happened in the last twenty-four hours. Best keep her occupied, I thought.

'Your bags are upstairs,' I said. 'Let's start unpacking and sort out what you need for tonight.'

Tilly gave a small nod and, still looking lost and bewildered, came with me upstairs. When she saw the long row of dustbin liners full of her belongings snaking its way around the landing she began to cry. 'I hate him! I don't feel like I've got a home any more.' I thought that Dave's actions had had the desired result and Tilly had got his message.

'This is your home now,' I said, putting my arm around her.

'He's such a bastard,' she said, weeping as I held her. 'I don't know why Mum stays with him.'

'I know.' I soothed and comforted her as best I could.

Lucy's bedroom door opened and she came out. 'What's the matter?' she asked Tilly, very concerned.

Tilly straightened and rubbed her hand over her eyes.

'I'll fetch some tissues,' I said, and went to the bathroom.

As I did, I heard Lucy tell Tilly: 'Your stepfather is a creep, but at least you won't have to do your own packing. I used to hate packing when I moved. I found it really upsetting.'

Lucy rarely talked about those times now, of when she had to move from one home to another – it was all so long ago – but clearly some memories remained. I passed Tilly the box of tissues and she wiped her eyes. Lucy's phone sounded from her room. 'Got to get that,' she said. 'I'll catch up with you guys later. It will get better,' she told Tilly.

'Yes, thanks,' Tilly replied, and looked a bit brighter.

A few words from Lucy acknowledging she knew how Tilly felt had helped.

'I've no idea what each bag contains,' I said to Tilly. 'We'll have to open them so you can decide what you need.' I went to the bathroom for the scissors, at the same time returning the tissues. I then snipped through the tape binding the top of each bag and Tilly began looking in them.

'This one,' she said, after a few moments. 'It's got my night things and underwear.' She heaved the bag into her bedroom and came out again. 'I'll need the one with my laptop.'

'That shouldn't be too difficult to find,' I said. A few moments later I'd identified the bag containing the laptop and dragged it into Tilly's room. She took out the laptop and set it on the small table, which acted as a desk.

As she began to unpack I saw that all her belongings had just been stuffed in, not folded or rolled, as though they had been grabbed in anger and shoved in. There was rubbish in the bags too, like sweet wrappers and empty cartons of juice, which you'd normally throw away when packing, not include. It was disrespectful of Dave and I wondered where Tilly's mother had been and what she'd said – if anything – when he'd been throwing all her daughter's belongings into these bin liners.

'I think he just tipped in the whole drawer,' Tilly said in dismay, and I agreed.

Halfway down the third bag was an open box of sanitary towels. 'I hate the thought of his hands on my personal things,' she said, disgusted.

'I know. Did you have any privacy at home?' I asked as we worked.

'Some. I could lock the bathroom door. He wasn't supposed to go in my bedroom, although I think he did when I wasn't there.'

'What makes you say that?'

'He wears a strong deodorant and I could smell it sometimes when I went in. I told Mum, but she stuck up for him as usual and said I must be mistaken.'

'Here we all respect each other's privacy,' I said, thinking it was a good time to explain a household rule. 'We don't go into each other's bedrooms. This is your space. If any of us wants you, me included, we will knock on your door and wait until you call "come in". I expect you to do the same to all of us.'

'Yes, of course.'

I helped Tilly unpack another two bin bags and at the bottom of one was a heap of ornaments. Like everything else, they had just been thrown in and some were chipped and broken. 'These were my gran's,' she said, and looked close to tears again. 'She gave them to me the last time I saw her.' At that point I loathed Dave for what he had done, unprofessional though that might have been.

We carefully took out the broken pieces and set them on the table. 'I should be able to glue some of these,' I said optimistically.

There was also a framed photograph, which thankfully hadn't been broken. 'That's my gran,' Tilly said.

I admired the photo of a white-haired lady sitting in a garden on a summer's day. 'Would you like to see your gran again if possible?'

'More than anything in the world,' Tilly said.

'I'll speak to Isa and see what can be arranged, although I'm not promising anything.'

'Thank you, Cathy. You are kind.' I could have wept.

Having unpacked four bags, Tilly had what she needed for tonight and tomorrow and said she was going to do some work on her laptop. I carefully gathered up the ornaments and took them downstairs where I glued them back together as best I could and left them to set overnight. I then went into the living room and wrote up my log notes. At nine o'clock Tilly came down and said she was going to have a shower and an early night and could she have a glass of water. I poured it for her, checked she had everything she needed and told her to call me in the night if she was upset. I knew from experience that the first few nights could be very difficult for a looked-after child, regardless of how old they were – alone in a strange room. Tilly promised she'd call if she needed me and, thanking me again, went upstairs.

Later I heard the shower running and then her cross the landing and return to her bedroom. It went quiet and I assumed she was asleep. However, when I went up to check if she was all right I heard her talking on her phone, so I didn't disturb her.

She was still on the phone when I went up to bed. I got ready, hoping she'd wind up the call before long, but half an hour later, at 10.45, when Lucy, Adrian and Paula were asleep or going off to sleep, I decided it was time to explain another household rule. Although I felt sorry for Tilly and what she'd been through, it was important I established our rules, as I do for all the children and young people I look after.

With my dressing gown on, I went round the landing and knocked lightly on her bedroom door. There was no reply. 'Tilly, can I come in?' I asked quietly.

'Yes,' came her small reply.

I opened the door. She was lying in bed, her phone in her hand.

'I think you should get some sleep now, love. It's late and I like all phones to be switched off for the night or left downstairs. It's a rule that applies to everyone in the house so we don't disturb each other and we all get enough sleep.'

'It's my friend,' Tilly said, as if that made a difference.

'But I'd still like you to say goodbye and then speak to her tomorrow. When school starts again you won't be up this late.'

'OK,' she said.

I returned to bed, her phone went silent and eventually I fell asleep. I never sleep well when there is a new child or young person in the house. I'm half listening out in case they wake, frightened, not knowing where they are and in need of reassurance. It didn't matter that Tilly was fourteen and had assured me she'd call out if she needed me; I was still worried about her, and when I wasn't, I was worrying about Lucy.

However, Tilly did sleep well and as far as I knew was still asleep the following morning. I was up first, as usual, followed by Lucy and Adrian, who had to go to work. At 8.30 Tilly came downstairs, dressed. The graze on her cheek looked much less angry. 'I don't think you'll need to see a doctor about that, do you?'

'No, and I've got to go out now.'

'Why?'

'Mum's just phoned me. She's upset. Dave's not there, he's gone to work.' One of the downsides of mobile phones for young people in care is that this type of contact cannot be controlled. I had concerns.

'Your social worker said she wanted you to meet your mother away from your home, and to wait until after she'd spoken to her.'

'I can't. Mum needs me now,' Tilly said, with an edge of desperation.

'Is she in danger?' I asked.

'No, but she's very upset.'

'I think you should wait until you've spoken to Isa. What if Dave comes home and finds you there?'

'He won't, he's at work. Mum needs me,' she said again. 'Don't worry, I can take care of myself.'

I wish I had a pound coin for every young person who'd told me that! I'd be very rich indeed.

'She really does need me,' Tilly persisted. 'Sorry, I need to go.' She turned and headed for the front door.

It was clear I wasn't going to be able to dissuade her and she was too big for me to stop, so reluctantly I had no choice but to watch her go. Foster carers are not allowed to lock doors to stop a child from leaving, but I was concerned that Dave might suddenly appear, and this type of contact was against her social worker's wishes. It also crossed my mind that this could be a trap to entice Tilly home. Her mother was in Dave's control and he was angry. I wouldn't have excluded any possibility. Years of fostering has taught me to expect the unexpected.

I now needed to report what had happened. As it was close to nine o'clock, I decided not to phone the emergency out-of-hours duty social worker, who probably wouldn't be familiar with Tilly's case, but to call Isa's work mobile, which would be on during normal office hours. It wasn't an emergency as such, as it is when a child goes missing. I knew where Tilly was going.

My call went through to Isa's voicemail and I left a message explaining what had happened. Ten minutes later Isa returned the call. 'I got your message. So Tilly's on her way home?'

'Yes. She seemed settled last night. She ate with us, did some unpacking and slept well, but then her mother phoned this morning, upset.'

'Do you know why she's upset?'

'No, Tilly didn't say, only that her mother needed her.'

'Has Tilly got her phone with her?'

'Yes.'

'I'll phone her now and try to persuade her to return to you, but I won't be able to do much more until this afternoon. I'm about to go into court for an emergency protection hearing.' I knew social workers often carried huge caseloads and were stretched to the limit.

I thanked her, and then waited for news.

Fostering a teenager is clearly different from fostering a baby or young child. Teenagers have the ability to make their own decisions, although they don't always have the life experience to make the best ones. I'd been anticipating a pleasant day helping Tilly unpack, spending time with her and getting to know her better. Now I was left with uncertainty, worry, a row of black bin liners on the landing and the ornaments I'd done my best to repair.

Half an hour later Paula came downstairs. 'Where's Tilly?' she asked. 'Her bedroom door is open but she's not there.'

'Against advice she's gone to her mother's,' I said. 'I've informed her social worker and I'm hoping to hear something before long.'

As Paula made herself some breakfast the landline rang and I quickly answered it, but it was my mother phoning for a chat. Since my father had died a few years previously, we spoke regularly on the phone and saw each other most weekends. We talked for a while, although I didn't tell her about Tilly as it would only have worried her and there was nothing she could do. She and my father, when he was alive, had always been very supportive of me fostering, and also when my husband had left me many years before. Mum would meet Tilly at some point, assuming Tilly returned to us. Once I'd finished talking to Mum, Paula spoke to her, then she returned upstairs to get dressed.

An hour passed and I assumed I wouldn't hear from Isa until this afternoon when she'd come out of court and had had a chance to speak to Tilly and her mother. However, five minutes later my mobile rang and to my surprise Tilly's number came up.

'Hello. Are you all right?' I asked.

'No. I haven't got my bus fare back.'

'Can't your mother give it to you?' Had Tilly not left in such a hurry, I would have checked she had enough for her return journey.

'I've already left and I don't want to go back and ask her.' Tilly sounded moody rather than upset.

'Where are you now?'

'At the petrol station at the end of my road, and I'm freezing.'

'I'll come and fetch you, but it's going to take me at least fifteen minutes to get there. Wait inside the shop.'

'Thank you,' she said, subdued.

She couldn't have been with her mother for very long before it had all gone wrong. Doubtless I would find out in time what had happened, and hopefully this had taught Tilly a lesson. I made a note of the postcode of her mother's home address from the essential information form, and then went upstairs and told Paula where I was going.

'Be careful, Mum,' she said, concerned. 'The roads are icy. There have already been some accidents.' She had newsfeeds on her phone.

'I will,' I said, and kissed her goodbye.

Downstairs I took my coat from the hall stand and went out into the cold morning air. The car still had a layer of frost on it. While I waited for the windscreen to defrost, I entered the postcode of Tilly's house into my satnav, then carefully pulled away. The side roads were treacherous, as they hadn't been gritted, but the main road was clear. I knew roughly where I was going but not the exact location. Although Tilly had disrupted my day, I was pleased she'd had the sense to phone me and hadn't panicked. Eventually I approached her road and saw the petrol station, and then Tilly standing outside. She looked very cold, coat collar up and stamping her feet to keep warm.

I pulled up and she got into the passenger seat. 'Couldn't you have waited in the shop?' I asked her.

'The guy in charge said if I wasn't buying anything I had to wait outside.'

I tutted. I would have liked to have gone in and given him a piece of my mind, but I didn't. I waited for Tilly to fasten her seatbelt, then drove off. Her hands were so cold they were trembling.

'Haven't you got any gloves?' I asked.

'I forgot them.' Here was something else I could have checked she had with her had she not left the house in such a hurry.

'Did Isa phone you?' I asked after a few moments.

'Yes, but I didn't answer.'

'Why not?' I glanced at her.

She shrugged.

'So what happened at your mother's?'

'We had another argument.'

'About what?'

'I don't want to talk about it.'

'Because?'

'I'll just get upset again.' Her voice caught.

'OK. You know you can tell me if you want to.'

She gave a small nod but was then silent for the rest of the journey, occasionally checking her phone.

Once home, I telephoned Isa and left a message on her voicemail saying I'd collected Tilly and she was with me. I made a hot lunch for us and Paula, which the three of us ate at the table in the kitchen-diner. Paula and I tried to make some conversation, but Tilly was very quiet. After lunch I gave Tilly the china ornaments I'd repaired and her allowance for the week, which she thanked me for. I suggested we did some more of her unpacking and she reluctantly agreed. We managed three bags before she said she'd had enough. I knew she was feeling very unsettled.

'Do you want to talk about what happened this morning?' I asked her.

'Not really. Nothing has changed at home. I just wish she'd leave him.'

'I understand, but that has to be your mother's decision. My priority is to keep you safe, so in future I don't want you rushing off home. Isa is going to speak to your mother about how the two of you can see each other. OK?'

She nodded.

'Good.'

But the following morning exactly the same thing happened. Tilly's mother phoned her, distraught, and Tilly rushed out of the front door.

CHAPTER FOUR

NEW YEAR

I hadn't heard any more from Isa, so at 9.a.m., with Tilly on her way to see her mother and not answering my call, I phoned her. If a looked-after child is away from the placement without authorization – as Tilly was – then their social worker needs to know.

'I got your message,' Isa said straight away. 'Thanks for collecting Tilly yesterday. I didn't have a chance to call you. It was too late by the time I'd placed the children we brought into care.'

'Tilly's gone again,' I said bluntly, 'despite all I said to her. Her mother phoned upset around eight-thirty this morning and Tilly is on her way there now. I've tried calling her mobile but she's not answering.'

Isa sighed. I guessed this was the last thing she needed to hear after a previously busy day. 'I'll phone her and ask her to return,' she said.

'Hopefully she'll answer. But, really, it's her mother who needs to stop putting her under pressure. Tilly is angry with her, but at the same time she can't ignore her cries for help. She's not going to settle like this. Doesn't Heather have any friends who can support her?'

'Apparently not.' Which is what Tilly had told me. 'She's very isolated. I'm trying to help her, but it is difficult. I'll call Heather as well as Tilly.'

'Thank you. Just one more thing. Tilly hasn't seen her maternal grandmother in a long time, and she would like to. I said I'd tell you.'

'I'll mention it to Heather. I must go. I'll phone Tilly now before my first meeting.' I could hear office noise in the background as the call ended.

I now faced another day of uncertainty and I couldn't go far from home in case Tilly suddenly reappeared. I purposely hadn't given her a front door key and I wouldn't until she had proved herself trustworthy and mature enough to own one. I'd learnt the hard way many years before, when I'd first started fostering. Wanting to make the young person feel at home, I'd given them a key straight away and they'd abused it by stealing from me. Now those I fostered who were of an age to have their own front door key had one when I could be sure they would use it responsibly. Some of the social workers didn't agree with this, but ultimately it was my house and I needed to keep us all safe. I always made sure I was home to let in the young person, so they were never left waiting on the doorstep. If they decided to return home unexpectedly then they knew they could phone or text me and I'd arrive very quickly.

I cleared up the breakfast things and then set about doing some administrative work that I did mainly from home for a local firm. As I sat at my computer filling in spreadsheets, Isa telephoned between meetings. She said she'd spoken to Heather and Tilly, and had agreed that Tilly could stay at her mother's for two hours and then she'd return to me. 'I've also suggested to them both we have a meeting to discuss contact arrangements,' she added.

'Good idea.'

'I've provisionally booked next Tuesday, the day before the new term starts. Nine o'clock, here at the council offices. Heather says Dave will want to be there.'

I made a note of this on the pad beside the phone. 'Shall I tell Tilly?'

'I think her mother will have done so already, but check.'

We said goodbye. I wrote the appointment in my diary and continued to work on the spreadsheets. I doubted Tilly would be pleased Dave was going to the meeting, but it might help calm the situation if we all got together and talked and agreed on contact arrangements.

As I continued with my work it occurred to me that I hadn't heard from Edith, my supervising social worker (SSW), for some time. All foster carers in the UK have a supervising social worker. Their role is to monitor and support the carer and their family in all aspects of fostering. They also act as a link between the child's social worker and the carer. Often the referral for the child comes through the SSW, although that hadn't happened with Tilly. I assumed Edith was still on holiday, as many workers had taken the whole week off between Christmas and New Year. I could manage fine without her, but new carers need the support and guidance of a good SSW.

Half an hour later the doorbell rang and it was Tilly, earlier than expected. She was clearly not in a good mood.

'Dave phoned Mum from work and said he was on his way back, so I left,' she said, scowling. 'He does it just to check up on her. He phones and she jumps.'

'Hopefully we can get some better contact arrangements in place at the meeting next Tuesday. Isa told you about that?'

'Yes, but I'm not going if *he's* there. My life has nothing to do with him.'

'Well, it does really, love,' I said. She took off her coat and threw it over the hall stand. 'Dave is your stepfather and is living with your mother. I know you don't like him, but it might help if we all sit down and talk.'

'I'm not talking to him,' she said fiercely. 'He's a control freak. Mum could have come to the meeting alone, but he has to be there. And the reason the meeting is so frigging early is because of him. So he doesn't have to miss work!' Which seemed reasonable to me. 'And he's stalking me online,' she added.

'What do you mean?' I asked, immediately concerned, and looked at Tilly carefully as she took off her trainers.

'He sent Facebook friendship requests to people in my class and some of them were stupid enough to accept. He's been messaging them and asking about me.'

'Have you told Isa this?'

'No, I only just found out. My friend Abby phoned me while I was on the bus.'

'We'll need to tell Isa.' I didn't like the sound of this. 'In the meantime, your friends could "unfriend" him and ignore or even block his messages.'

'They could if they wanted but he's charming to them. Some of them like the attention. Abby sees through him because she knows what he's like. Can I have some lunch, please? There was nothing at Mum's. He hasn't taken her shopping.'

'Yes, of course. But doesn't your mother go food shopping alone?' I asked, surprised.

'There wouldn't be any point as she never has any money. Also, she gets very anxious about going out alone. She never does it. He makes sure of that.'

'I see.' The more I learnt about Dave the more I disliked him and the more worried I was for Heather. 'Does your mother not realize his behaviour is very controlling?' I asked Tilly.

'I'm not sure. He's always been like it – well, for as long as I can remember. Can I have a sandwich?'

'Yes.'

I called up to Paula, who was in her bedroom doing some college work, and asked her if she'd like lunch too. 'Yes, please. Toasted cheese sandwich,' came her reply.

Tilly said she'd like the same and came with me into the kitchen. As I made the toasties I said to her, 'I know it's difficult for you at present, but I don't think running to your mother every time she phones is good for either of you.'

'She won't be phoning me again,' she returned. 'Dave checked the calls on the house phone and saw my mobile number come up. He has banned her from calling me again. He checks bloody everything she does!'

'It is abusive control,' I said, horrified by what Heather was going through. 'Does he hit her?'

'Sometimes.'

'Did he hit you?'

'No, but he threatened to.'

'He sounds nasty. I know you worry about your mother and I'm worried about her too, but there's nothing much you can do. It will need to come from her.'

'She won't do anything. She's too scared of him,' Tilly said. 'Pity she can't come here to live.'

I smiled weakly. Of course that wasn't an option. 'Isa is giving your mother some support, so let's hope that helps.' But I could tell from Tilly's expression she was very doubtful. She'd lived with her mother and stepfather so knew them better than Isa or me. I felt sorry for Heather, but helping Tilly and keeping her safe was my priority.

Once the toasties were ready, Paula, Tilly and I sat at the table and had lunch together. In the afternoon Paula went to see a friend who was having a New Year Eve's party at her parents' house and wanted some help getting it ready. I suggested to Tilly that we unpack some more of her bags and she sighed but agreed to do a few. As we worked, I asked her if she had any plans for tomorrow – New Year's Eve. I wasn't just making conversation; if she was going out, I needed to know where she was going and how she was getting home. Tilly said she hadn't any plans to go out and didn't really feel like partying.

'We could see in the New Year together,' I offered. 'I expect Adrian and Lucy will be out.'

'Do they have lots of friends?' she asked as we set about the second bag.

'I suppose they do. We've lived in the same area since they were little, so we know a lot of people.'

'I've got friends at school, but I never felt able to invite them home,' Tilly admitted sadly. 'It would have been too embarrassing with Mum and Dave the way they are.'

'That's a shame.'

'I've been to some of my friends' houses, but it's awkward if you can never invite them back.'

I understood. 'Well, if you want to invite a couple of your friends here to see in the New Year, that's fine with me as long as their parents agree.'

She stopped what she was doing and her eyes rounded in amazement. 'Do you mean it?' she exclaimed.

'Yes, of course. Your friends are welcome here, although I would like some notice if they are staying for dinner any time.'

She smiled. 'Fantastic! Thank you so much! I'll ask Abby.

She's my best friend and she knows I'm in care and living here. Shall I phone her now?'

'Yes, love, if you wish. Suggest she stays the night and I'll take her home in the morning. If her mother wants to speak to me then put her on.'

I was pleased. It was important Tilly felt she could invite friends back. It was her home while she was with us. She phoned Abby straight away. She hadn't any plans for New Year either and jumped at the idea of joining Tilly. 'I'll call you later,' Tilly told her. 'I've got to finish my unpacking now.'

Which is exactly what we did. Spurred on by wanting her room to look nice for when Abby stayed, Tilly worked diligently. An hour later we'd unpacked all the bags. Her clothes were hanging neatly in the wardrobe or folded in the drawers, and her books and knick-knacks were on the shelves with the ornaments I'd repaired, together with the photograph of her grandmother. It was starting to look like home. I got rid of all the dustbin liners. If and when Tilly eventually left us it would be with her belongings packed in cases, not thrown in bin bags.

Tilly spent the rest of the afternoon on her phone to Abby planning their New Year's Eve celebration, which I understood included pizza, popcorn, ice cream and soft drinks. It was lovely to see Tilly so enthusiastic and happy. My own children took it for granted that their friends were always welcome, but for Tilly, like many children I'd fostered, inviting friends home was a first for her.

After dinner Tilly spent some time choosing what she was going to wear the following evening. Although it was just her and Abby, planning the event and dressing up gave it a sense of occasion. She had plenty of clothes to choose from and she told me that Dave had given her a generous clothing allowance as he liked her to look nice.

'What about your mother?' I asked, feeling slightly uncomfortable about this remark. 'Does she have a clothing allowance, too?'

'No. He buys what she needs.'

I didn't say anything as I didn't want to dampen Tilly's spirits with talk of Dave, but here was another example of coercive control. I was sure Heather was a victim of domestic abuse whether she knew it or not.

As I thought might happen, Adrian was seeing in the New Year with his long-time girlfriend, Kirsty, and Lucy with Darren. They were both spending the night with their partners, so I wasn't expecting them home until New Year's Day.

'Remember, we're going to have *that* chat tomorrow,' I reminded Lucy before she went out in the evening.

'Yes, I know,' she said and, kissing my cheek, left.

Abby's parents dropped her off at 7.30 on their way to a party. They didn't come in and Abby said one of them would collect her the following morning at 11 o'clock. Tilly had their evening planned so I left them to it. Paula was at a friend's party and I sat in the living room and telephoned my mother to wish her a Happy New Year, as I knew she wouldn't be staying up until midnight. I then settled down to watch a film. I'd received invitations to a couple of parties, but I'd sent my apologies when Tilly had arrived. It wouldn't have been appropriate for me to leave her and Abby in the house alone, and it was more important that Tilly had a good time after all she'd been through. However, ten minutes later a friend of mine, Marie, who lived in the next road, texted:

My plans for the evening have fallen through. 🙁
If you are in, I could come round with a bottle of wine? 🙂

I texted back: *Yes. Great. See you soon.*

Twenty minutes later Marie arrived, dressed up, with two bottles of wine, one red and one white, and in the mood to party. We went into the living room where I put on some music and opened the first bottle of wine. Tilly and Abby were in Tilly's bedroom with their music on loud, laughing and having fun. Halfway through the first glass of wine Marie told me that the reason she was suddenly free was because the guy she'd been dating had just dumped her.

'That wasn't very nice of him on New Year's Eve,' I said.

'Never mind, there's plenty more fish in the sea,' she said brightly, refilling her glass. 'You should try online dating.'

'I don't go looking for trouble,' I joked. 'It comes to me.'

Marie found dates online easily, but all her romances seemed to end the same way. A few months of intense dating and then it was all over. My feeling was that it had something to do with the nature of online dating. It was so easy to find a date that no one was interested in building and sustaining a relationship. She already appeared to be over this one and moving on, and proved it by messaging a guy who'd been in touch using the website's dating app on her phone. She showed me some of the guys' profiles she thought might interest me. It was a laugh if nothing else and she refilled her glass again.

Marie and I joined up with Tilly and Abby to eat pizza and ice cream, and then later at midnight to see in the New Year. We gathered in the living room with the television on so we could see and hear Big Ben. We counted down to midnight and as the clock struck we sang 'Auld Lang Syne' together with the revellers gathered in London. My children and I texted each other 'Happy New Year', as did some of my other friends. Marie's phone was busy too, and not just with messages from her family and friends, but guys from the dating website. By the time she left at one o'clock she was very tipsy as she'd drunk most of the wine, but we'd had fun.

Before I went to bed I checked on Sammy, as fireworks were going off outside, then I went upstairs. I lay in bed listening to the fireworks, party-goers on their way home, and Tilly and Abby laughing. We'd all had a good evening. I've found before that often these small impromptu get-togethers are just as much fun as big organized events.

Then my thoughts turned again to Lucy. It was now New Year's Day and she'd promised that when she returned she would tell me her decision. I was filled with dread and longing.

CHAPTER FIVE

LUCY'S DECISION

The following morning, I briefly met Abby's father when he collected her at eleven o'clock. He was very pleasant and thanked me for having Abby and wished me a Happy New Year. Tilly then came with me to collect Paula from her friend's house. Paula could have caught the bus home, but it was a bank holiday so there was a reduced service and she might have ended up waiting a long time. Paula had had fun but was very tired, as was Tilly, so once home, both girls went up to their rooms for a lie-down. It wasn't long before they were asleep.

An hour passed and I was sitting in the living room with Sammy when Lucy let herself in the front door. Immediately my heart rate increased. 'Hi, love, I'm in here,' I called, my voice unsteady.

I heard her take off her coat and shoes, and then she came into the living room.

'Did you have a nice evening?' I asked her.

'Yes, although I fell asleep before midnight. I've been quite tired lately. I think it's the –' She stopped, leaving the sentence half complete. 'Darren and I stayed in and had a takeaway,' she said. 'I didn't have any alcohol. It's not good for the –' Another unfinished sentence, but I could guess what she'd been going to say.

She sat down beside me on the sofa. 'You look worried, Mum,' she said, taking my hand between hers.

'I am.'

'Because of me?' I nodded. 'I'm sorry, but I needed time to think, to be certain I am doing the right thing. I know what it feels like to be an unwanted child.'

'Oh Lucy,' I began.

'No, don't get me wrong, I know I'm wanted now, but all those early years before I came to you. I didn't want to bring a child into the world unless I could commit to it unconditionally, one hundred per cent. It's not fair on the child. That's why I needed time to think.'

'I understand, and presumably you needed to discuss it with Darren too?' I said.

'Yes, that as well, but I felt the decision ultimately had to be mine, as we hadn't been going out for very long. I thought if I went ahead, the child would be my responsibility. I mean, I couldn't expect Darren to commit after we'd only been in a relationship for a few months.'

I nodded sombrely.

'So we've done a lot of talking,' Lucy continued, 'and he's saying he does want to commit. But even if he drops out along the way, it won't affect my decision. Mum, I'm going to have the baby. I'll give them all the love and care in the world. I know how to be a good mother thanks to you.' She kissed my cheek.

I felt so emotional I couldn't speak, and while I was pleased, I could also see all the problems that lay ahead. I hugged her.

'So you are going to be a grandma,' Lucy said after a moment. 'What do you think about that?'

'I think I'm too young,' I replied, laughing, and blinked

back a tear. 'I am pleased for you and Darren as long as you're sure this is what you want.'

'Yes. We are.'

'Have you told his parents?'

'He's doing it now.'

'It will be nice for us to meet before long,' I suggested.

'Yes, once they're over the shock. Darren wasn't looking forward to telling them. His sister is a single parent and they hoped he would get married first and then have children.'

'Will you get married?' I asked tentatively.

'It's not something that's top of our agenda. We'll see how things work out between us first.'

'Where will you live?'

'We'll find somewhere to rent, not far from here. I'll take maternity leave from work, but I'll have to return at least part-time.'

Clearly Lucy had thought this through.

'I'm proud of you,' I said. 'And I am happy. New life in our family is just what we need.'

'Do you think Nana will be pleased?' Lucy asked, stroking my hand as I used to do to her when she was little. 'Things were different when she was my age.'

'I think she will be delighted, although it will come as a surprise.'

'You tell her so she has time to recover before I see her,' Lucy said with a smile.

'We'll also need to tell Adrian, Paula and Tilly,' I said, thinking aloud.

'Yes. I'll do that. And my work will have to know.'

'When is the baby due?'

'The doctor said 26 July, but that could change once I'm seen at the hospital and have a scan.'

'Will Darren go with you for the antenatal appointments?' I asked. There was so much to consider.

'Yes. I think so. If not, will you come with me?'

'Of course, love.'

'There is something else I need to talk to you about,' she said seriously.

'Yes, what? You're not expecting twins, are you?'

She laughed, 'No, not as far as I know. It's about Bonnie. Do you think I should tell her?' Bonnie was Lucy's birth mother and she saw her once or twice a year at the most. I hadn't seen her in years and she was rarely mentioned now.

'What do you think? What is your heart telling you to do?' I asked Lucy.

'To tell her.'

'Then do so.'

'You don't mind?'

'No, of course not, love. Does Darren know about Bonnie?'

'Yes. He assumed I was your daughter to begin with.'

'You are, and always will be. I love you.'

'I love you too.'

I slipped my arm around her and we sat quietly for some time, as close as any mother and daughter can be, enjoying the moment. Then our peace was shattered by Tilly's bedroom door flying open and her running downstairs. 'Cathy!'

'In the living room!' I called, wondering what on earth was the matter.

Lucy eased away from me as Tilly ran into the living room.

'Hi, Lucy,' she said quickly. Then, 'Cathy, look at this message!' She pushed her phone towards me so I could read the text. It was from Dave. *Happy New Year. As you are not answering my calls I've stopped your clothing allowance.*

46

'Is that it?' I asked, thinking I must have missed something.

'He's stopped my allowance!' Tilly exclaimed indignantly.

'I'm not surprised. Don't worry. I'll give you your clothing allowance.'

'Can I have it now?' she asked.

'Yes, shortly.'

'It's all right, Mum,' Lucy said. 'You sort out Tilly's allowance. I can remember how important clothes were at her age.'

I smiled at her and was reminded of the huge difference in maturity between a fourteen- and twenty-four-year-old.

'Are Adrian and Paula in?' Lucy asked.

'Paula is, she was having a sleep. Adrian will be back later.'

'I'll see if she's awake.'

Lucy went upstairs as I took my purse from my handbag. I heard Lucy knock on Paula's door and ask if she was awake. She must have been for her bedroom door opened and Lucy went in. I gave Tilly her clothing allowance.

'Thank you,' she said.

'Remember, that's for the month,' I reminded her. 'Are you planning on going shopping today?'

'No. But I'll tell Dave to stuff his allowance.'

'I don't think that's a good idea – best not to antagonize him.'

'Why?' Tilly asked with attitude. 'He thinks he can control me just like he does Mum.'

'I know, but let it go. It won't do your mum any good if you wind him up. She has to live with him.'

Tilly looked at me thoughtfully. 'You could be right. I won't say anything.'

'Wise choice. Does he still text you a lot?' I asked.

'A bit.'

'Are you happy with that?'

She shrugged. 'Not bothered. I don't reply unless I want to.'

I supposed that, as Dave was her stepfather, it was reasonable he maintained some contact with her, as long as it wasn't threatening or abusive.

'Let me know if it becomes a problem and I'll speak to Isa,' I said.

'OK,' Tilly replied and returned upstairs.

It's usual for a young person of Tilly's age to be given their clothing allowance if they are responsible enough to spend it reasonably wisely. Tilly was used to having an allowance and buying her own clothes, so I thought she could manage it. The money I'd given her was in addition to her weekly pocket money. Children in care often receive more cash than the average child of their age, which can cause a problem with the carer's own children, who may receive less and be on a tight budget.

Fifteen minutes later Paula came downstairs. 'I'm going to be an aunt!' she declared, delighted.

'Yes, and I'm going to be a grandmother,' I said.

'Lucy and I think "Nana" sounds better.' I wasn't so sure. I was starting to feel much older since I'd learnt I was going to be a grandmother, lovely though it would be.

'I can babysit,' Paula said happily. 'It'll be fun. We can all help Lucy.'

'Yes. We will,' I agreed.

Presently Lucy appeared and said she'd told Tilly her good news but she hadn't been interested and was too busy texting to say much. I think she was a bit hurt.

'Tilly has only recently joined our family,' I said. 'We can't really expect her to appreciate just how much this means to us. And of course she's got her own family to think about.'

'I know,' Lucy said. 'Have you told Nana yet?'

'No, I will this evening.'

Adrian arrived home just before six o'clock. I was in the kitchen preparing dinner and he came to find me.

'Did you and Kirsty have a good New Year?' I asked him as he kissed my cheek.

'Yes. It was great, thanks. And you?'

'Marie came round with a bottle of wine.'

'I'm pleased you had some company. I telephoned Nana this morning and wished her a Happy New Year. She was fine.' Adrian is a thoughtful, sensitive, level-headed and sometimes conservative young man. Thankfully, his father leaving us when he was young didn't appear to have harmed him, although my father, when he'd been alive, had stepped into that role and more than compensated as a good male role model.

Lucy must have heard Adrian arrive home, for she joined us in the kitchen. 'Guess what, big brother,' she said playfully. 'You're going to be an uncle. I'm expecting.'

'What? A baby?' Adrian said, taken by surprise. The look on his face was priceless!

'Well, I assume it's a baby,' Lucy laughed. 'Although I don't know if it's a boy or girl yet.'

I could see Adrian was struggling with what he should say. 'Right. I see. Goodness. Well, that's a surprise. When?' he asked.

'July, but don't worry, you won't have to be there, and I'll have moved out by then.'

'Oh, OK. Will you? You don't have to go, do you? I suppose you do. Well, congratulations,' he finished, and kissed her cheek. 'I am pleased for you if this is what you want.'

'It is. I'm happy,' Lucy said. 'I knew before Christmas, but I told Mum not to say anything as Darren and I had a lot of talking to do.'

'Christmas. You kept that quiet,' he said to me. I nodded. 'So I can tell Kirsty then?'

'Yes, of course,' Lucy said. 'Now the decision is made the news is on general release.'

'Decision?' Adrian queried.

'As to whether to have it or not,' Lucy replied.

'Which is why I couldn't say anything until now,' I explained.

'Oh, I see.' Adrian paused and looked at Lucy thoughtfully. 'I think you made the right decision. You'll be a good mum. I'm happy for you both.'

'Thank you,' she said, clearly touched. 'And maybe one day I'll be an aunty.'

It took Adrian a moment to realize what she meant. 'Not just yet,' he said with an embarrassed laugh. 'I'm saving up first.'

That evening, when everyone else was occupied, I sat in the living room, telephoned my mother and gently broke the news to her. 'It wasn't planned, but we're pleased,' I explained. 'We'll do as much as we can to help Lucy.'

'And the young man?' Mum asked. 'You say you've only met him twice. Can he be relied upon to support the child and look after Lucy?'

'I hope so, but time will tell.'

'Why aren't they getting married?'

'It's different now, Mum. Lots of couples live together and have families without getting married.'

'I know, but marriage gives you security.'

'That wasn't my experience,' I reminded her. My ex had run off, leaving me with a young family, a large mortgage, little income and a divorce bill from my solicitor. The children and I had recovered and done all right since then, and I'd always made sure they hadn't missed out, but in terms of marriage offering security, it hadn't.

'Let's hope Lucy's young man is committed, then,' Mum said, and I agreed.

Now Lucy had made her decision I was looking at her slightly differently – as an expectant mother, although of course she was no different physically to the day before. I think Paula and Adrian were viewing her in a different light too. Their sister, my daughter, had suddenly blossomed into a woman. It was a strange feeling and one it would take time to adjust to, but that's the cycle of life: our parents grow old and a new generation is born.

The following day, 2 January, Adrian and Lucy were both back at work after the New Year. Tilly said she was going clothes shopping with Abby and would be back in the afternoon. Around 3 p.m. she texted to say she was going to see her mother but would leave before Dave returned at 5 p.m. I was concerned that, against advice, she was going home again but pleased she'd followed my instructions and told me her plans had changed.

She arrived home just before six o'clock. 'Everything all right?' I asked her as I let her in and closed the front door against the dark, cold evening.

'Yes, I'm fine,' she said.

'Did you have any success shopping?' I asked. She wasn't carrying any bags.

'I didn't buy clothes,' she admitted.

'OK, never mind. I expect you'll have more luck next time.' I appreciated what it was like to go clothes shopping but not find anything suitable. Tilly would keep her clothing allowance for another time.

However, that evening, as I was working at the computer in the front room, Tilly came down from her room, phone in hand. 'Mum's upset and needs me,' she said anxiously. 'Could I have some money for a cab so I can go to her?'

I stopped typing and looked at her. 'Why is she upset?' I asked, concerned.

'Dave's been horrible to her.'

'Is he there now?'

'No, he's gone out, but she needs me.'

'Has she just phoned you?' I asked, mindful that Dave had forbidden Heather to use the landline.

'Yes, but she used the mobile I –' Tilly said, and stopped, realizing her mistake.

'The mobile phone you bought with your clothing allowance?' I asked.

'Yes, I'm sorry, but she can't use the landline and I hated the thought of her being all alone. I bought her a pay-as-you-go phone today and showed her how to use it.'

I nodded. I'd fostered children before who'd felt so responsible for their parents that they'd secretly given them their allowances, sometimes after the parent had asked them for money, although that didn't appear to be the case here.

'I understand why you did that,' I said. 'But I don't want you going to your mother's now. Would it help if I spoke to her?'

'It might,' Tilly said. She was about to call Heather when her phone buzzed as a text came through. 'No, you can't phone her now,' she said anxiously. 'He's come back. I'm so worried for her.'

So was I.

CHAPTER SIX

THE MEETING

There was no point in telling Tilly again that she wasn't responsible for her mother. Of course she worried about her and wanted to help, but if Heather – an adult – didn't want to make changes to her life there was little Tilly, Isa or anyone could do. There is support available for victims of domestic violence wanting to flee their abusive partners, but the victim has to make the decision to leave, with all the emotional and financial implications that accompanies it. Heather would have little confidence from years of abuse and didn't have an income so relied heavily on Dave. I appreciated what a mammoth decision she faced. It's said in fostering that you don't just take on the child but the problems of the whole family. It was certainly true now.

That evening Tilly and I talked for over an hour about her mother's options. I said I'd email Isa an update as I wouldn't have a chance to speak to her before the meeting at 9 a.m. the next day. Once Tilly had gone to her room, I returned to my computer and sent an email to Isa. I also emailed an update to Edith, my supervising social worker, who I still hadn't heard from. She would have been notified that Tilly was with me.

To my surprise Isa replied almost immediately, although it was out of office hours.

Hi Cathy. Thanks. I'll talk to Heather again. Sorry, it was me who advised her to buy a pay-as-you-go phone for her own safety. I should have realized Heather would ask Tilly to get it. Don't mention the phone at the meeting. Dave mustn't know about it.

I replied, confirming I wouldn't mention it.

'I hope Dave hasn't found Mum's phone,' Tilly said the following morning as I drove us to the meeting at the council offices. 'She hasn't been in touch since yesterday.'

'She won't dare use the phone while he's there,' I replied, concentrating on the traffic. The roads were busy at this time in the morning.

'I got rid of all the packaging,' Tilly said. 'She's just got the phone and charger. I set it on silent and put it at the back of her wardrobe.'

'That should be fine.' Although it was appalling that such steps needed to be taken, and indicative of the fearful situation her mother lived in. 'Isa is going to have another chat with your mother,' I said.

'And say what? She's not going to leave him.' Which was probably true, for now at least.

Tilly fell silent as I parked outside the council offices. I felt apprehensive too. It would be the first time I met Heather and Dave, although I'd formed impressions of them both from what I knew so far. The parents of a child in care are often angry to begin with that their child is in care. They can take out their anger on the foster carer, who they see as being part of the system and who has usurped their role as parents. I knew Dave could be violent and controlling, and I thought there was a good chance he would vent some of his anger at me and Isa.

If a parent has a history of threatening social workers, the security guard – usually positioned in reception at the council offices – stands outside the meeting room for the duration of the meeting. As far as I knew that wasn't true of Dave.

With some trepidation, Tilly and I registered at reception, hung our ID passes around our necks and went upstairs to the meeting room. It was just before nine o'clock. I knocked on the door and opened it. Isa and another, older woman, who Isa introduced as her manager, Nikki Bets, were already there. 'Nice to meet you,' Nikki said to us. 'Come and sit down.'

We sat opposite them. Apart from the table and chairs, there was no other furniture in the room. It was used purely for meetings.

'How are you settling in with Cathy and her family?' Nikki asked Tilly.

'All right, thank you,' she replied. 'Are both Mum and Dave coming?'

'I think so,' Nikki said. 'We're aware of your concerns and Isa is doing all she can to help your mother.'

'She won't help herself,' Tilly said passionately. 'Dave controls her.'

'Can you give me your mother's mobile number,' Isa said, opening her notepad. 'In future I'll phone her on that, so my call won't show up on the statement for their landline.'

Tilly told her the number.

'Thank you. Try not to worry. Have you got everything you need for school tomorrow?'

'Yes,' Tilly said, then started as the door suddenly opened.

I looked over as a man I assumed to be Dave came into the room first, followed by a woman – Heather. He was tall, heavily built, with fair hair thinning at the front. Heather was short and gaunt, and her dark hair was streaked with grey.

They were both dressed smartly, although Heather's shapeless woollen dress suggested comfort rather than attractiveness. Dave, by comparison, was dressed to impress and wearing a smart light-grey tailored suit, presumably because he was going to work after the meeting. I knew from the placement information forms that he held a middle-management position with a local company. He had the presence of someone used to being in charge. He said a confident hello to everyone and then shook my hand. I caught a strong whiff of the deodorant Tilly had told me he used. He went to kiss Tilly, but she moved away. Unfazed, he went to the other side of the table and shook hands with Isa and Nikki, while Heather slid unobtrusively into the chair on my left at the end of the table. I noticed she had a small cut and a bruise just below her right eye. Nikki noticed it too.

'That looks painful,' she said to her as Dave sat beside his wife.

'It's nothing,' Heather said quietly. 'I tripped and fell.'

'Too much gin,' Dave joked, but he was the only one who laughed.

I saw Tilly looking at her mother, concerned. 'Would you like to swap seats with me so you can sit next to your mother?' I offered.

'Yes, please.' We changed seats and Tilly reached for her mother's hand and held it protectively. Isa and I exchanged a glance.

'Thank you, everyone, for coming,' Nikki said, starting the meeting. 'Let's begin by introducing ourselves.' Introductions are usual at most social services meetings even if there are just a few present and they know each other. 'I'm Nikki Bets, Isa's manager. I'll take some notes of our meeting but I'm not planning on circulating formal minutes.'

'Why not?' Dave asked.

'I don't think it's necessary,' Nikki replied. 'This is a short, informal meeting to give us the chance to get to know each other and decide on contact arrangements that will suit everyone.'

'You won't mind if I take notes, then,' Dave said, and set his phone on the table in front of him.

'Not at all,' Nikki replied, unfazed. 'Shall we continue with the introductions.'

I was next. 'Cathy Glass, Tilly's foster carer,' I said, as Dave made a note on his phone.

'I'm Tilly Watkins,' she said. Then to Dave, 'You're not going to note that too, are you?' He ignored her.

Heather was next. 'I'm Heather Mitchel, Tilly's mother,' she said in a quiet, self-effacing manner as if she had no right to that title or to be here.

'Thank you,' Nikki said with an encouraging smile, and looked at Dave.

He took a moment before he said in a confident voice, 'Dave Mitchel, Tilly's stepfather.'

'Not any more,' Tilly said under her breath but loud enough for him to hear.

He didn't respond, but I could see from the tightness in his jaw he was struggling to maintain his composure.

Isa introduced herself and then said, 'Mr and Mrs Mitchel, is there anything you would like to ask Cathy or tell her about Tilly's care that might be of help.'

Silence, then Heather said quietly, 'I don't understand why my daughter can't come home.'

'Because we have safe-guarding concerns, regarding her emotional and physical wellbeing,' Nikki said. 'I believe Isa has explained this to you.'

'I'm assuming these so-called concerns are a result of the silly argument between my wife and myself,' Dave said haughtily, pausing from typing on his phone. 'I'll admit it got out of hand, but no harm was done.' I was amazed he could think that.

'Tilly was hurt,' Nikki said bluntly. 'She had a graze on her cheek from something that you threw at your wife. And the emotional damage of living in a violent household cannot be overstated.' Nikki wasn't mincing her words. I guessed as a senior social worker she would have seen too many cases of the damage done to children living with domestic violence, as indeed I had as a foster carer.

'All couples argue sometimes,' Dave said dismissively. 'I seem to be the villain in this, but I've always provided well for Tilly. She's never wanted for anything – clothes, the latest phone. I probably indulged her too much and spoilt her. Now, for reasons I don't understand, she has turned against me and her mother.'

'Just you,' Tilly said angrily.

Dave shrugged. 'Well, if she wants to stay in foster care that's fine with me, but I object most strongly to her carer allowing her to stay out all night on New Year's Eve. She's fourteen, a minor. An all-night party isn't appropriate at her age. I shall be lodging a formal complaint.'

Isa and Nikki looked at me for an explanation and Tilly was staring daggers at Dave.

'Tilly wasn't at a party,' I said. 'She was at home with me. She invited a friend to see in the New Year and stay the night, but they didn't go out. They were at my house.'

'What made you think Tilly had been to a party?' Nikki asked Dave.

'There was a photo.' He stopped. 'It doesn't matter,' he added, backtracking.

'You've been stalking me online again,' Tilly snapped at him. 'Leave me and my friends alone.' Then to the rest of us, she said, 'I took some selfies of Abby and me on New Year's Eve and put them on Facebook.'

Tilly had shown me the photographs she'd taken on her phone, of her and Abby glammed up and with raised glasses (of fruit cocktail). Dave had mistakenly believed they were at a party rather than at my home. But more worrying was that it seemed he had been actively looking for Tilly on social media again. She wasn't Facebook friends with him and neither was Abby, but clearly someone had shared the photo with him.

'My mistake,' Dave said. 'Shall we move on? I've another meeting to go to after this one.'

'I'd like to establish some regular contact,' Isa said.

'Tilly is welcome to come to my house anytime,' Dave said, sounding very reasonable.

'I think it would be more appropriate for Tilly to see her mother either at Cathy's home, in the community or at the Family Centre.'

'That would be difficult for me,' Heather said in a small voice. 'I don't go out much.'

'She has agoraphobia,' Dave said.

'Because of you,' Tilly snapped.

'Has it been medically diagnosed?' Nikki asked, making a note. There'd been no mention of it so far.

'We don't need a doctor to know what is wrong with her,' Dave retaliated. 'She hardly ever leaves the house.'

'Because of you,' Tilly said again, which he ignored.

'Are you receiving help?' Nikki asked Heather.

'Yes, I help her,' Dave said before she could answer.

'How do you suggest Tilly sees her mother, then?' Nikki asked him curtly.

'Tilly will need to come to our house. If you like, I will give you an undertaking that I won't be there.' Which made Dave appear very reasonable and helpful. 'I only want what's best for my stepdaughter,' he added. Tilly gave a snort of derision.

'Heather,' Nikki said, looking at her, 'if we booked a cab to take you to Cathy's for contact and to collect you at the end, would you feel able to go?'

She shook her head.

'I've told you Tilly can see her mother at my house and I promise I won't be there,' Dave said firmly. 'I can't be more reasonable than that, and realistically it's the only way they will be able to see each other, as my wife doesn't go out.'

Nikki said something quietly to Isa, who then said, 'OK. We'll see how it goes. The new school term starts tomorrow so I suggest Tilly visits her mother after school for an hour three times a week, perhaps Monday, Wednesday and Friday. Would that suit everyone?'

Heather, Tilly and I nodded, and Dave typed. 'So just to confirm, it will be four to five?' he said.

'Yes,' Isa said.

'I'll make sure I don't return from work early on those days.'

'Thank you,' Nikki said.

'And what about phone contact?' I asked. I was hoping we could firm up some rules, as it was unsettling for Tilly to have her mother keep phoning, often upset. She needed to be able to concentrate on her schoolwork and get on with her life.

'Shall we set phone contact for the days Tilly doesn't see her mother?' Isa suggested. 'Tuesday, Thursday and once over the weekend.' This level of contact wasn't unusual.

'That's fine with me,' Dave said as he typed. Then, looking at Tilly, he added, 'You can phone the landline. Your mother won't know how to use the mobile. It was a waste of your money.' I went cold.

'Arsehole,' Tilly snapped, as Nikki and Isa exchanged pointed looks.

'See what I have to put up with,' Dave said disparagingly.

'Couldn't your wife be shown how to use the mobile phone?' Nikki calmly asked him.

'No,' he said flatly.

I glanced at Heather and saw the fear in her eyes. Was the injury to her face a result of Dave finding her phone? Tilly had dropped her mother's hand but now took it again.

Isa wisely changed the subject. 'As it's Tilly's first day back at school tomorrow, I suggest contact starts on Friday,' she said.

'Agreed,' Nikki said. 'Is that all right with you, Tilly?'

She nodded.

I made a note of the contact arrangements, aware Dave was staring at Tilly as if he had scored a point. The tension in the room was palpable. Isa asked if there was anything else anyone wanted to raise. There wasn't, at least not in front of Dave. 'Thank you all for coming,' she said, and ended the meeting.

Dave tucked his phone into his jacket pocket and stood. 'I'll take you home,' he said to Heather, and cupping her elbow drew her to her feet.

'Keep your hands off her,' Tilly said angrily and, leaning over, pushed his hand away.

'Grow up,' Dave sneered. Taking his wife's arm, he steered her out of the room. The door closed and I allowed myself to breathe. Nikki and Isa visibly relaxed too.

'He's such a bastard,' Tilly said, seething. 'I hate him, but Mum won't leave him.'

'I know it must be difficult for you,' Nikki said. 'Isa is doing what she can to help your mother.'

It would be difficult to explain to Tilly at her age all the reasons that could be keeping her mother in the abusive relationship, including fear of leaving Dave and what he might do to her, the prospect of becoming homeless and low self-esteem from years of being a victim.

'I'm going to contact our local police safeguarding unit,' Isa told Tilly. 'They provide support and practical assistance to victims of domestic abuse.'

'Dave mustn't find out,' Tilly said anxiously. 'He'd go ballistic and take it out on Mum.'

'Don't worry. They have specially trained officers who are used to dealing with those in your mother's situation. They won't do anything that could jeopardize her safety.'

'In the meantime, I suggest you're careful who you share things with on online,' Nikki added.

'I will be, but I shouldn't have to be,' Tilly said. 'It's him who needs to be stopped. They're my friends.'

'If the police find evidence he is grooming your friends he will be stopped, trust me,' Nikki said with feeling.

It seemed that everything that could be done was being done to help Heather and protect Tilly. Isa said she'd be in touch, and we all stood and left. Tilly and I went out of the room first and made our way downstairs to reception where we handed in our ID badges. I could see Tilly was still anxious, angry and worried about her mother, so I suggested that rather than go straight home we should go into town. I needed to get a few things, and it would give Tilly something else to think about. She agreed and said she'd like to buy her mother a little present, but then added that she didn't have any money as she'd spent it all on the phone. I said I'd advance her next week's allowance.

Tilly was quiet as I drove to the shopping centre, but once there and we were wandering around the brightly lit shops among other shoppers, her mood lightened. She spent some time choosing a gift for her mother and settled on a spa gift-box set, which included jasmine-scented bath oil and candles, designed to help you unwind and relax at the end of the day. It was an attractive gift that I was sure her mother would appreciate, although I knew it would take more than a few scented baths before Heather truly relaxed. Victims of domestic violence are continually on guard, waiting for the next attack.

We had lunch in the shopping centre and on the way home Abby phoned. Tilly told her about the meeting; that Dave had found her mother's phone and seen the photograph of them on New Year's Eve online. Abby must have apologized for sharing it, as Tilly said, 'It's not your fault. It's him.'

Once home, I checked Tilly's school uniform was ready for the following morning and that she had her bus pass, and I gave her some lunch money. That evening I heard her talking to Abby again. She was a good friend and a similar age so could offer empathy and understanding in a way I couldn't. Tilly slept well and the following morning I saw her off to school. She seemed in a positive frame of mind and was looking forward to seeing her friends again. However, the next time I saw her it was very different. She was so angry and upset she could barely speak.

CHAPTER SEVEN

GOOD AND BAD NEWS

I knew something was wrong with Tilly as soon as I opened the front door. 'My phone, I don't believe it!' she cried, coming in. She had her phone in her hand and I thought Dave must have terminated the contract so it had stopped working, just as he'd stopped her clothing allowance. I'd warned her that might happen.

'It's not a problem, love,' I said. 'We'll change the contract to pay as you go and I'll give you the money to cover it.'

'No, it's not that! It's still working. But look at this.' Coat and shoes still on, she thrust her phone towards me. I looked at the screen showing where the apps and programmes were stored. 'See that?' she said, pointing to an icon with a picture of an eye on it. 'It's a tracker. Dave knows exactly where I am all the time and he can read my messages without me knowing.'

'How do you know that's what it is?' I asked her sceptically.

'I came back with a guy on the bus I know from school. He's a techie. I was texting Abby and he noticed my screen took a long time to close after each message. He asked if my battery ran down quickly and I said it did. And if my phone screen lit up when my phone was idle and took a long time to close down. Which it does. He said he thought there could be a tracker on my phone and asked to look at it. I thought he was being silly, but he found this! Dave must have put it on there when he bought the phone.'

'Just a minute,' I said, still not fully believing what she was telling me.

I picked up my own phone from the table in the front room and googled the name on the app she was pointing to. Sure enough, it went to a website that sold tracking devices for mobile phones. Designed for parents to keep their children safe, it tracked the child's movements and allowed the parents to read their messages and monitor their activity on social media. Used correctly, it could help keep children safe, but in Dave's hands it felt anything but safe.

I looked at Tilly, unsure of what to say or do for the best. 'I'm sorry, I've never come across this before.' Technology is moving at such a pace that sometimes it's a struggle to keep up. If Dave had been a loving, concerned parent then it would have seemed reasonable for him to track Tilly's phone and read her messages, but this felt more like stalking. 'It must be possible to disable it,' I said.

'Yes, my friend did it for me on the bus. He said I should remove the software completely, but I wanted to show you first.'

'That was sensible. Can you take a screen shot before you remove it and I'll send it to Isa. Although I'm guessing Dave will say he just wanted to protect you.'

She scoffed. 'Watch me, more like it!' She took the screen-shot I'd asked for and sent it to me, then removed the app from her phone.

'My friend told me to check every so often to make sure it doesn't reappear,' Tilly said. 'It's possible to put this type of stuff on remotely. I wouldn't put anything past Dave.'

'Tell me straight away if it does reappear or if he tries to contact you,' I said, very concerned.

'Yes, I will.'

I then asked Tilly about her first day back at school, and we talked about that for a while before she went up to her room.

Later that evening, after I'd written up my log notes and sent Isa an email updating her, I spent some time researching the type of app Dave had placed on Tilly's phone so I had a better understanding of what we were dealing with. Sometimes as a foster carer you have to be a detective too. I discovered there are a variety of different apps on the market, from simple tracking devices based on a GPS signal, to those like the one that had been placed on Tilly's phone, which could allow a third party to read messages and monitor social media activity. Some of the software even allowed the user to spy through the phone's camera, which I thought was going too far even for a concerned parent. I also found out that these apps were being used by those who suspected their partners of being unfaithful, as well as unscrupulous users spying on others for illegal purposes. In the wrong hands they could do real harm and I doubted Dave's motives, just as Tilly had.

On Friday Tilly visited her mother. She caught the bus there straight after school, stayed for an hour and left before Dave returned. She was home by 5.30 and I asked her how it had gone. She told me her mother had been pleased to see her and loved the gift she'd bought, but she was unhappy and lonely now Tilly was no longer living there, which had made Tilly feel guilty. She said a police officer from the domestic violence unit had phoned Heather, but they hadn't spoken for long as her mother had been worried Dave would find out. Heather had told the officer she didn't want to do anything at present. I was aware that victims of domestic violence try to leave their abusers many times before they succeed and leave for good. I reassured Tilly that at least her mother now had a contact number and knew where to find help when she was ready. I just hoped she didn't leave it too long. Domestic violence tends to escalate – it rarely goes away by itself – and who knew what Dave was capable of?

Tilly also said her bedroom was bare since Dave had packed and sent all her belongings. Only the bed, stripped of linen, and the wardrobe remained. She said it looked as though she'd never lived there.

'Who owns the house?' I asked.

'He does. It's in his name. He pays the mortgage and all the bills, as he keeps telling Mum. She hasn't got anything. It's her third marriage and she's had nothing but heartache.'

'Is that what she told you?'

'Yes, a while ago.'

I felt sorry for Heather, but it was a shame she confided so much in Tilly, who at fourteen didn't need the burden of her mother's misery. I assumed Heather leant on Tilly because she didn't have a good friend or support network. She had also told Tilly that the injury to her face we'd noticed at the meeting was caused by Dave after he'd found the mobile phone Tilly had bought her. I tried to reassure Tilly it wasn't her fault, as she was feeling even more guilty.

On a lighter note, on Saturday we went to visit my mother. Paula, Lucy and Tilly came. Adrian was going to see her with Kirsty another day. It was the first time Mum had met Tilly and seen Lucy after she'd announced she was pregnant. Mum was at the door as soon as she heard our car pull up and welcomed us in with hugs and kisses. 'Lovely to meet you,' she said to Tilly as she followed me in. 'How are you, dear?'

'Good, thank you.'

Then to Paula, 'Lovely to see you again. And how are you?' she pointedly asked Lucy, looking her up and down.

'I'm very well, thank you, Nana.'

'You look it. How's your young man?'

'Fine. You'll meet him before long.'

'I'll look forward to that,' Mum said easily.

Ice broken, we all settled in the living room and talked. Mum used to cook for us, but now she was in her eighties we usually ate out at a local pub restaurant. It was a treat for us all. I'd booked the table for one o'clock and we walked there.

Lucy ate ravenously – starter and main course.

'Eating for two?' Mum asked, with a smile.

Lucy laughed. 'I'm permanently hungry,' she admitted, which I'd started to notice at home.

'I remember when I was pregnant I had a craving for dry cornflakes. I ate them straight from the box,' Mum said.

'Mine was tomato ketchup,' I said. 'I poured it over everything and normally I rarely have it.'

Lucy said she wasn't having cravings yet, and we then chatted about what could cause cravings, which many women experience in pregnancy. Tilly, who'd previously been too involved in her own problems to say much about Lucy being pregnant, also joined in, as did Paula. She said she had cravings for chocolate but didn't have the excuse of being pregnant!

After lunch we returned to Mum's house for the rest of the afternoon. As usual when we left it was with that warm glow that comes from spending time with a much-loved and cherished grandparent. My family and I knew how lucky we were to have her.

That evening Tilly telephoned her mother. It had been agreed at the meeting she'd phone her once at the weekend and then on Tuesday and Thursday evening – the days she wasn't seeing her. Contact for younger children is more regulated and often supervised, but at Tilly's age there had to be some flexibility, for in practice, if she had a mind to, she could visit and phone her mother whenever she pleased. However, they only spoke for a minute or so and then Tilly came to find me.

'Dave was there, listening,' she said, annoyed. 'I'll have to phone Mum straight after school on Tuesday and Thursday before he gets home.'

I agreed, but again I felt this was no way for Heather to be living – with her life so curtailed and controlled by Dave that she couldn't even speak to her daughter on the phone.

On Sunday I was presented with another problem after Lucy had spent the day with Darren. She returned home preoccupied and worried.

'Is everything all right?' I asked her.

'I think I made the wrong decision,' she said.

For one horrible moment I thought she meant having the baby. 'About what?' I asked.

'I told Bonnie I was pregnant and she wants to be involved.' Lucy pulled a face. 'She even offered to be my birthing partner!'

'That's not going to happen, is it?'

'No. I told her Darren would be with me and she said she could come as well!'

'Lucy, I think she will have lost interest long before then, don't you, love?'

'I hope so.'

I knew so. Bonnie breezed into Lucy's life a couple of times a year at the most and then out again. I felt no animosity towards her; I recognized – as did Lucy – that she had no more commitment now than when Lucy had been little. While being involved in the birth of her grandchild might have fleeting novelty value, I was sure it wouldn't last. I'd lost count of all the promises Bonnie had made to Lucy over the years – presents and meetings – that she hadn't fulfilled. Lucy usually enjoyed the hour or so they spent together, but she didn't expect any more so was rarely disappointed. It had been very different when she'd been little, before she had come to me and had needed a mother. But that was all history now. Lucy had never known her father. She'd asked Bonnie about him once and she'd laughed it off and said she couldn't remember who he was.

The following morning Lucy suffered her first bout of morning sickness. She'd been lucky so far and escaped it, but just before seven o'clock, as she woke she rushed out of her bedroom and was sick in the toilet. I fetched her a glass of water and then made her the slice of dry toast she asked for. She felt a bit better once she'd eaten and went to work. She texted an hour later to say she'd been sick again and had told her manager she was pregnant. She was all right by dinnertime that evening, but the next morning she was sick again. Although it's called morning sickness it can last all day and is common in early pregnancy. It's thought to be a reaction to the high levels of pregnancy hormones and usually clears up between sixteen and twenty weeks. However, it is very unpleasant, like bad seasickness, only you can't get off the boat.

Tilly's visit to her mother after school on Monday went as planned. Isa telephoned me on Tuesday afternoon, having spoken to Dave about the tracking software. He admitted he'd put it on Tilly's phone and said it was to keep her safe. He was aware it had stopped working and complained that I was acting irresponsibly and compromising Tilly's safety by allowing her to remove it. Isa explained to him that Tilly felt very uncomfortable with him knowing where she was every minute of the day and reading her messages. She said it was reasonable for Tilly to remove it, given the situation between them at present. Dave wasn't happy, to put it mildly, and said Heather knew about the tracker and had agreed it was a good idea. Considering how few opinions Heather was allowed and the level of control Dave asserted over her, I felt this was him talking, not Heather, as did Isa. I added that I didn't think Tilly was aware her mother knew of the tracker, for I felt sure she would have mentioned it when she'd seen her the day before.

But that afternoon Tilly arrived home angry and upset, having just learnt that her mother did know.

Tilly had telephoned her mother after school, as she wasn't seeing her that day, and Heather had confessed she'd known all along Dave was tracking her movements and reading her messages. She hadn't told Tilly before because Dave had told her not to and that the tracker was for Tilly's good, but now it was out in the open she felt bad for lying to Tilly.

'I asked Mum yesterday if she knew about it and she told me she didn't!' Tilly exclaimed, hurt. 'I wonder what other secrets she and him have. Neither of them can be trusted. They're as bad as each other!'

I calmed her down and tried to explain why her mother – a victim of years of domestic violence – wouldn't dare cross Dave and risk incurring his anger. I'm not sure it helped, and part of me felt Tilly was right and Heather couldn't be trusted. She was so controlled by Dave, she could be coerced into just about anything. Perhaps I was being unfair and Dave had simply wanted to protect Tilly and keep her safe, but from what I'd seen so far I doubted it.

Lucy was sick every morning that week, on waking and when she got to work, then her body seemed to settle down for the rest of the day and she ate well. On Friday she told me she was having her first ultrasound scan the following week and Darren would go with her. The scan, also known as the dating scan, confirms how far advanced the pregnancy is and checks the baby's development. They had both booked the time off work.

Also on Friday I received notice in the post of Tilly's first review for the following Thursday, together with a review form for me to complete. There were two identical envelopes, one addressed to me and the other to Tilly, which would contain her review form. Children in care have regular reviews, the first being within a month of their arrival. The child's parent(s), social worker, teacher, foster carer, the foster carer's support social worker and any other adults closely connected with the child meet to ensure everything is being done to help the child, and that the care plan (drawn up by the social services) is up to date. Very young children don't usually attend their reviews, while older children are expected to. I put Tilly's letter to one side and completed mine while I had the chance, and when Tilly came home from seeing her mother that afternoon I gave it to her. As she opened the letter, I explained what the review entailed, about the reviewing officer who would chair and minute the meeting and the review form. I could have guessed her response.

'*He* won't be there, will he?'

'Dave is your stepfather, so I think he will be invited,' I said. 'But if you really don't want him to attend, I suggest you tell Isa.'

'I will!' she said vehemently. 'I'll call her now.'

'OK, but it's five-forty-five so she might not answer, in which case you can leave a message on her voicemail.'

I could have contacted Isa and told her Tilly's views, but I thought it would be better coming from her. If I'm fostering a young child, I liaise with their social worker on their behalf, but at Tilly's age it was reasonable for her to do it herself. Isa had given Tilly her work telephone numbers – office and mobile.

Tilly telephoned Isa's mobile straight away and left a message, saying in no uncertain terms she didn't want Dave at her review. Ten minutes later Isa texted Tilly saying she'd received her message and would get back to her.

'If he's going, I'm not,' Tilly said bluntly.

'Just wait and see what Isa says, and in the meantime you can fill in your review form so it doesn't get forgotten,' I suggested.

'Who sees it?' she asked.

'The reviewing officer. They will ask if you want it read out at your review.'

She went off to her room to fill in the form. The review forms are standard and ask questions about how the young person feels being in foster care, contact with family and friends, school, if they are happy or sad, and if they have any problems or questions. I help young children and those with learning disabilities fill in their review form, but Tilly was capable of doing it by herself. Twenty minutes later she came downstairs with the form sealed in the envelope provided and handed it to me. 'Can you post it, please?'

'Yes, of course.'

'The last question asked if I wanted to add anything,' she said, 'so I put, *I want Mum to leave Dave.*'

My heart went out to her. She suddenly seemed so young and vulnerable. 'I know you do, love, but I'm afraid reviews can't make that happen, only your mother can.'

'Yes, I know that really,' she said sadly, and gave me a hug.

'It's not so bad living here, is it?'

'No, it's nice, but I worry about Mum. I feel guilty for not being there for her.' As do many children who come into care. They feel guilty they are no longer at home and able to help or protect the parent(s), and that they didn't do enough while they were living there. Some children believe it's their own fault they were brought into care. Of course, they have nothing to feel guilty about, but it is often a long time before they start to accept this.

CHAPTER EIGHT

CAN'T LEAVE MUM

On Saturday Adrian and Kirsty went to see my mother, Tilly went shopping with Abby, Paula stayed in and chilled, and Lucy went flat hunting with Darren – once she'd got over her morning sickness.

'There is no rush to find a flat,' I told her.

'We want to be settled before the baby is born,' she said, which made sense.

On Sunday Adrian and Paula went out for lunch with their father, my ex-husband, John. When they were little I used to make the contact arrangements on their behalf, but now they were young adults they made their own arrangements. They usually saw their father for a few hours every couple of months. I was always civil to John if he came to the front door, but he rarely did now, preferring to wait in his car and text either Adrian or Paula to say he'd arrived.

'Enjoy,' I said to them as they kissed me goodbye.

'We won't be long,' Adrian said.

'See you soon, Mum,' Paula added.

The door closed behind them.

I'd been hurt and angry when John had first left us, but it was a long time ago and at some point you have to let go of anger and move on, otherwise it eats you alive. I wrote my self-help guide, *Happy Adults*, partly based on what I learnt at that difficult time. I now thought it was his loss that he hadn't played a bigger part in the lives of my wonderful children. Did he regret it? I've no idea. He remarried soon after our divorce came through.

Tilly decided not to telephone her mother over the weekend, as Dave would be there, listening. She also said she was going to ask him for her mother's phone back, as she'd paid for it. I thought this was likely to antagonize him, so I suggested she made the request through Isa, which she did, leaving another message on her voicemail.

On Monday Tilly went to see her mother straight after school as planned but returned home upset and angry. Heather had confided that she'd had a dreadful weekend. Not only had Dave been cruel and threatening to her, but she also suspected he was having an affair. Tilly didn't need to hear all this, and again I reassured her as best I could. On Tuesday, when Tilly telephoned her mother on the bus coming home from school, Heather confided more tales of misery, and when she visited her on Wednesday it was no better. Tilly arrived home distraught, saying she was thinking she should move back home so she could protect her mother. I calmed her down and sent Isa an email telling her what was going on. She phoned me the following afternoon.

'Tilly is not going home,' she said. 'It would be very damaging for her, and it's not a safe place. If necessary, I'll apply for a court order to return her to care.'

I agreed and shared my concerns about the negative impact contact was having on Tilly.

'I phoned Heather this morning,' Isa said. 'She didn't appreciate how upsetting it was for Tilly to hear all of her problems. Tilly seems to put on a brave face in front of her mother. Heather has promised she'll try not to share so much with Tilly in future. I told her I could arrange supervised contact at the Family Centre, but she said she couldn't go there without Dave. Also, if Dave doesn't come to the review tomorrow, Heather says she won't be coming either. I've told Tilly.'

The good news on Wednesday was that when Lucy arrived home she had the ultrasound scan photos of her unborn baby. 'That one's for you,' she said, proudly handing me the glossy black-and-white scan photo. 'We had extra printed. Darren's got some too.'

A lump rose in my throat. Even at thirteen weeks, the outline of the baby was clear, curled snugly in the womb, warm and protected. This was the first glimpse of my grandchild and it was a moment to be treasured.

'My due date has changed slightly to 28 July,' Lucy said. 'It could change again.'

I nodded as I gazed in awe at the photo. 'Lovely, just like you.'

She laughed. 'At the next scan we can know the sex of the baby if we want to.'

'And do you?'

'Yes. It makes sense and then we can prepare. I want a girl and Darren wants a boy.'

'The most important thing is that the baby is healthy,' I said. 'It will be nice to meet Darren again soon. Perhaps he and his family would like to come to dinner?'

'I'll ask them,' she said, and went off to show the photos to Paula, who was upstairs.

I placed the scan photo in pride of place on the mantelpiece and then stood back for a moment to admire it. A new life had begun, and technology was allowing me a glimpse of that incredible journey of creation. I felt very blessed to be a mother to three wonderful children, a foster carer to many, and shortly a grandmother too.

Tilly's review was the following day and I had expected to hear from Edith by now. Part of the supervising social worker's role is to attend reviews, and if she wasn't coming then I would have expected to be told. That hadn't happened. However, the morning of the review, I received a phone call from Jaclyn Pearson, Edith's manager. I didn't usually have much to do with her.

'Edith has left us,' Jaclyn said flatly. 'She didn't return in the New Year and is using her leave to work out her notice.'

'Oh, that's a bit sudden,' I said.

'Yes, we were surprised too. We are advertising the position this week, but it may be a while before we fill it. I don't really have anyone spare to attend Tilly's review with you. I could come if you need someone there.'

'No, it's OK, I'll be fine.'

'Good. As you can imagine, this has left us a bit short.'

'Why did Edith leave so suddenly?' I asked.

'"Change of career," was all she said.'

'Where shall I email my reports?' I asked. 'I've been sending them to Edith.'

'Yes, I've been reading her emails but address them to me in future until we appoint someone. I'll give you my email address.'

I wrote it down.

'Anything urgent you need help with now?' she asked. 'I read your email about the issues around contact. I'm assuming Isa is dealing with that?'

'Yes, trying to.'

'OK. Keep me informed, and hopefully you'll have a new supervising social worker before long.'

We said goodbye. Of course, it wouldn't just be me who was affected by Edith's sudden departure, but the dozen or so other foster carers she was responsible for. Some of them would be new carers who needed support and guidance more than I did. While I was surprised Edith had left so abruptly, I wouldn't lose any sleep over it. I'd felt for some time her heart wasn't really in her job, unlike Jill, my previous supervising social worker, who'd been incredibly passionate and committed to her work.

I added Jaclyn Pearson's email address to my contact list and then set about some admin work. I'd arranged to collect Tilly from school at 3.30 – the end of school – and then drive straight to the review at the council offices. Her review had been arranged for four o'clock so she wouldn't miss any school. I didn't know if Tilly's mother and stepfather would be attending, as Isa had said that Heather wouldn't go without Dave, and Tilly didn't want him there. Generally it is important the parent(s) attend the child's reviews, as it gives them a voice, and most do.

At 3.20 I parked where there was a space a little way from Tilly's school and then stood near the main gate, waiting for her to come out. It was a cold but bright day with a wintery sun low in the sky. The bell inside the school rang and after a few minutes the students began to stream out. Tilly appeared with Abby. I said hello to Abby and asked her how she was before she headed home.

'Mum's definitely not coming,' Tilly said to me as we went to my car.

'Did Isa phone you, then?' I asked.

'No. I called Mum. I thought I might be able to persuade her to do something by herself for once, but she won't come without him.'

'Because she's afraid of him,' I said.

'Yeah, whatever.' Tilly shrugged dismissively, clearly annoyed.

There wasn't much more I could say in addition to what I'd already said about Dave's control over her mother, which had effectively stamped out any will or personality of her own. Tilly was silent as I drove and then said, 'Miss Jenkins is coming.'

It's usual for someone from the school to be invited to a review. 'She's not your form teacher, though?' I knew this from what Tilly had told me about school.

'No, she's the deputy head.'

'She'll be the designated teacher for looked-after children,' I explained. 'All schools have one.'

'She spoke to me when I first came to live with you and said if I had any problems or just wanted to chat, I could go to her. I wondered how she knew I was in care.'

'The social services work closely with schools,' I said. 'Don't worry, it's all confidential.'

'Good. I don't want my friends knowing what's going on. Only Abby knows.'

This wasn't unusual. Many children and young people in care don't want their classmates to know they are living with a foster carer, especially when they first come into care. Sometimes they say they are staying with an aunt or family friend. When the truth eventually comes out, which it usually does, they are often pleasantly surprised to find that being in care doesn't have the stigma they thought, and other children take it in their stride or are interested. A friend of one boy I fostered told his mother he wanted to go into care as it sounded fun and could he come and live with me to see what it was like!

As I parked outside the council offices, Tilly spotted Miss Jenkins getting out of her car. She and I introduced ourselves and then went into the building together. Having registered at reception, we continued upstairs to the room where Tilly's review was being held. I knocked on the door and led the way in.

I stopped dead. Dave was sitting at the table with a woman I took to be the Independent Reviewing Officer (IRO).

'What the fuck are you doing here?' Tilly cried as she saw him.

'Language,' Dave chastised. 'I thought one of us should be here and your mother didn't want to come.'

'She wouldn't come without you!' Tilly shouted angrily. 'I told my social worker I didn't want you here. Where is she?'

'Isa should be here soon,' I said, and looked at the IRO, wondering what to do for the best.

She was clearly taken aback and confused by this outburst, apparently not understanding what was going on. 'Is there a problem?' she asked Tilly. 'I've just been talking to your father.'

'He's not my father!' Tilly shouted. 'He's my bloody stepfather and I don't want him here!'

'Shall Tilly and I wait outside while you sort this out?' Miss Jenkins suggested to me, touching Tilly's arm.

'Yes, please,' I said.

Tilly didn't move but was staring so hard at Dave I thought she was going to hit him, while he sat, passive-aggressive, with his back to her, arrogant and unfazed.

'Tilly, wait outside with Miss Jenkins, please,' I told her.

She stamped her foot but left the room with the deputy head teacher. Miss Jenkins was a mature woman, and I guessed a highly experienced teacher, who had instinctively known what to do.

Without Isa present, it was up to me to explain the problem.

'You're the IRO?' I clarified first.

'Yes, Joanna Hargreaves,' she replied.

'I'm Cathy Glass, Tilly's foster carer. Tilly specifically asked that her stepfather wasn't present,' I said. 'She even wrote it on her review form.'

'I haven't read that yet,' the IRO said, and took the form from a folder that was on the table beside her laptop. 'Perhaps we should wait for the social worker,' she said. 'It's four o'clock, so she should be here soon.'

'I don't understand what the problem is,' Dave said, irritated. 'I'm Tilly's stepfather. I have a right to be here, and why is the social worker late?'

'I expect she's been held up,' the IRO said in a conciliatory manner.

'It wouldn't be acceptable in my line of work,' he huffed, then folded his arms across his chest to wait.

I sat at the opposite side of the table to him as the IRO read Tilly's form. There were a few minutes of uncomfortable silence before we heard footsteps outside the door and then the low hum of voices. The door opened, and Isa and her manager, Nikki, came in.

'Sorry we're late,' Isa said.

Tilly and Miss Jenkins followed them in.

'Mr Mitchel, could we have a chat outside?' Isa asked him.

'No,' he said. 'I've wasted enough time. I've come for the meeting so can we just get on with it?'

Nikki, Tilly and Miss Jenkins sat at the table while Isa remained standing. She rested one hand on the table as she spoke to Dave. 'Tilly has asked that you're not present for her review and I think we should respect her wishes.' Nicely put, but I could see the anger in his eyes as his jaw set. 'You will be sent a copy of the minutes,' Isa added. 'So you'll know what has been discussed.'

There was a moment before Dave suddenly stood and, snatching his phone from the table, hissed angrily, 'You'll be hearing from my solicitor!' He stormed out of the room and slammed the door behind him with such force the clock on the wall jumped.

'Someone who likes his own way,' the IRO remarked dryly.

'Yes,' Isa agreed quietly. She looked a bit shaken. It's unsettling to witness an adult angry and out of control.

'Are you OK?' I asked Tilly, who had obviously seen Dave's anger many times before.

'What did you mean about the minutes?' she asked Isa.

'The minutes are a record of what is discussed here,' Isa explained. 'We take them at all reviews, and then copies are sent to those who have been invited, whether they attend or not.'

'It's part of my job to take the minutes,' the IRO added.

'I don't want Dave to see them,' Tilly said. 'My life has nothing to do with him now.'

'We can address them to your mother,' the IRO suggested.

'He opens her mail,' Tilly replied anxiously.

'Is there a solicitor involved?' the IRO asked Isa and Nikki. 'We could send them there.'

'We're not aware of a solicitor,' Isa said.

'In that case I suggest we advise Heather when the minutes

are available and she can decide what she wants to do,' Nikki said. 'Could you make a note that the minutes are not to be sent to Mr and Mrs Mitchel for the time being. If a solicitor makes contact, they can have a copy.'

The IRO nodded as she typed this into her laptop. Isa wrote on her notepad.

'Let's begin the review now,' the IRO said as she finished typing and looked up. 'Welcome to your first review, Tilly. I'm sorry you had to witness all that. How are you?'

'OK.'

'Good. Let's begin. It's usual to start with introductions. I am Joanna Hargreaves, the Independent Reviewing Officer. I shall be chairing and minuting this meeting. Would you like to state your name, please?'

'Tilly Watkins.'

'Thank you.' The IRO smiled and then looked at Isa, who was on her right, to continue.

'Isa Neave, social worker for Tilly,' she said.

'Nikki Bets, team manager.'

'Faith Jenkins, deputy head of Tilly's school, with additional responsibility for looked-after children.'

'Thank you,' the IRO said. 'What is the name and address of Tilly's school?' Miss Jenkins told her.

'Cathy Glass, foster carer,' I said. 'My supervising social worker won't be attending as she has resigned,' I added. 'I wasn't sure if you knew.'

'Yes, her manager replied to the invitation, thank you. Are we expecting anyone else?' she asked Isa.

'No.'

'Let's begin then. Tilly this review is about you. I'm sure your social worker or foster carer has explained why we have them and what happens, so perhaps you'd like to start by telling us a bit about yourself and how you're settling in with Cathy?'

I threw Tilly an encouraging smile, but her face crumpled and tears filled her eyes. 'I'm all right, but my mum isn't. I can't just leave her there.'

CHAPTER NINE

THREATENING BEHAVIOUR

Tilly was so upset that we spent the first part of the review talking to her and trying to reassure her. While she wiped her eyes, Isa fetched her a glass of water. Usually reviews are quite formal and the IRO asks all those present to take a turn to give their report while they minute and chair the meeting. However, given what had happened at the start and how upset Tilly was, it seemed more appropriate to discuss her worries first. They kept coming back to the same point: that Tilly wanted her mother to leave Dave, but until Heather felt able to, there was little anyone else could do. Eventually Tilly dried her eyes and accepted it wasn't advisable for her to return home to protect her mother, although I wondered how long that would last. Probably until the next time Heather confided in her, which I was sure wouldn't be long.

'I am concerned Tilly is finding it difficult to settle because of the constant worry of her mother,' I added.

The IRO nodded. 'Perhaps this would be an appropriate time for everyone to give their reports,' she said, getting the meeting back on track. 'Cathy, would you like to go first?'

'Yes.' I glanced at the notes I had in front of me on the table, and began with the positives, as I always like to do.

'Tilly is a lovely young person, polite and kind, and a pleasure to look after. She has a good circle of friends at school and a special friend, Abby, who has been to our house. Tilly's dental and optician check-ups are up to date, and she is eating and sleeping well. No accidents or injuries since she's been with me.' These were all things the IRO would expect to be included.

'Tilly is going to school each day,' I continued. 'But she is weighed down with the problems at home between her mother and stepfather. Mr Mitchel appears to be very controlling. For example, unknown to Tilly, he placed tracking software on her phone so he knew where she was all the time and could read her messages.'

'Really?' the IRO said, raising her eyebrows and glancing up from typing.

'Some parents use these apps to help keep their children safe,' Nikki explained.

'Tilly was very upset when she found the app,' I said. 'It's been removed from her phone now.'

'Does Mr Mitchel know?' the IRO asked.

'Yes,' Isa said. 'And he wasn't happy.'

'And contact? How is that going?' the IRO asked me. It was a standard question at a review.

'Tilly sees her mother for an hour after school on Monday, Wednesday and Friday and phones her on Tuesday and Thursday. She sees her mother at home as her mother doesn't go out.'

'Why not?' the IRO asked.

'Dave says she has agoraphobia,' Isa said. 'But it's never been diagnosed. It appears to be more about Heather not being able to go out without Dave.'

'He won't let her go anywhere without him!' Tilly blurted, her voice unsteady.

'It must be very worrying for you,' the IRO sympathized.

'It is,' I said. 'Tilly often arrives home from seeing her mother upset and angry as a result of what Heather has told her about the way Dave treats her. I console her as best I can. I understand Heather has promised Isa she will try not to share so much with Tilly in the future.'

'I don't mind,' Tilly said quietly, and the IRO threw her a reassuring smile.

'Tilly is allowed to phone her mother over the weekend as well,' I said. 'But she doesn't because Dave is always there, listening. Tilly bought her mother a mobile phone but unfortunately he found it and took it away from her.'

'Can I have it back?' Tilly asked the IRO. 'I bought it with my own money – the allowance Cathy gave me.'

'I asked Dave if it could be returned to you,' Isa said. 'But he claims he doesn't know where it is.'

'Bullshit!' Tilly exclaimed. 'Of course he knows where it is. He took it!'

'Very likely, but I don't think he'll be giving it back,' Isa said.

'You have a phone of your own, though?' the IRO asked Tilly.

'Yes.'

The IRO looked to me to continue.

I glanced at my notes. 'Tilly would like to see her maternal grandmother. She used to speak to her on the phone when she lived at home, although she hasn't seen her in a long time.'

'If Tilly wants to go, I don't have a problem with that,' Isa said. Then to me, 'Can you arrange a visit and stay with her?'

'Yes, of course. Do we know the address?'

'I do,' Tilly said.

'I'll arrange it,' I confirmed as Isa and the IRO made a note. 'I think that's all I wanted to say,' I concluded.

'Thank you. And Tilly is getting home on time?' the IRO asked.

'Yes. If she is going to be late, she texts.'

'Good. Does she have her own front door key? I know this can be an issue with some young people.'

'Not yet. But I am happy for her to have one.'

'Would you like your own front door key?' she asked Tilly.

'Don't mind. Cathy is always home, like my mum was.'

'I'll leave it with you, then,' she said to me. 'Any complaints from anyone?' she asked. This was a standard question. Isa, Nikki and Miss Jenkins shook their heads. 'Tilly? Do you have any complaints?'

'Only about Dave.'

'I know, I've noted what you have said,' the IRO said kindly. 'You're happy with the care you are receiving from Cathy?'

'Yes.'

'Isa, would you like to speak next?'

Isa straightened in her seat and, with a folder open in front of her, began. 'Tilly is in care under a Section 20 and the care plan is that she will remain in care until the age of eighteen. I've visited Tilly in placement and I've also spoken to her a number of times on the phone. She has my contact details and has phoned my mobile. I've talked to Tilly about contact and offered supervised contact at the Family Centre, but because her mother doesn't go out without Mr Mitchel, and Tilly doesn't want to see him, my manager and I agreed contact should take place at the family home. But that will be reviewed. Mr Mitchel has given an undertaking not to go to the house while Tilly is there and so far he has kept to it. If that changes, we will have to reconsider the contact arrangements.'

'If Mrs Mitchel won't leave the house, you aren't left with many options, are you?' the IRO said, glancing at Isa.

'No, exactly,' Isa agreed, then continued with her report. 'Heather is aware of the help available and a police officer from the domestic abuse unit has been in touch with her, but she doesn't feel able to access that help yet.'

'Apart from the maternal grandmother, are there any other family members?' the IRO asked.

'Tilly has an older stepbrother and stepsister, but they don't see each other.'

'Thank you, please continue.'

'Tilly will remain in her present placement while in care. It appears to be working well,' Isa said. 'She is able to catch the bus to school and to visit her mother. Tilly is an only child, but she likes having older foster siblings.'

'So no issues, then?' the IRO asked.

'No.'

'And health?' the IRO prompted.

'Tilly is in good health. I've asked her if she would like to see a therapist at CAMHS [Child and Adolescent Mental Health Service], but she doesn't want to at present. I can make a referral if she changes her mind, although there is a waiting list.'

'All right. Thank you. Tilly, do you have anything you want to add to what your social worker has said, or any questions?' the IRO asked her.

'If Mum leaves Dave, will I be able to live with her again?'

Nikki replied, 'It's possible. It will depend largely on where your mother is living. But as far as we know your mother hasn't any plans to leave, unless you know something we don't?'

Tilly shook her head. 'I tell Mum to leave, but she won't. She hasn't got anywhere to go.'

'There are refuges for victims of domestic violence,' Nikki said. 'Isa has talked to your mother about them and I'm sure the police officer would have done too. Their locations are secret, but Isa has given your mother the telephone numbers for Women's Aid and the domestic violence helpline.'

Tilly nodded.

'Do you have any other questions?' the IRO asked her.

'I don't think so,' she said quietly. 'I love my mum.' Which was touching in its simplicity.

'You're doing very well,' I said to her.

Everyone agreed Tilly was doing well apart from Miss Jenkins, the last to give her report. Nikki was there primarily to support and monitor Isa, who I guessed was probably a newly qualified social worker.

Miss Jenkins was clearly used to addressing groups and spoke confidently without looking at her notes. But what she said was worrying, even though it began and ended positively. 'Tilly is a pleasant member of her class and is liked by pupils and staff,' she began. 'She can participate sensibly in group discussion but is underachieving in all subjects and not fulfilling her potential. I've spoken to her subject teachers and she is well below average. At her age she should be working at Key Stage Four and taking her GCSE examinations next year. However, at present she is unlikely to achieve any grade fours or above – which are generally accepted to be a reasonable pass and are required for higher education.

'When Tilly first joined the school aged eleven,' Miss Jenkins continued, 'the report from her primary school was promising, and to start with she made reasonable progress. However, that has gradually fallen away and she has been struggling to keep up. Her work is often unfinished or done to a poor standard, and she lacks concentration in class. She has a good attendance record, but her thoughts are elsewhere. We were not aware of any problems at home until Tilly was taken into care. Now it's obvious why she has been so distracted and failing in her work. Last year her form teacher felt there might be something wrong at home, but when she asked Tilly she said she was fine. I've now spoken to Tilly and she knows where to find me in school if she wants to talk. Hopefully, now she is in care and has some stability in her life she will make good progress.'

She stopped. There was silence. It was the first I'd heard of Tilly failing at school and I was shocked. 'I will do all I can to help her,' I said, already feeling responsible for her underachieving so badly.

'Didn't you feel you could confide in a teacher?' the IRO asked Tilly.

'No, only Abby. I knew she wouldn't tell. Dave would have been furious if I'd said anything. I kept hoping it would get better or he would go, or Mum and me would leave. But it got worse.' Her voice shook.

'I understand,' the IRO said kindly.

'Is there any work outstanding from this term?' I asked Miss Jenkins.

'Yes.'

'I'll make sure Tilly does it,' I said. 'I usually give responsibility for homework to the young person when they are Tilly's age, although I'm on hand to help if necessary. Tilly has been going to her bedroom in the evening to do her homework, but clearly that hasn't been happening.'

'I can't concentrate,' Tilly protested.

'I know it must be difficult, but we'll work together on this,' I told her.

'Thank you,' Miss Jenkins said. 'The school library is available until six o'clock each school day for students to study if there isn't a quiet place at home.'

'I don't need the library,' Tilly said. 'I've got my bedroom at Cathy's and the front room. It's just that I keep thinking about Mum.'

'Do your mother and stepfather know you are struggling at school?' the IRO asked her. 'It's been going on for some time.'

'No,' Tilly replied.

'What about parent–teacher evenings?' the IRO asked. 'Weren't they told then?'

'They didn't go,' Tilly said.

'They attended in Tilly's first year with us,' Miss Jenkins added. 'I checked. But that was the only time.'

'Don't schools follow this up?' the IRO asked.

'They do if the invitation to the consultation isn't returned, but Tilly's were returned, signed, and with an apology saying they couldn't attend.'

'I signed them,' Tilly admitted. 'I didn't want Dave going to my school. My life has nothing to do with him.'

'What about the end-of-year school reports?' Nikki asked, puzzled. 'I have to sign and return a tear-off slip to say I have received my children's reports.'

'I forged a signature on those too,' Tilly said.

'But didn't your parents think it odd that they never received a school report or invitation to attend a parent–teacher consultation evening?' Nikki asked.

Tilly shrugged. 'Dave asked once, and I said it was in the

post, and then he forgot. He only thinks about himself, and Mum is so wound up in her own problems she didn't notice.'

'We'll revise our policy in view of this,' Miss Jenkins said stiffly, and made a note. 'It reflects badly on the school. Who should we send Tilly's reports to in future?'

'One copy goes home with Tilly to Cathy,' Nikki said. 'And one to us, please.' Miss Jenkins wrote this down.

'And Tilly's next report will be much better than the last,' I added positively.

'Thank you, Cathy,' the IRO said with an appreciative smile.

'Where are we with the PEP?' Nikki now asked Isa. PEP stands for Personal Education Plan. Children in care between the ages of three and eighteen have a PEP. It's a document that forms part of the care plan and contains goals and achievements to help the child or young person reach their full academic and life potential.

'I need to arrange a PEP meeting. I haven't had time yet,' Isa said. Ideally the child's PEP should be available at the review, but that isn't always possible. 'I'll look at some dates for the PEP meeting,' Isa said, making a note. At the meeting Isa, Tilly, a teacher and myself would draw up the PEP for the coming academic year.

With no further matters to discuss, the IRO wound up the meeting and set the date for Tilly's next review in three months' time. We stood, but Miss Jenkins held back, wanting to speak to Isa and Nikki, so Tilly and I left the room first.

'I will do all I can to help you with your schoolwork,' I said to Tilly as we made our way downstairs. 'I know you have a lot on your mind, but education is so important. It opens gates and allows choices and opportunities.'

'Abby is doing well,' Tilly said despondently.

'And so will you.'

We returned our ID badges to reception and Tilly took her phone from her pocket. We had both set our phones to silent before going into the meeting. I would check mine once in the car. Just as we moved away from reception Tilly exclaimed, 'The bastard! He's cut off my phone. It's not working.'

Tilly showed me the text message from the service provider. 'Dave was bound to stop paying for it at some point,' I said. 'It's not a problem. We'll change your contract to pay as you go.'

'When?' Tilly asked, still pushing buttons on her phone to try to make it work. 'I can't even send a frigging text.'

I glanced at my watch. 'The shop should still be open if we hurry. If you promise to do your schoolwork, we'll go there now and I'll set up a pay-as-you-go phone for you.'

'Deal,' Tilly agreed with a faint smile.

'Good girl.'

Yet Dave's actions had left me with a feeling of disquiet. While I'd been expecting him to stop paying the contract on Tilly's phone, I was sure the timing of it wasn't pure chance. He'd left Tilly's review very angry. I thought this was his way of getting his own back – revenge, tit-for-tat. It was juvenile, but also threatening and sent a clear message that he still had control over Tilly. Perhaps I was reading too much into it, but instinct from years of fostering told me I wasn't.

CHAPTER TEN

A SHOCK

We got to the phone shop in time and converted Tilly's phone to a pay as you go. It needed a new SIM card, which came with a different number. Had she wanted to keep the same number, it would have required an authorization code that the assistant told us could take twenty-four hours. Not wanting to be without her phone, Tilly opted for having the new number. This, of course, had the advantage that Dave didn't know it. I paid and we left the shop with Tilly happily texting her friends.

It was too late for Tilly to call her mother as she usually did on the days she didn't see her. Dave was likely to be home by now, so Tilly said she'd give her mother the new number when she saw her tomorrow.

'Make sure she knows Dave mustn't have it,' I said. 'And put your phone on "private number" when you call her so it doesn't show on their phone bill.'

'I will.'

Once home, I made dinner and then sat with Tilly and went through the schoolwork that she'd fallen behind with, prioritizing what needed to be done first, both on her laptop and in her exercise books. As well as unfinished work from previous weeks, there was also current homework. Clearly

Tilly couldn't be expected to catch up in a few days, so I suggested that rather than get further behind, she completed the current work first and then spent some time each evening catching up. It would show the school she was making an effort and was sincere in her wish to do better. I also suggested that in future she did some homework when she first arrived home, before dinner, and then another two hours after dinner, stopping for a break halfway through, which is what my children had done when they were studying. Tilly pointed out straight away that it wasn't going to work on Monday, Wednesday and Friday when she saw her mother.

'OK, so use the time on the bus to research and plan your work, then you can write it up when you return. You're usually back here by five-thirty, so plenty of time.'

'I'll need time to talk to Abby as well,' she sighed, a bit disgruntled.

'Of course, and to see her sometimes. Abby is doing well at school so I'm sure she'll appreciate that you need to catch up. I expect she spends quite a bit of time studying in the evening too.'

'Yes, and at weekends,' Tilly admitted.

'So when you are both free she could visit us again and maybe stay overnight? Half-term holiday isn't far away.'

'I'll ask her.'

It is important for children in care that they live as normal a life as possible, although there are obstacles in their way that the average child doesn't face. Meetings, for example, reviews and PEPs, visits from their social worker, not to mention contact, which can be very disruptive. It is vital that schools are aware of this and make allowances where necessary. Sometimes there is the feeling among teachers that once the child is in care all their problems vanish. But for many it's just the beginning of a very long journey of adjustment, missing loved ones and coming to terms with a difficult past and uncertain future.

That evening Tilly worked until nine o'clock and then came downstairs for a drink before going to bed. 'Can we arrange to see my gran soon as well?' she asked me.

'Yes, of course, we'll need to phone her first to find out when is convenient. Can you give me her contact details? I don't have them.'

A few minutes later Tilly reappeared and handed me a piece of paper with her grandmother's address and phone number on it. I was taken aback when I read where she lived. 'Your gran only lives a few miles away,' I said. 'When was the last time you saw her?'

'Two years ago.'

'And your mother hasn't seen her since then either?'

'No. Dave wouldn't take her.'

'And she couldn't go on the bus or use a taxi?'

'Not without him.'

'But you've spoken to your gran on the phone?' I asked.

'Yes, a few times last year, but not for about six months.'

'Oh dear.'

When I thought of all the times my family and I saw my mother and telephoned her in between, I struggled to appreciate why Heather hadn't found a way to see her mother or at least speak to her on the phone. But then I wasn't a victim of intimidation and control by an abusive partner as she was.

'It's a bit late to phone your gran now,' I said. 'We'll call her tomorrow when you get back. Or you could phone from your mother's, then she can talk to her as well,' I suggested.

'Mum won't in case Dave finds out.'

'He won't know if you use your phone rather than the landline. There's no tracker on your phone now and it's a new SIM, so he has no control over it.'

Tilly's face lost some of its seriousness as she realized the truth in what I was saying.

'You're a genius!' she said, and kissed my cheek. 'Mum can speak to whoever she likes on my phone and he won't know.'

'That's right, but make sure she knows not to divulge the number to Dave,' I reminded her.

'I will.'

'It might come as a shock to your gran to suddenly hear from you both after all this time and to learn you're in care,' I cautioned. 'She may be upset to begin with.'

'I'll explain what's happened. When shall I tell her we will be going to see her?'

'This Sunday if that suits her.'

The following morning Tilly was happier than I'd seen her in a while. She looked as though a huge weight had been lifted from her shoulders, which it had. She was safely away from Dave, catching up on schoolwork and was going to see her gran and invite Abby back for another sleepover. Tilly hadn't been with me a month, yet already I was seeing a difference. It was at times like this I knew why I fostered. Before she left for school, I gave her a front door key.

'Thank you,' she said. 'Dave would never let me have one in case I lost it.'

'You're responsible enough to keep it safe,' I said. 'I trust you.'

Isa telephoned later that day to let me know the date and time of the PEP meeting the following week and I wrote it in my diary. I told her about the new SIM in Tilly's phone and gave her the number. I said Tilly was planning on calling her gran from her mother's house that afternoon to arrange a visit. Isa didn't have Mrs Watkins's contact details so I gave them to her. It was important that, as Tilly's social worker, she had the contact details of those in Tilly's extended family who she was seeing.

I thought about Tilly that afternoon and wondered how she was getting on as she phoned her gran. I imagined it would be a shock for Mrs Watkins to suddenly hear from her daughter and granddaughter after so long, but I hoped it was a pleasant one. At 5.30, when Tilly arrived home, she let herself in with her front door key and I went into the hall to greet her. 'How did it go?' I asked her eagerly.

'All right. Sunday is fine, but Gran's not well. We didn't speak for long. She started coughing and couldn't get her breath.'

'What's the matter with her?' I asked, concerned.

'She said she'd tell us when she saw us.' Which I didn't like the sound of.

'She feels well enough for us to visit on Sunday?' I checked.

'Yes. She was pleased. She said to arrive between one and two o'clock, as that would be best for her. Then she started coughing.'

'I expect she's picked up a winter virus,' I said. 'Lots of people have coughs and colds, even flu, at this time of year. Did your mother speak to her?'

'A little. It was awkward. Mum didn't know what to say and Gran asked her why she wasn't coming to see her on Sunday. Mum lied and said Dave was ill. I think Gran knew she was lying because she said he couldn't have been ill for over two years. Mum went quiet and didn't say any more.'

'I suppose it's not possible for your mother to come with us on Sunday? If we collected her in the car and dropped her off after?' I suggested.

'No. Dave will be there. She wouldn't dare.'

I didn't say anything further on the matter. Tilly knew it wasn't right that Heather couldn't visit her own mother, even though she was ill, but there was nothing I could do about it. Tilly was pleased she'd made the call and was looking forward to seeing her grandmother. She'd had some other good news too. Miss Jenkins, the deputy head, had spoken to her and said she'd had some feedback from staff and was pleased with the improvements she'd already made in her attitude to her work, and to keep it up. I praised her, and then she went to get a drink, which she took to her room.

I updated my log notes. Not just about school, but the phone call to her gran and that Heather wouldn't be visiting her mother on Sunday because Dave wouldn't let her. It affected Tilly and there was no way of knowing where this could lead in the future. If ever evidence was required in court to show that Tilly shouldn't return home to live then details like this could form part of the case. My log had been used in care cases before, so I knew how important it was to keep accurate, detailed and objective notes, using the child or young person's words as much as possible.

I'd just finished writing when Lucy came home, looking very pale.

'The morning sickness is getting worse,' she said. 'I've been sick three times today and still feel sick. The smell of coffee in the staffroom made me retch.'

I sympathized. 'Lots of women seem to have an aversion to coffee when pregnant. Have a lie-down before dinner.'

'I don't want any dinner,' she said, pulling a face. 'I can smell fish.'

'I'm making fish pie, but you don't have to have that. What do you fancy?'

She thought for a moment. 'Cheese on crackers, and a glass of water. But I'll have it in my bedroom so I don't have to watch everyone else eat.'

'OK, love.' I gave her a hug. 'It will pass.'

I made Lucy the cheese on crackers and took it up to her room with a glass of water and then finished making our dinner. Lucy was asleep by eight-thirty and the following morning I heard her dry-retching in the bathroom as soon as she got up. Then she bravely went to work. Like most women who suffer from sickness in pregnancy, Lucy carried on as best she could while feeling completely awful. If the sickness didn't pass or got significantly worse, she'd need to see a doctor for a check-up to make sure she wasn't getting dehydrated, which would be bad for her and the baby.

On Saturday I went to see my mother. Lucy stayed at home. She was going to rest in the morning and then see Darren in the afternoon. Adrian was going to see Kirsty. Paula and Tilly did some homework before we set off in the car. I think having the examples of Abby and Paula studying helped Tilly focus, although I'd never underestimate the struggle she faced trying to concentrate on schoolwork with her homelife in turmoil.

Mum welcomed us with hugs and kisses, and it wasn't long before Tilly told her she was going to see her grandmother the next day and that she hadn't seen her for over two years. Mum knew better than to ask why.

'I'm sure your grandmother will be overjoyed to see you,' Mum said. 'As you get older, spending time with your children and grandchildren becomes even more special.' Bless her, I thought.

'I'm going to start seeing my gran every week,' Tilly said. 'I couldn't before because of *him*, but now I'm at Cathy's I can go whenever I want.'

'Good,' Mum said, without asking who *he* was. 'That will make your gran very happy, I'm sure.'

Although I was taking Tilly to see her grandmother this weekend as Isa had asked, it occurred to me that if Tilly began going every weekend it would be difficult for me to commit to that level of contact. I thought that, if all went well tomorrow, I'd suggest to Isa that some weeks Tilly could catch the bus to visit her gran. It was only a short journey, about the same as it was to Tilly's school, just in a different direction.

As usual we had a lovely time at Mum's. When we said goodbye she said to Tilly, 'Don't forget to tell your gran and your mother you love them. You may think they know, but it's nice to hear it.'

'Very true,' I said as I kissed her.

We were a family who said 'I love you', but I knew many families didn't, assuming they knew they were loved. I'm sure they do know, but it's still nice to hear. 'Bye, Mum. Love you,' I said as we left.

The following day, after lunch, having reminded Adrian, Lucy and Paula where I was going, I set off with Tilly in the car to visit her grandmother. We stopped off on the way to buy some flowers and arrived at one-fifteen. Mrs Watkins lived in a bungalow in a street of similar properties, but unlike her neighbours, whose front gardens were neatly tended, her garden was mostly weeds. They had also grown up through the cracks in the path. 'It didn't used to look like this,' Tilly said as we went to the front door. 'Gran used to keep it nice.'

'I expect it got too much for her,' I said. Mrs Watkins was in her seventies and a widow.

Tilly pressed the doorbell and we heard it ring inside but it was a few minutes before the door opened. I knew straight away Tilly's grandmother had more than a cold. She had the classic appearance of someone undergoing chemotherapy.

'Gran, what's the matter?' Tilly asked, clearly shocked.

'Don't you worry about me,' she said. 'Lovely to see you both. Come in out of the cold.'

'I'm Cathy, Tilly's foster carer,' I said, closing the door behind us.

'I'm Nancy.'

Tilly's grandmother used a walking stick and had lost large patches of her hair. Her face had that bloated look that can result from taking steroids – often given with chemo.

'Sit yourselves down,' she said, hobbling into her living room at the rear of the bungalow.

'I bought these for you,' Tilly said awkwardly, holding up the flowers as her gran eased herself into an armchair.

'They're lovely, dear. Thank you,' she said breathlessly. 'There's a vase in the kitchen, in the cupboard below the sink. Could you put them in some water, please?'

'Sure,' Tilly said, and left the room, pleased to be occupied and of some help.

I met Nancy's gaze. 'How are you?' I asked.

'Not too wonderful,' she said, lowering her voice. 'I was diagnosed with lung cancer at the end of last year. They operated, took out half a lung, and now I'm on chemo. I wanted to explain to Tilly in person.'

'Yes, I understand. I am sorry.'

'I'm determined to fight this, but the chemo knocks the stuffing out of you.'

'Yes. I have a friend who's just been through similar, but it'll be worth it in the end,' I said positively.

'Let's hope so. It's my own bloody fault for smoking. I stopped years ago but the damage must have been done.'

'It's not your fault,' I said firmly. 'Back then no one knew the dangers of smoking.'

She nodded and coughed.

'You didn't tell Heather you were ill?' I asked.

'No. She hadn't been in touch for ages, so I thought it best not to worry her. She's got enough problems of her own and our relationship is strained, to put it mildly.'

'But you don't mind her knowing now?' I asked. 'Tilly is bound to tell her.'

'Yes, although I'm not sure what Heather can do apart from worry. She never leaves the house without him.'

'You're aware of the problems at home then?' I asked carefully.

'Some of it. I've surmised the rest.' She coughed and cleared her throat again.

Tilly appeared, carrying the vase of flowers.

'They're beautiful. Thank you, love,' Nancy said. 'Can you make room for them over there on the sideboard?' She pointed.

The glass-fronted sideboard, like the other furniture in the room, was of an older style but built to last with the wood polished and the glass gleaming. The three-piece floral suite – a sofa and two armchairs – was the same fabric as the curtains, and a rug was positioned in front of the hearth. The room was typical of an era and as you may find in the homes of many older people. The coal fire was no longer in use, having been replaced by central heating and an arrangement of dried flowers sat in the grate. Tilly set the vase on the sideboard and then joined me on the sofa. She looked at her gran, concerned.

'I've had lung cancer, dear,' Nancy told her. 'But I'm getting better. I'll have to get myself a wig if my hair doesn't grow back. Perhaps blonde?' she added with a smile.

'But you *are* going to get better?' Tilly asked, clearly worried.

'Yes, of course. Don't look so sad.'

'But you never used to use a walking stick. Is that to do with the cancer?'

'No. I tripped and fell and pulled a ligament in my ankle. They gave me the crutch at the hospital to use until it's healed. Nothing for you to worry about. How are you and your mother?'

Tilly clearly didn't know what to say for the best.

'You can tell me,' Nancy said. 'I've been through a lot with your mother in the past.' She coughed again.

'Can I get you a drink?' I offered.

'Good idea. Let's have a cup of tea,' Nancy said. Then to Tilly, 'I bought some of your favourite biscuits. Well, my neighbour, Babs, did. She's been helping me with the shopping.'

'Are they Jammie Dodgers?' Tilly asked, referring to the popular round biscuits with jam in the middle.

'Yes,' her gran replied. 'You can take home what you don't eat. I'm not supposed to be having too much sweet stuff.'

I offered to make the tea, but Nancy insisted, so the three of us went into the kitchen. It was only when we returned to the living room with Tilly carrying the tray of tea and biscuits that the conversation turned serious.

'Tilly, I might be getting old,' her gran said, lowering herself into her armchair. 'And I'm not in the best of health, but I'm not stupid. You need to tell me what's been going on in your home. I haven't seen you or your mother for over two years and then I find you're in foster care.'

'I'm sorry, Gran,' Tilly said, her voice catching. 'It's been dreadful. I'm so pleased to see you.' As she set the tray on the coffee table, a tear slipped from her eye.

CHAPTER ELEVEN

GRANDMOTHER

'It's Dave,' Tilly said. 'He's been horrible to Mum. They argue and he throws things at her and he is really cruel. I feel sorry for Mum, but I'm angry she won't help herself. I stayed at home for as long as I could, and now I've put myself in care. I can't go home, but I worry about Mum. She won't leave him. Why is she like this, Gran?'

'Come and sit down, love,' I said to Tilly, and drew her to the sofa.

'Does he hit your mother?' Nancy asked.

Tilly nodded and another tear slipped down her cheek. I passed her a tissue.

'Sometimes,' she said, 'but he controls her in other ways. She's so scared of him now he only has to raise his hand or voice and she jumps. She daren't do anything, not even come and see you.'

'Dear me,' Nancy said, frowning with anguish. 'The last time she and I spoke on the phone was the middle of last year and I thought she sounded desperate then. I told her the two of you could come to live with me here, but she said Dave would come after her. I haven't heard from her since. She never answers my calls. What if I went to see her when Dave was at work? Perhaps I could persuade her to leave.'

'I don't think Mum would dare let you in, and you're not well enough,' Tilly said, wiping her eyes.

'Why doesn't she answer the phone?' Gran asked. 'I've tried phoning during the day when he's not there.'

'He's been monitoring our calls,' Tilly said. 'Mum's not allowed to speak to you. Dave says bad things about you, which I know aren't true. Mum needs help, but she's too scared to get it.'

'What are the social services doing?' Nancy asked me. The tray of tea and biscuits remained untouched on the coffee table. 'I assume they are involved if Tilly is in care?'

'Yes, they've put Heather in touch with the domestic violence unit at the police station,' I said. 'But the onus is on her to follow it up. They can't force her to leave or press charges if she doesn't want to.'

'Why is she like this, Gran?' Tilly asked again, desperation in her voice.

'Life,' Nancy said with a sigh. 'Has your mother ever talked to you about when she was young and the time before she met Dave?'

'Not really,' Tilly said. 'She said she made some bad decisions, and she was lucky Dave wanted her. But I don't think she's lucky at all. He's horrible.'

Gran looked thoughtful. 'I can see why she might say that, though,' she said. Leaning forward, she picked up her teacup, took a sip and replaced it on the tray. 'You're old enough to know,' she said, looking at Tilly. 'And it might help you understand your mother. Some of what happened was my fault and, looking back, I probably should have done things differently. I spoilt her. Your mother was my only child and I gave her everything she wanted and rarely told her off. When I talked to her it was more like a friend than a child. Your grandpa used to tell me I wasn't firm enough with her, but I didn't take any notice. I loved her to bits and thought I was doing the right thing.' She paused reflectively.

'It started to go wrong when your mother was a teenager,' Nancy continued, catching her breath. 'Heather wanted to go out a lot and I never stopped her or put rules in place for when she had to be home. I suppose I was worried she might not like me if I stopped her doing things, but when she was fifteen she got in with a group of lads a lot older than her. At seventeen she was pregnant. She didn't find out until it was too late.'

'My mother had another child?' Tilly asked in amazement.

'Yes, for a while, but hear me out, please. Your grandpa and I were shocked, but we stood by her. The baby's father wanted nothing more to do with her or the baby. She never saw him again. We turned the spare room here into a nursery and supported Heather through her pregnancy, but towards the end the doctors warned us there might be something wrong with the baby. We hoped for the best, but when he was born he was very poorly and had a lot of things wrong with him. Heather was advised to have him christened and I knew then they didn't expect him to live. We had a little service in the hospital chapel and she named him Peter after your grandpa.' Nancy's eyes filled and it was a moment before she could continue. I was feeling choked up too, and Tilly looked close to tears again.

'The doctors were marvellous,' Nancy continued. 'They did all they could to save Peter, but he only lived twelve days. We were all heartbroken and Heather blamed herself and felt she was being punished. She was in such a state I had to arrange the funeral. It was the most upsetting thing I've ever had to do. The coffin was so small. No one should have to bury a child. The funeral directors asked if there was a special outfit we wanted them to dress Peter in. Heather chose one of the knitted sets I'd made for him and I took it in. She wanted to see Peter one last time. I didn't think it was a good idea, but I went with her. Your grandpa drove us to the funeral parlour, but he couldn't come in. He waited outside. That little coffin. I'll never forget it. But Peter looked very peaceful. Lying there in the white outfit I'd made against the white satin lining of the coffin, he looked like a little angel. God rest his soul.' She paused again. I swallowed hard and fought back tears. Tilly was wiping her eyes. It was one of the most difficult and moving stories I'd ever heard. After a moment Nancy continued.

'There was just Heather, your grandpa and me at the funeral. I let the father know – I thought it was only right – but he didn't come. So we buried Peter in the cemetery and I visited his grave and kept it nice. I don't know if Heather ever went, but your grandpa used to take me in the car. Heather slept with the little white booties Peter had worn in hospital under her pillow. I think she still has them somewhere. There was nothing I could say or do to console her. She was heartbroken and spent days in bed crying. Eventually your grandpa lost patience with her. He was a good man but didn't really understand the agonizing pain a woman feels at losing her baby. He told Heather she needed to get herself up and running again. She did. The following day she packed a bag and left.

'Mum ran away?' Tilly asked.

'Yes. I don't know where she went, but she phoned from time to time over the years and occasionally I saw her. I always gave her some money. She wouldn't talk about her life. I asked her to come home, but she wouldn't. I think she felt ashamed, but Grandpa and I just wanted her back safe and happy. She seemed to go from one bad relationship to another and was always moving. Then she met your father and I was pleased. She seemed to be getting her life back on track. He'd been married before. However, it turned out he was no angel. Heather suspected he was having an affair and eventually he left her for another woman. It was only then she discovered the debt they were in. She was left with nothing, so the two of you came to live with me and your grandpa. You were about four then.'

'I vaguely remember that,' Tilly said. 'I think I saw my father sometimes.'

'Yes, you did. He used to come here and take you out and spend money he didn't have. You'd only been here for a few months when your mother met Dave. Her self-esteem was at an all-time low then and Dave told her everything she wanted to hear. How beautiful she was and so on. He can be a real charmer when he wants to be. Three months later they were married, and you went to live in his house. I knew three months wasn't long enough to get to know someone, but I hoped and prayed it would be all right. The poor girl deserved a break. But it wasn't long before the cracks appeared. He was jealous and manipulative and had a bad temper. He stopped you from seeing your father, then I couldn't see your mother without him being there, and she wasn't allowed to come here either. He never said it outright, it just happened, and quickly got worse. When your grandpa died you were all late for the funeral. I found out after it was because of Dave. The times I was able to see or speak to your mother became less and less. I'm glad you had the sense to get out. I love your mother, but I don't know what else I can do to help her, especially now I'm unwell.' Nancy stopped and the tears she'd so bravely held back escaped and ran down her cheeks.

Tilly immediately went to her and put her arm around her gran and held her close. 'I could die without ever seeing my daughter again,' Nancy said, which made Tilly cry too.

I looked at them holding each other, their upset raw, and I blinked back my own tears. It was so sad and moving. 'I'll do everything I can to help you see Heather,' I said, and I meant it.

'Thank you, love,' Nancy replied, and reached for a tissue. 'You are kind.'

But I was only doing what any compassionate person would do.

While Tilly and her gran dried their eyes and had another cuddle, I took the tray of cold tea into the kitchen and made fresh cups. Nancy thanked me as I returned and set the tray on the coffee table. I then offered around the biscuits she'd bought especially for Tilly.

Feeling a bit better, we drank our tea and tried to talk about other things. Nancy asked Tilly about school and her life with me. But talking for so long and so emotionally had exhausted her. Nancy looked pale and drawn. Once we'd finished our tea, I said I thought we should go soon and she didn't protest. I asked her if there was anything she needed before we left, but she said there wasn't as her good neighbour, Babs, helped her out. I washed up the tea things and she saw us to the front door.

'You will come again soon?' she asked Tilly.

'Yes, next weekend, Gran, I promise.'

'I'll look forward to it,' Nancy said. A lump rose in my throat as I saw my own mother in her: a kind, elderly lady eagerly looking forward to seeing her grandchild again.

'Give your mother my love,' she said, hugging Tilly. 'Tell her I need to see her. If my time is up, I don't want to die with things being difficult between us.'

'I'll tell her,' Tilly said, her voice faltering.

I kissed Nancy goodbye and said I'd be in touch. She thanked me for bringing Tilly.

The door closed slowly behind us as we returned to the car. I didn't immediately start the engine. Tilly and I sat for a few moments, deep in thought. Then Tilly suddenly said, 'I'm going to phone Mum now and tell her.'

'Dave will be there,' I said, glancing at the dashboard clock.

'I don't care. Mum needs to know Gran is very ill. She must see her soon.'

I didn't try to stop her calling. I felt it should be her decision, and she was right, Heather should see her mother while she had the chance. Tilly engaged the speaker on her phone and then pressed the number for the landline at their home. Dave answered.

'It's Tilly. I want to speak to my mother,' she said curtly.

'Yes, of course,' he replied politely, perhaps aware I was listening. 'Can I ask what it's in connection with? I don't want your mother upset any more than she already is.'

'If she's upset, it's because of you,' Tilly snapped. 'Gran could be dying! Put Mum on now!'

I touched her arm, cautioning her to stay calm. I thought Dave was less likely to cooperate if she was rude to him. 'I'll see if she's free,' he said haughtily, and the line went quiet. When he returned he said, 'Your mother is in the bath so can't speak to you right now. Shall I give her a message?' Courteous and respectful – Mr Nice Guy if you didn't know the back story.

'Fuck off!' Tilly yelled and, cutting the call, burst into tears.

I spent some time calming her down and talking to her, then told her not to call the landline again if there was a chance Dave could be there.

'Wait until you see your mother tomorrow and tell her then,' I said. 'Also tell her we'll find a way for her to see her mother.'

'Thank you,' Tilly sniffed.

At that point I didn't know how or when Heather was going to see her mother, only that she should. However, that night as I lay in bed thinking about the problem, I had an idea. Dave worked Monday to Friday and didn't get home until five o'clock. Half-term holiday was in two weeks. Could Heather be persuaded to go behind Dave's back and visit her mother with Tilly one day during that week if I collected her and dropped her off? She might once Tilly had told her how ill Nancy was. While taking a parent of a looked-after child to visit their mother wasn't part of my role as a foster carer, it certainly was as a human being. I doubted Heather would ever get on a bus and go by herself, despite her mother being so unwell – she was far too frightened of Dave – but with Tilly and me by her side I thought she might possibly be persuaded to.

The following morning, I told Tilly of my plan and she liked the idea. She was seeing her mother after school and said she would suggest it to her then. I had foster-carer training that day from nine-thirty to four o'clock, but I struggled to concentrate with everything else that was going on in my life. Foster carers are expected to attend a minimum number of training sessions each year, regardless of how experienced they are. This one was about cognitive behavioural therapy in managing challenging behaviour in looked-after children, but my thoughts wandered. Not only to Tilly, Heather and Nancy, but to Lucy, who'd been very sick again that morning. She'd texted me from work saying she felt so rough she was leaving early.

When I returned home, Lucy was lying on her bed with a bucket beside her. She looked pale and I was worried she wasn't keeping enough food and fluid down to support her and the baby. I suggested she get checked over at the doctors if the sickness didn't pass in the next few days or got worse. She hadn't had any lunch and said she didn't want any dinner, but I persuaded her to have a slice of toast, which I made and took up to her with a glass of water. 'Make sure you drink it,' I said.

When Tilly returned from seeing her mother, I was in the kitchen preparing dinner for the rest of us. I heard her let herself in and I went into the hall.

'How did it go?' I asked.

'Mum's not sure,' she said, annoyed, dropping her school bag on the floor. 'I told her how ill Gran was and we phoned her using my phone. Gran told Mum she needed to see her to put things right between them, but she wasn't sure she could go. I mean, what does it take for her to see her mother! I got angry with her – I know I shouldn't, but I feel sorry for Gran.'

'So do I, love,' I said. 'They need to see each other. Your mother could regret it if she doesn't. Would it help if I spoke to her?'

'It might, but Dave will be there now. I saw his car pulling into the road as I was leaving.'

'And tomorrow you phone your mother from the bus,' I said, thinking aloud. 'So how about if I speak to her on your mobile on Wednesday when you see her again?'

'Yes, that should work.'

'OK, try not to worry.'

But clearly she was very worried indeed.

It might seem ridiculous that we had to go to such lengths to cover up even a phone call, but this wasn't only about trying to help Heather see her mother; it was about keeping her safe. The voluntary work I'd done in a women's refuge had shown me the lengths it was sometimes necessary to go to in order to cover tracks and protect victims of domestic violence.

Tilly said she had a lot of homework that night, although how she was going to concentrate I couldn't imagine. But, to her credit, after dinner she went to her bedroom and worked until 9.30 p.m. when I went up and said I thought she'd done enough. I made her a hot drink and she had a shower before going to bed.

On Wednesday morning I telephoned Tilly's school and asked to speak to Miss Jenkins, who as well as being the deputy head was also the designated teacher for looked-after children. I told her that Tilly was in touch with her grand-mother but we'd discovered she was ill and fighting cancer. It was important the school knew so they could make allow-ances for Tilly if necessary. She thanked me, wished Mrs Watkins a speedy recovery, and said she'd speak to Tilly's subject teachers and advise them.

That afternoon Tilly telephoned me around 4.15 p.m., shortly after arriving at her mother's. They'd already had cross words. 'You try talking to her!' Tilly exclaimed angrily. 'She won't listen to me.' She passed the phone to her mother.

'Tilly doesn't understand,' Heather said in a small, plain-tive voice.

'She's very worried about you and so am I,' I said. 'You can tell me it's none of my business if you wish, but I think you should see your mother as soon as possible. She's not at all well.'

'I know, but it's difficult for me.'

'Why? Your mother doesn't hold any grievance. She just wants to see you again.'

'It's not that, it's Dave. He'd be angry if he found out.'

'Has Tilly explained my suggestion for half term?'

'Yes, but it's not that simple. I'll have to think about it. I'll put Tilly back on.' She returned the phone to her daughter.

'Sorry,' I said to Tilly.

'Thanks for trying. See you later.'

I assumed I'd failed in my attempt to persuade Heather to see her mother, but when Tilly returned that afternoon she sounded surprisingly upbeat and positive. 'Cathy!' she called from the hall. 'Mum has agreed to go in half term.'

'Fantastic,' I said, going to meet her. 'Well done you.'

'I put her on the biggest guilt trip ever, but it worked. I thought we'd go on Wednesday, if that's OK with you. It's one of the days I see Mum, so Dave won't be home until after five o'clock.'

'I'll check in my diary but I'm sure it's clear. Have you asked your gran if that suits her?'

'Yes. She can make Wednesday. She said early afternoon is good for her as it takes her a while to get going in the morning. Mum says she wants you to stay with us in case Dave turns up.'

'All right, but he won't as long as your mother doesn't tell him we're going.'

'That's what I said, but he has such power over her, it's like she thinks he can see through walls.'

It wasn't so unusual for victims of abuse and coercive control to feel this way, such is the power their abuser has over them. I also knew that abusers could be very devious and relentless in finding out what their victims were doing, even following them for days, or setting traps to catch them out. But I didn't tell Tilly that.

I made a note of our intended visit in my diary and also in my log – saying only that Tilly had arranged to see her gran with her mother and I was taking them. I would give a more detailed account after the visit, if it went ahead. I had doubts, but all I could do now was wait for half term and hope Heather didn't lose her nerve.

CHAPTER TWELVE

THE VISIT

The following day Lucy was still being sick, so she made an appointment so see the doctor that morning and I went with her. The doctor examined her and took blood and urine samples. She said Lucy was a little dehydrated and should drink more. She offered to sign her off sick from work, but Lucy said she wanted to go in as she'd feel worse lazing around at home with nothing else to think about but feeling ill. The doctor told us to make a follow-up appointment for the next week.

On Friday Heather began to falter in her decision to see her mother. When Tilly arrived home after visiting her, she said she'd had to persuade her to go all over again. I wasn't wholly surprised and still had big doubts she'd go at all. On Saturday I saw my mother. Adrian and Paula came with me. Lucy was resting and Tilly had gone to see her gran, having telephoned her first to make sure it was OK.

On Monday I attended Tilly's school for her PEP meeting. Miss Jenkins, Tilly and I sat in the meeting room, discussed Tilly's achievements and set targets and goals for the coming year. The student's parents can be invited to the PEP meeting, but it wasn't appropriate in Tilly's case. Her mother would never have attended without Dave and Tilly was adamant she didn't want him there. Miss Jenkins took the opportunity to praise Tilly again for the improvements she was making.

'My gran says it's important I do well in my exams,' she said. And there was me thinking it was because of what I'd been doing!

'How is your gran?' Miss Jenkins asked.

'OK, I guess,' Tilly said. 'I'm going to see her every week now and I'm hoping Mum will see her soon.'

That afternoon Tilly had contact, but when she returned home she was angry with her mother, as she was having doubts again. Tilly said she'd spent most of her time there trying to convince her mother Dave wouldn't find out unless she told him. Then, over the following days in the run-up to half term, Heather kept changing her mind. One day she was going and the next she wasn't. It was all very stressful and eventually Tilly declared, 'It's up to her if she goes. I'm done!'

'Let's just wait and see,' I said. 'You can't do any more.'

As Tilly was now going on the bus to see her gran every weekend and phoning her during the week, I updated Isa. She replied saying she was due to visit Tilly again soon and would like to come at 11 a.m. on the Thursday of half term – the day after Tilly and I were supposed to be taking Heather to see her mother. I emailed back confirming the appointment, made a note in my diary and informed Tilly.

Tilly went to see her mother earlier than usual on Monday. It was the half-term holiday so with no school she arrived at three o'clock instead of four. She returned at the normal time of 5.30. 'Gran spoke to Mum on my phone and she's going to see her,' Tilly told me.

'Excellent.'

However, the following day when Tilly telephoned her mother – as she did on the days she didn't see her – Heather had changed her mind again. Tilly was furious and yelled at her down the phone.

'Leave it for now,' I said. 'We'll go as planned tomorrow. Hopefully when she sees us in the car she'll come. I think she's had too much time to think about it and worry.'

There was nothing more I could say. I felt sorry for Nancy, who must have been even more unsettled by her daughter's indecision than Tilly or I were. The last thing she needed while battling cancer was stress. I decided that if Heather didn't come with us this time, I wouldn't suggest it again. It wasn't fair on Nancy.

Tilly didn't sleep well that Tuesday night and the following morning, while Lucy was being sick, I heard her on the phone confiding in Abby. Tilly tried to phone her mother mid-morning, but she didn't answer. At 12.30 we set off in the car and at that point we really didn't know if Heather would be coming or not. Tilly was very quiet and kept chewing her lip and checking her phone. She tried calling her mother from the car, but she didn't answer.

I parked outside their house just before one o'clock and Tilly got out. I watched her walk up the front path to the door and ring the bell. As she waited and the seconds ticked by, she turned and, looking at me, shrugged a gesture of uncertainty, for clearly her mother had to be in – she never went out alone. She rang the bell again and waited some more. I was worried, imagining all sorts of scenarios involving Dave hurting her. Tilly took out her phone, presumably to call her mother, but before she got the chance the front door finally opened. I caught a glimpse of Heather, then Tilly went in and the door closed. I waited again – five minutes, ten minutes passed. I assumed Tilly was having to persuade her mother to come.

I was about to get out of my car and find out what was going on when their front door opened, and to my surprise Heather came out, followed by Tilly, who slammed the door shut behind them. I could see from their expressions they'd had cross words. Tilly's face was set in frustration and Heather, handbag over one arm, was looking down, agitatedly pulling her coat together at the front. Tilly opened the rear car door and her mother got in. I turned in my seat.

'Hello, Heather, nice to see you again.' I smiled encouragingly.

She nodded and grappled with her seatbelt, tense and nervous. Tilly got in the front passenger seat and let out a heartfelt sigh.

'Well done,' I said to them both, and started the engine.

They were both silent for some time as I drove and the atmosphere was awful. 'Your mother will be pleased to see you,' I said, glancing in the rear-view mirror at Heather.

'Yes,' she said flatly but didn't meet my gaze.

'Cheer up, Mum,' Tilly said brusquely. 'Gran is looking forward to seeing you. Don't spoil it for her. We'll be back long before the pig is.'

'I hope so,' Heather said, her voice slight.

'We will,' I reassured her.

'What time will we leave?' Heather asked, clearly very worried.

'It's up to you,' I said. 'But the latest should be four o'clock so you will be home and settled in plenty of time.'

'Let's make it three o'clock to be safe,' Heather said.

'OK.'

As I pulled up outside Nancy's bungalow, Heather was looking through her side window. 'She's let the garden go,' she remarked as Tilly had.

'Gran's ill, Mum,' Tilly said. 'She can't do it any more.'

'I thought I might tidy it up once I've seen you both in,' I said, releasing my seatbelt.

'But you will stay to take me home?' Heather asked anxiously.

'Yes, of course.'

Nancy must have been watching out for us. As we walked up the path, the front door opened and she stood leaning on her walking stick, ready to greet us.

'Hi, Gran,' Tilly said easily, giving her an affectionate kiss and hug as she went in.

'Mum,' Heather said flatly, and kept going as if to walk by her.

'Don't I get a kiss?' Nancy asked her.

Heather paused and gave her mother a small peck on her cheek and continued down the hall. I thought it was a really odd – cold – reaction. She hadn't seen her mother for two years and the woman was clearly ill. But Heather had the appearance of someone who'd shut off their emotions, presumably in order to cope with living with Dave.

I went in, kissing and hugging Nancy as I went.

'Thanks for bringing them,' she said quietly to me.

'You're welcome. I'm pleased we made it.'

'So am I.' She threw me a knowing look, as if she'd guessed what it had taken to get Heather here.

We went into the living room and Nancy lowered herself into her armchair. Heather perched on the edge of the sofa.

'Take off your coat, Mum,' Tilly said, slipping off her own coat. Heather did as she was told and Tilly draped both coats over the armchair that wasn't being used.

'Would you like to make us some tea?' Gran said to Tilly. 'And there's a lemon sponge cake in the tin. I bought it specially as well as some more of your Jammie Dodgers.'

Tilly went into the kitchen. She seemed quite relaxed and at home here now, while Heather was looking very awkward.

'Sit yourself down,' Nancy told me.

'I thought I might tidy up your front garden while the three of you have a chat,' I said. 'If you tell me where your gardening tools are.'

I think Nancy appreciated they needed some time together. 'That's very kind of you,' she said. 'It could certainly do with weeding. The gardening tools are in the shed at the bottom of the garden. It's unlocked. There are some green bags in there for garden waste.'

'OK. I'll see you later, then,' I said.

I went into the kitchen where the door to the back garden was.

'Shall I bring your tea and cake out to you?' Tilly asked me.

'Yes, please.'

I unlocked the back door and went down the garden to the shed. The rear garden, although bigger than the front, was mainly lawn with shrubs around the edge, and didn't need much tending in winter. Opening the shed, I checked there weren't any spiders about to pounce, and then found a trowel, gardening gloves, kneeling mat and the green sacks for the weeds. As I returned up the garden, I could see Heather and Nancy in the living room to the right of the bungalow and Tilly in the kitchen on the left. It appeared a cosy family scene if you didn't know their history. I hoped Heather and her mother were talking and starting to repair the damage done to their relationship so they could move on. How, I wasn't sure. It was going to be difficult if Heather could only see her mother in the school holidays. The next one wasn't for another seven weeks.

Rather than traipse through the bungalow and let in cold air, I used the side passage to access the front garden. It was a cold, bright day and I was happy to work outside and help Nancy. I began pulling up weeds. I like gardening because you can see immediate improvement. It says thank you. After a few minutes Tilly opened the front door, holding a tray with my tea and cake. 'I'll put it down here,' she said, placing the tray in the porch.

'Thanks, love. How's it going in there?'

'They're starting to talk to each other,' she said.

'Good.' I smiled.

I pulled up some more weeds and then paused to drink my tea and eat the cake. I heard a door to a neighbour's bungalow open and then a woman of a similar age to Nancy appeared over the hedge.

'I'm Babs,' she said. 'Nancy and I are good friends.'

'Hi, I'm Cathy. Nice to meet you.' I put down my cup and plate and went over. 'Nancy has mentioned you.'

'You're Tilly's foster carer?' she asked.

'Yes.'

'Nancy said you might be coming. I'm so pleased you managed to persuade Heather to come.'

'So was I. It was thanks to Tilly, really. It's nice of you to do Nancy's shopping and help her out.'

'I'd do anything for her. She's a lovely person and was very good to me when my husband died three years ago. I was shocked when she told me she had cancer.'

'Yes, but she's doing OK, isn't she? I mean, the treatment is working?'

'I think so. As far as I know. She never complains, but she's had more than her fair share of problems with Heather. That awful husband of hers has stopped her from coming to see her and made things really bad between them. Nancy thought she might die without ever seeing her daughter again.'

'Thankfully she's here now,' I said.

'Yes. You're doing a good job there,' she said, leaning over the hedge for a better view of the garden. 'I can't help Nancy with that, I'm afraid. It takes me all my time to do my own. I have a gardener who comes to do the heavy stuff.'

We chatted for a while longer – about gardening and the weather – and then Babs, who'd come out without a coat, shivered and said she was going indoors. I finished my tea and cake and then continued with the weeding. I worked for over an hour and by the time I'd finished the front garden looked much better. I was pleased with my efforts. I stacked the green bags along the side way, ready for collection, returned the gardening tools to the shed, and then took the tray with my empty cup and plate into the kitchen. As I entered through the back door, I heard Heather crying in the living room and Nancy talking to her in a low, gentle voice. Although I couldn't hear exactly what they were saying, I heard the name Dave mentioned.

I took off my coat, pushed the door to and then washed up my cup, saucer and plate. As I was drying them Tilly came in.

'Mum wants to go now,' she said.

'It's not three o'clock yet,' I said, glancing at the wall clock. 'We can stay for a while longer if she wishes.'

'She's worried Dave will come home early. I think Gran is tired anyway.'

'All right.'

I returned the tea towel to its hook and, picking up my coat, went into the living room with Tilly. Heather was sitting on the sofa wiping her eyes, and while not crying, Nancy looked close to tears.

'Bye, Mum, I have to go,' Heather said, and immediately stood. 'You understand why?'

'Yes,' Nancy replied stoically. 'But you can't carry on like this. It will be the death of you.'

Heather looked at her mother. Overwhelmed and not knowing what to say, she fled the room. We heard the front door open and shut behind her. 'I'll go to her while you say goodbye to your gran,' I said to Tilly. Nancy had made no attempt to get out of her chair and looked physically and emotionally drained.

Slipping on my coat, I said goodbye to Nancy and let myself out the front door. Heather was standing by my car. I pressed the fob to open the doors and she slid into the rear seat. I got in beside her.

'Are you OK?' I asked, concerned. She wasn't crying now but looked very anxious.

She shook her head and stared straight ahead.

'Do you want to talk about it?' I asked.

'No. I need to take one of my pills.'

'Shall I get you a glass of water?' I asked, thinking the pills were in her handbag.

'I haven't got them with me. They're at home.'

'Oh. How often do you have to take them?' I asked, wondering if they had to be taken at regular intervals, in which case we would need to leave straight away.

'I take one when I'm not coping or I'm very unhappy,' she said, so I assumed they were antidepressants.

Not wanting to leave Heather alone, I sat with her, and then a few minutes later the door to the bungalow opened and Tilly came out. I immediately got out. 'Is your gran all right?' I asked.

'Yes, she's going to have a lie-down. I said I'd phone her later.'

I got into the driver's seat and Tilly into the passenger seat, then I began the drive home. The atmosphere was heavy again. Every so often I glanced in the rear-view mirror at Heather. She was looking agitatedly out of her side window.

'We've got plenty of time,' I said. But I was relieved when I drew up outside her house.

'His car's not here,' Tilly said.

Heather seemed reassured, but I felt bad returning her to a house that held nothing but misery and abuse, as if I was complicit in allowing it to continue. But what else could I do?

'Will you be all right?' I asked her.

She nodded and got out.

'Are you staying?' I said to Tilly. It was only 3.30 and according to the contact arrangements she could stay until five o'clock as Dave wouldn't be home until then.

'No, I've had enough today,' Tilly said. 'I'll see Mum in. Will you wait for me?'

'Yes, of course.'

I watched them disappear into the house and finally allowed myself to breathe. We'd done it. Nancy had seen her daughter and gone some way to mending the past. Whether they would get the chance to see each other again I didn't know, but I agreed wholeheartedly with what Nancy had told Heather: 'You can't carry on like this. It will be the death of you.' I'd just learnt that Heather's life was so awful she relied on antidepressants to get her through. It was sad and shocking. So often in fostering the child arrives with one set of problems, then you discover that's the tip of the iceberg and worse is going on in their family.

CHAPTER THIRTEEN

'I CAN'T BELIEVE IT!'

'Did you know your mother takes antidepressants?' I asked Tilly as I drove us home, having taken Heather home.

'Yes. Dave got them for her from the Internet.'

'From the Internet?' I asked, shocked.

'He said it was a proper pharmaceutical website.'

'I hope it was. Didn't she go to the doctor and get diagnosed?'

'No. He told Mum it would look bad on her if she did and called her mental. He scared her off going to see the doctor.'

'Probably because he knew the doctor would ask your mother some questions about why she was depressed.'

'I know,' Tilly said despondently. 'I told Mum I would go with her and we could make an appointment during the day when he was at work. But she was too scared and thought he'd find out.'

I nodded. This wasn't unusual for a victim of domestic violence. They are often petrified into inaction like a rabbit caught in a car's headlamps and can't make even the most basic decisions for themselves.

'Thanks for taking us to see Gran,' Tilly added.

'You're welcome, love. I'm pleased your mother came. Will she be able to go again?'

'I don't know. I don't think so. While you were doing the garden, Gran was trying to persuade Mum to stay and live with her, but she just kept crying and saying it was impossible and Dave would find her. It was very upsetting and frustrating. I could shake Mum sometimes. I mean, I got away from him, so she should.'

'Yes, I know.' But I was aware of all the reasons why Heather felt trapped. Tilly was younger, free-spirited and hadn't been subjected to the years of abuse Heather had, which had worn her into the ground.

That evening, before dinner, Tilly telephoned her gran but didn't talk for long, as Babs was there. Tilly said her gran sounded quite cheerful and Babs sent her love.

'That's nice,' I said. 'It's so important to have good friends, especially in times of difficulty.' With the help of Babs, Nancy was managing to remain upbeat and positive, despite her illness and worries about her daughter. Tilly had Abby, while Heather, through no fault of her own, was socially isolated and had no one apart from her daughter and possibly her mother – if she dared to see or phone her again, which I doubted. While family support is invaluable, so too I think is a really good friend who is likely to be of a similar age and on the same wavelength, and therefore able to empathize in a way that a parent may not.

We all ate together that evening. Lucy felt able to join us, as she was feeling a bit better, having only been sick once when she first woke in the morning. I was still waiting to meet Darren again, and his parents for the first time. Lucy said she was 'on it' and also that she and Darren were viewing some more flats on Saturday, one of which seemed promising.

* * *

The following day Isa visited us as arranged. It's a requirement of the child's social worker to visit a looked-after child in placement at least every six weeks. During their visit they spend time alone with the child in case they want to discuss issues they don't feel comfortable talking about in front of their foster carer. However, to begin with, Isa wanted me present, so the three of us settled in the living room. Tilly and I began by updating Isa about our visit to Tilly's gran the day before, as Isa took some notes.

'Are there any plans for your mother to see your gran again?' Isa asked, as I had done.

'No,' Tilly replied. 'She's too scared of Dave.'

'I don't want you placing yourself in danger with him,' Isa warned.

'I won't. He doesn't scare me,' Tilly replied.

'And the contact between you and your mother is going well?' Isa asked.

'Yes, although I get angry with her sometimes. I know I shouldn't,' Tilly admitted.

'What makes you angry with her?' Isa asked.

'Just the way she is. She won't help herself.'

Isa nodded as she wrote. 'And your stepfather hasn't been at the house while you've been there?'

'No.'

'Good, so contact with your mother is working,' she said as she wrote. 'And telephone contact? How is that going?'

'OK, I guess. I call her from the bus so Dave's not there.'

'I don't think I need ask but is contact with your gran going well?' Isa asked with a smile.

'Yes, I love her so much!' Tilly declared. Her face lit up, as it always did when she mentioned her gran.

Tilly continued by telling Isa how much she enjoyed seeing her gran and how she made her tea and did some housework – dusting and vacuuming her bungalow. Isa asked about the treatment Nancy was receiving and we told her what we knew. Isa then asked Tilly about her own health, and school, and praised her for the changes she was making. She asked me in passing if I had a new supervising social worker yet and I said I didn't. She continued by asking Tilly about her routine, bedtime, meals, what she liked to do in her spare time and so on. These were standard questions asked by the social worker as part of their visit. With a younger child the foster carer supplies most of this information, but clearly Tilly was of an age where she could answer for herself. I either nodded in agreement or commented when appropriate – for example, in respect of our mobile-phone policy.

'I've had to remind Tilly a few times to switch off her phone at night,' I said.

'But I like talking to Abby,' Tilly complained.

'I know, but you need your sleep,' I said, and thankfully Isa agreed.

Isa then asked for some time alone with Tilly and I left them in the living room.

After about fifteen minutes they appeared, and Isa completed her visit by having a look around the house – part of each social-worker visit. We saw her to the door where she said goodbye and wished us a nice afternoon.

Tilly had arranged for Abby to come round that afternoon and sleep over, as it was the half-term holiday. I made Tilly and myself a soup and sandwich lunch, and then Tilly telephoned her mother earlier than usual. They didn't speak for long and, once they'd finished, I asked her to check her bedroom was tidy, as I knew she and Abby would want to spend time there, as young people do.

Abby arrived at two o'clock with an overnight bag, having caught the bus. I told her to make herself at home and left the two of them in the kitchen pouring drinks, which they took up to Tilly's bedroom. With Adrian and Lucy at work and Paula at college – it didn't close for half term – I made the most of my free time and set about doing some admin work on the computer in the front room. Once I'd finished, I began preparing dinner for later, including an apple crumble, which I'd serve with hot custard.

We ate at 6.30 p.m. and it was a lively meal with six of us all talking and eating. Sammy sat under the table waiting for titbits. I love these meals when all my family plus any friends are together. I hoped that when Lucy moved out she and Darren would join us regularly, and eventually their little one too. Lucy ate a small amount of the main course but plenty of crumble and custard, and drank two glasses of water, which was good.

Everyone helped clear the table and load the dishwasher, then Tilly and Abby disappeared up to Tilly's room again. They had their music on, not excessively loud, but the rest of us could hear it. Lucy went to bed at nine o'clock, so I asked them to turn it down. They appreciated why. Later I checked Abby had everything she needed for the night and then I went to bed around 10.30. By eleven o'clock the house was quiet – even Tilly and Abby were asleep, having worn themselves out from talking and laughing. The temperature had dropped outside and flurries of snow were forecast in some areas.

* * *

The following morning I woke to the sound of Lucy in the bathroom suffering from morning sickness again. I checked she was coping all right and then opened my bedroom curtains to find a thin layer of snow covering the landscape outside. Not enough to cause disruption, but sufficient to smooth away the edges of reality and paint everything a dreamy white. I told Lucy, who managed a small smile, and Adrian and Paula admired it as they got up.

Adrian was using his car to go to work and I assumed the main roads had been gritted. Paula and Lucy were catching buses and I warned them to be careful, as the pavements could be slippery – especially Lucy, who shouldn't fall over in her condition. I told them to text me if the buses weren't running and I'd take them in the car, but they texted to say they were running, although a bit later than timetabled.

Abby and Tilly surfaced around ten o'clock. I made them some breakfast and Abby left at 11.30 to catch the bus home. By then the snow was melting fast. Tilly was due to see her mother that afternoon and I asked her if she was planning on going earlier, as she had done on Monday. I thought it was a good idea, as there was a chance of more snow later.

'Yes, I'll phone her now to let her know,' Tilly said. 'Otherwise she won't open the front door.' Tilly had never had a front door key to her house, as her stepfather had said she might lose it. Personally, I thought this was more about control than the key being misplaced.

Tilly went up to her room to make the call. She did most of her phoning from there. Adrian, Lucy and Paula usually went to their rooms to make and take calls too, partly for privacy, but also because it would have been impractical for all of us to be downstairs talking on our phones.

Ten minutes later Tilly came to find me, looking worried. 'Mum's not answering,' she said. 'She never goes out. Where can she be?'

'Try again later,' I said. 'She might be in the bathroom or putting out the rubbish. There are plenty of reasons why she might not be answering.' Although I was concerned. Tilly was right, her mother didn't go out, and there were other, more sinister possibilities for why Heather wasn't answering the phone. For example, it crossed my mind that, depressed, she'd made an attempt on her life, or Dave had assaulted her so badly she couldn't get to the phone or was in hospital. The last of these occurred to Tilly when ten minutes later she came to me again, as her mother still hadn't answered.

'I bet that pig has hurt her,' she said. 'I'm going to go to the house.'

'No, you're not,' I said. 'It might not be safe and you can't get in.'

'I'll climb in through a window.'

'They're not likely to have left windows open in the middle of winter,' I pointed out. 'And I still think there could be a rational explanation for why your mother isn't answering. Perhaps she's having a sleep. Wait until one o'clock and if she still hasn't answered, we'll do something.' Although I wasn't sure what. Were there grounds for calling the police and asking them to check on Heather and break in if necessary? They would do if an elderly or vulnerable person could be at risk. Or should we go there and see if there was anything amiss? It wasn't really a matter for Isa, so I didn't phone her.

Tilly agreed to wait until one o'clock. I busied myself as the minutes ticked by while Tilly periodically phoned her mother, without any reply. I was painfully aware that if Heather was lying unconscious from an overdose or a severe beating, we could be losing valuable time. They don't tell you about situations like this when you first sign up to foster or in training, but I'd found before – as I'm sure other foster carers have – that circumstances sometimes arise that are outside our remit or experience, so we rely on common sense.

'OK, let's go to the house,' I said. It was one o'clock and Heather still hadn't answered the phone. 'If your mother doesn't come to the front door, we'll call the police.'

'What do you think could have happened to her?' Tilly asked, panicking.

'Possibly nothing, but let's check.' I was trying to stay calm and keep an open mind for Tilly's sake, so I could think rationally, although I felt anything but calm.

Thankfully the roads were clear of snow. Tilly was quiet as I drove, sitting tense and upright, her phone in her hand and staring straight ahead. I was still clinging to the hope that there was a rational explanation for Heather not answering the phone, but like Tilly I couldn't think of one. Tilly called her mother again en route and once more as we entered her road, but she still didn't pick up. My concern was growing – I was really worried now.

I parked outside the house and we got out. All the windows at the front were closed and net curtains covered them. Tilly pressed the doorbell, long and hard, sufficient to wake anyone who might be sleeping. But not if they were unconscious, I thought. And realistically, if Heather had been asleep, surely all the phone calls would have woken her, unless the phone had been unplugged. All sorts of possibilities were racing through my mind. I tried to peer through the letter box but the draught excluder covering it stopped my view. Tilly looked through too and then shouted, 'Mum! Are you there?'

There was no reply.

'Can we get round the back of the house?' I asked her. It was a semi-detached house with a side passageway. I'd already noticed the six-foot-high wooden gate.

'The gate's bolted, but I can climb over,' Tilly said, heading towards it. 'I've done it before.'

'Tilly, be careful,' I warned her.

With trepidation, I followed her to the side of the house where she pushed the refuse bin up against the gate, then jumped up onto it. My heart lurched. 'Be careful,' I said again, trying to reach up and steady her as much as I could. 'I'm sure you shouldn't be doing this.' I had a sudden flash of her falling and hurting herself and me trying to explain to the paramedics and her social worker why she'd been on the bin.

I hardly dared to breathe as Tilly grabbed the top of the gate and hauled one leg over and then the other. She dropped to the ground on the other side with a small cry.

'What's the matter?' I asked, horrified.

'It's OK, I've just got a splinter from the gate.'

Thank goodness that was all, I thought. I heard two bolts slide and then the gate opened. Tilly was sucking her finger. 'I'll get the splinter out later,' I said.

I followed her round to the back of the house. All the windows were closed here too. She tried the back door, but it was locked. However, unlike the front there weren't any net curtains here, so we peered through the glass of the kitchen window and then the living room. Both rooms were neat and tidy, with no sign of a disturbance or Heather. Tilly banged on the glass of the living-room window and then rattled the back door as I peered through the windows again. We waited and listened, but there was no sound or sign of life inside the house. Both rooms were meticulously tidy. The work surfaces, sink and draining board in the kitchen gleamed as if they hadn't been used.

'Is your house always this tidy?' I asked Tilly.

'Yes. Dave doesn't like a mess. What are we going to do?'

'Call the police,' I said. I stepped away from the window, glanced up at the back of the house again and took my phone from my pocket. I was about to press 999 for the emergency services when Tilly's phone began to ring. I paused as she quickly checked her caller display.

'It's Gran!' she cried, even more worried. 'Why's she calling? Oh no, what's happened!'

She put the phone to her ear and listened. I watched her expression change from blind panic to incredulity, and then something that looked like relief.

'What is it?' I asked as she listened.

'Mum's with Gran,' she said.

'What?' I asked, astounded and thinking I had misheard.

'Mum is at Gran's,' she repeated.

I continued to watch Tilly's expression as she listened to what she was being told, and I struggled to make sense of what was happening.

After a few minutes she moved the phone slightly away from her ear and asked me, 'Can we go to Gran's now?'

'Yes. I suppose so.'

She put the phone to her ear again. 'Gran, Cathy will bring me,' she said, and ended the call.

'Mum has left Dave!' she cried, elated. 'I can't believe it.'

Neither could I!

CHAPTER FOURTEEN

REVENGE

Struggling to believe what had happened, Tilly and I returned down the sideway of her parents' house and closed the gate behind us. We couldn't lock it, as the bolts were on the inside. Stunned into silence, we got into my car. As I drove, heading towards Nancy's bungalow, two miles away, Tilly told me what her gran had said on the phone about how her mother had arrived at her home. It seemed Dave had been particularly vindictive that morning, following Heather around and shouting abuse at her until she'd finally snapped. Realizing she had nothing to lose, she had waited until he'd gone to work and then fled the house.

'Why now?' I asked.

'Gran said it was a combination of losing me and seeing her again.'

I nodded. It made sense. I knew that victims of sustained and long-term domestic violence could suddenly snap, sometimes with devastating and irreversible results – when losing control, they turned on their abuser and killed them in a fit of rage. Thankfully Heather hadn't done that but run away instead; something she should have done years ago.

I drew up and parked outside Nancy's bungalow where only a couple of days before I'd brought Heather. How much had changed in just forty-eight hours, I mused. From what Tilly had said, it seemed our visit might have been the catalyst for Heather leaving Dave. As soon as the car stopped, Tilly released her seatbelt, jumped out and ran up the garden path. I joined her at the door as we waited for the bell to be answered. It was some moments before Nancy opened the door, steadying herself on her walking stick.

'Where's Mum?' Tilly asked, slightly panicky, perhaps thinking she'd gone again.

'Calm down, love. She's in the living room,' Nancy said. 'She didn't want to answer the door in case it was Dave.'

Tilly rushed down the hall, crying, 'Mum!'

'You could do with a security spyhole in your door,' I said to Nancy as I went in.

'I usually check who's there from the bedroom window,' she said. 'But I guessed it was you. If Dave does turn up here, I'll hit him with this,' she said, raising her walking stick. I smiled.

'You will stay for a while?' she asked, closing the door. 'At least for a cup of tea.'

'Yes, thanks. And I'll need to firm up the contact arrangements for today so I can tell Tilly's social worker. As far as she's aware, Tilly is seeing her mother at her house this afternoon, so I'll need to let her know.'

I followed Nancy slowly down the hall and into the living room. Clearly her ankle was paining her today. Tilly was sitting with her mother on the sofa and Heather had her head resting on Tilly's shoulder like a child might.

'Hello, how are you?' I asked her.

She raised her head. 'I don't believe I've left him,' she said, bemused.

'Neither do I, Mum,' Tilly declared, elated. 'And you're never going back!'

'No, I wouldn't dare go back now. He'd kill me for sure,' Heather said. 'But I haven't any clothes with me.'

'I'm sure that can be sorted,' I said.

'I've told you already, I've got some money put away for a rainy day,' Nancy said to Heather. 'It's enough to buy you what you need.'

'And Heather might be entitled to some welfare assistance if she has nothing,' I added.

'I'll make us a cup of tea,' Nancy said, but she sounded breathless.

'Shall I do it?' I offered.

'Yes, please. I'll have a glass of water too, if you don't mind.' She made her way across the room and sat heavily in her armchair. She looked rather red in the face.

I went into the kitchen, poured a glass of water and handed it to her. 'Are you feeling all right?' I asked.

'Yes, just a bit out of breath. It's all the excitement.'

'Just sit there for a bit and take it easy.'

I returned to the kitchen and made the tea. I was worried about Nancy and the effect all of this was having on her. She was undergoing chemotherapy and had clearly had a huge shock this morning when she'd opened her front door to find Heather there, on top of their emotional reunion on Wednesday.

I carried the tray of teas into the living room and handed them out, then I sat in the other armchair across from Nancy. I looked at Heather. 'Well done,' I told her.

'Yes, well done, Mum,' Tilly said.

Heather gave a small, nervous laugh and I noticed her hand shook as she took a sip of tea. 'I can't believe I've done it,' she said with a mixture of apprehension and relief. 'But he'll come looking for me, for sure. He won't let me go that easily.'

'As I said before, if he does, we'll call the police,' Nancy said firmly.

'If necessary, you may have to take out an injunction,' I added.

'We'll do whatever it takes,' Nancy said, and drank her water.

'I walked all the way here,' Heather said with a touch of pride, setting down her cup. 'I've only got these clothes and my coat and shoes. I haven't even got a toothbrush.'

'I've got a spare one,' Nancy said. 'And later, Tilly can help me make up the bed in the spare room for you. That hasn't been used in a long while.'

'Not since I stayed here with you and Grandpa when I was a child,' Tilly said.

Nancy smiled at the recollection. 'Dear me, how much has happened since then,' she sighed.

'I still can't believe I've actually done it,' Heather said again, her voice unsteady.

'Well, you have, Mum, and I'm proud of you,' Tilly said, giving her another hug.

'After you brought me here on Wednesday,' Heather said to me, 'I spent all night lying awake thinking about my dear mum and all the things she's done for me over the years, and that she was ill now and I couldn't see her. I haven't had any sleep for two days. Then Dave started having a go at me first thing this morning, shouting, pushing me around and threatening me. Suddenly I heard a buzzing noise in my head and something snapped. I locked myself in the bathroom and waited until he'd gone to work, then I went downstairs, put on my coat and shoes, picked up my handbag and walked out. Just like that. I was like a zombie and just kept walking. I didn't think about what I was doing.' Her whole body shuddered as she spoke. 'I was terrified he was coming after me and that Mum wouldn't be in. I don't know what I'd have done if she'd been out.'

'But I was in,' Nancy said. 'So you're safe now, Heather.'

'I've only got these clothes,' Heather said again, still in a state of shock.

'Do you need anything today?' I asked her practically. I was used to children arriving in what they stood up in.

'Just some clean underwear,' she said. 'But I daren't go out to the shops today. He might see me.'

'Tell me your size and I'll buy what you need and bring it here when I collect Tilly.'

'Thank you. I'm not sure what I need. I can't think straight, really. A face flannel maybe.'

'OK, I'll get one and some toiletries. What about a nightdress?'

'Yes, please. Thank you, that is kind of you,' Nancy said. 'Tell me what I owe you.' But I wouldn't be asking her for payment. Heather had arrived with nothing and Nancy only had her pension and a few savings.

'We could go clothes shopping tomorrow, Mum,' Tilly suggested eagerly.

'I don't think I'll be up to that,' Heather replied quietly.

'And I'm not sure it's a good idea to go out yet,' Nancy said. 'Give it a few days. Dave is bound to be angry when he finds you've gone.'

'You could order some more clothes online for your mother,' I suggested to Tilly. 'To see her through until she can get her belongings from home.'

'I'll bring my laptop with me tomorrow,' Tilly told her mother.

I drank my tea and then, before I left, I arranged to come back to collect Tilly at six o'clock unless Isa told me otherwise, in which case I'd telephone. I let myself out and as I went down the path Babs, Nancy's good neighbour, was coming up her path. We both paused.

'Everything all right?' she asked.

'Yes, Heather is here.'

'I know. I dropped off some bread and milk earlier. Heather had just arrived. I got the shock of my life. So she's finally left him. Good for her. Let's hope she doesn't go back.'

'Absolutely,' I agreed.

We exchanged a few more words and then I returned to my car but didn't start the engine. I needed to phone Isa first and let her know. Her voicemail was on, so I left a message saying Tilly was spending the afternoon at her gran's and her mother was there, having left Dave. I said I would collect Tilly at six o'clock and asked that she phoned me to confirm contact arrangements for next week when Tilly would be at school again. Clearly Tilly wouldn't be visiting her mother at home again, but at her grandmother's.

I drove into town, bought Heather plenty of underwear, socks – as it was winter and she was wearing trousers – a nightdress, face flannel and toiletries. I also bought the groceries we needed. I returned home, unpacked our food and began to prepare some vegetables for dinner later.

Isa returned my call. She was relieved that Heather had left Dave and said she would speak to her later when she telephoned Nancy. She confirmed it was all right for Tilly to stay there this afternoon, and to visit one afternoon over the weekend as she had been doing. Isa assumed, as I had, that future contact would now take place at Nancy's, in which case she'd need to visit Nancy next week to assess her and her bungalow and make sure it was suitable. We said goodbye and I finished making the casserole.

Paula arrived home at 5.30 and I briefly explained what had happened and then left her in charge of dinner, which was in the oven, while I went to collect Tilly. As I entered the road where Nancy lived I found myself watching out for any sign of Dave, probably much as Heather had done. Nancy had been right when she'd said it would be wise for Heather to stay indoors for a few days to give Dave time to cool off. He would be furious when he found out she'd escaped, and the weekend was coming up when he wouldn't be at work. However, if he did come to the bungalow, I knew Nancy wouldn't hesitate to call the police.

Tilly answered the door. 'Everything all right?' I asked as I went in.

'Yes. Mum's having a lie-down. I made up the bed in the spare room.'

'Here are the things your mum needs,' I said, passing her the carrier bag.

'I'll leave them outside her room,' Tilly said, and propped the bag against a closed door to our right.

'Are you ready to go?' I asked her.

'Can't I stay the night? Gran says I could sleep on the sofa.'

I'd been half expecting this. 'No, love, I've spoken to Isa and we've agreed I'm taking you home. I'll explain it to your gran.'

Tilly came with me into the living room where Nancy was in her armchair, clearly also very tired.

'I won't keep you,' I said. 'But I thought I should explain. I've spoken to Isa and she's said I should take Tilly home with me now. She can visit you again over the weekend. Isa is going to see you next week to clarify contact arrangements.'

'Yes, she telephoned,' Nancy said, stifling a yawn. She could barely keep her eyes open.

'I'm going to see Mum here from now on,' Tilly added. 'Monday, Wednesday and Friday.'

'Yes, the same times as before,' I said.

'I want to come here tomorrow and Sunday.'

'No, just one day for now,' I said. 'That's what has been agreed so far.'

'Make it tomorrow, love,' Nancy said wearily. 'But I'm worried about you coming on the bus. It's the weekend, so Dave won't be at work.' Clearly we were thinking the same.

'I'll bring and collect Tilly tomorrow,' I said.

'Thank you,' Nancy replied, her eyes beginning to close.

'We'll leave you to it,' I said, and she nodded.

Tilly kissed her gran goodbye and we quietly left the room. Tilly didn't want to disturb her mother, so we let ourselves out. I checked the front door was properly shut.

'What a day!' I said to Tilly, as we got into the car.

'I hope Mum's OK. What do you think Dave will do?' she asked, worried. 'He'll be home by now.'

'I expect he'll be very angry, but try not to worry. Your mum is safe with your gran.'

I started the car and pulled away. 'He'll know Mum is at Gran's,' Tilly said, still concerned. 'She doesn't have anywhere else to go.'

'If he goes there making trouble, your gran will call the police. If he should arrive tomorrow while you're there, don't confront him. Just keep the doors locked and call 999.' Tilly could be feisty at times and I knew she'd stood up to Dave in the past. I didn't want her doing it again, for her own safety.

She hadn't replied. Head down, she was concentrating on her phone.

'Tilly, are you listening to me?' I asked.

'Yes,' she said a little curtly. 'But I'd really like to see him suffer for all the pain he's caused Mum.'

'I know, but you are not the person to punish him. Keep right away from him. He's dangerous. Do you understand?'

'Yes,' she said testily, and continued texting.

The casserole was ready when we arrived home and Paula had laid the table and was warming the bread rolls to go with it. We all had dinner together, including Lucy, who for the second day in a row was feeling a bit better, having only been sick once in the morning. We talked about our day as we ate, although Tilly was subdued. She told everyone her mother had left Dave and was now living with her gran, but that was all she said.

After dinner everyone helped clear away the dishes, then went off to do their own thing. Tilly went to her room to phone Abby. I telephoned my mother and arranged to visit her on Sunday, weather permitting. She worried if bad weather was forecast and preferred us not to go. There was no snow or ice forecast for the weekend, but I said I'd make a final decision on Sunday morning and call her. I then wrote up my log notes before trying to unwind by reading a book. Tilly spent all evening in her room on her phone, talking to Abby, her mother and gran. She finally came down at nine-thirty for a drink of water to take up to bed.

'Mum says thanks for the things you bought her,' she said. 'Can we go there straight after breakfast tomorrow?'

'We'll leave around eleven-thirty so you are there for midday. Contact is set for the afternoon,' I said.

'But I want to see them for longer. I can go on the bus if you like,' she persisted.

'No. I'm taking and collecting you tomorrow for everyone's peace of mind.'

'I'll be going on the bus on Monday,' she said, wanting her own way.

'That's different. Dave will have had time to calm down by then, and he'll be at work.'

She huffed, pulled a face, looked as though she was going to argue the point, but then thought better of it and accepted what I was saying. 'I'm going to bed,' she said brusquely and left the room.

'Good night, love,' I called after her, but she didn't reply.

Young people of Tilly's age are responsible in many ways, but don't always have the experience or maturity to spot danger, and can sometimes act impulsively without due consideration for their or others' safety. It's more difficult to put boundaries in place for older children, but it's just – if not more – important. They have greater freedom and are therefore exposed to more danger.

I thought about Dave that evening and how he would be reacting to finding Heather gone. Perhaps he'd be relieved and not seek revenge, although I didn't think so. Tilly had escaped from his grasp and now Heather had too. From what I knew of him, I thought he was likely to be very angry, although how that would manifest itself I didn't know.

It was Sunday before we found out.

CHAPTER FIFTEEN

'WHAT A DREADUL WORLD WE LIVE IN'

O n Saturday, as I took Tilly with her laptop to her gran's, it occurred to me they would need a credit or debit card to buy clothes online for Heather. I knew she didn't own any cards – Dave had seen to that – and I doubted Nancy had shopped online before. So rather than just dropping off Tilly, I went in to check. Both Heather and her mother were look-ing much brighter after a good night's sleep. Heather told me she hadn't slept so well in years, although she had woken a couple of times wondering where she was. I explained to them both about online shopping. They were aware of it, but, as I thought, neither of them had actually shopped online. Nancy said she had a credit and debit card they could use.

'Use the credit card,' I said. 'It's more secure.' Then to Tilly, 'Make sure you ask your gran before you buy anything.' I didn't want her racking up a big bill.

I said goodbye and returned home. Lucy and Darren had been viewing a flat that morning, and Lucy telephoned as they left the letting agent and said they'd really liked the flat and had put down a deposit. They would know for certain it was theirs once the agents had completed their checks. I could hear the excitement in her voice and I was pleased for her, although I was also sad. Lucy was the first of my children to be leaving home for good. Adrian had gone away to university but had returned home once he'd completed his degree. I reminded myself that Lucy was an adult now; she was expecting a baby and setting up home with her partner.

'Fantastic,' I said. 'I'll look forward to seeing it.'

'As soon as we sign the lease and have the keys you will be the first to see it,' she said. 'The agent told us it should be about two weeks.' She then said goodbye and that she would be back this evening.

I'd seen the estate agent's photos of the flat on their website and it looked very nice. Modern, freshly decorated; it was in a small block only a mile or so away. It had two bedrooms and was on the first floor. It was being let unfurnished so I would help buy furniture and baby equipment nearer the time.

I collected Tilly from her gran's at six o'clock. I didn't go in. I rang the bell and Tilly let herself out, calling goodbye as she left. She seemed very relaxed and at home there now. As I drove, she told me she'd spent about eighty pounds on clothes for her mother, which Nancy had said was fine. Heather now had another complete change of clothes so she could wash what she was wearing. Hopefully she'd be able to collect her other clothes from home before too long. If not, Nancy had said they would replace everything a few items at a time. All that mattered was that Heather was safe now.

On Sunday we all went to see my mother, including Adrian, who often went there separately with Kirsty. It felt like a proper family outing and my mother was delighted to see us all.

'You look very well,' she said to Lucy as she welcomed us at the door with kisses.

'I feel fine, Nana,' Lucy said brightly. She hadn't been sick at all that morning and I was hoping that was the end of it now.

I'd booked a table at a local pub restaurant for lunch. As we couldn't all fit in my car, I took Mum, Lucy and Tilly, while Adrian and Paula walked there. They set off first. We met up in the foyer, were shown to our table and ordered drinks. As we waited for our food to arrive, we talked and Mum went out of her way to include Tilly. She was very happy to tell Mum about her gran, how her mother was living there now and she would be soon.

'I'm not sure that is an option, love,' I said gently, not wanting her to raise her hopes unrealistically.

'Why not?' she asked.

'There are only two bedrooms for one thing and –' I didn't get any further.

'There's a dining room that Gran doesn't use any more. She said we could turn it into a bedroom for me. She's going to tell my social worker when she sees her next week.'

'OK, but we'll have to wait and see what Isa says.'

Apart from the matter of the bedroom, Isa would need to be satisfied that Heather was capable of looking after her daughter and that the family set-up – as well as the bungalow – was suitable for Tilly. Nancy was elderly and battling cancer, while Heather was struggling with her own problems. Would they be able to provide what a fourteen-year-old needed or would it be too much for them? Even if Isa felt that living with her gran and mother was in Tilly's best interest, it wouldn't happen overnight. She'd have to complete various assessments, police-check Nancy and Heather, and be as sure as she could be that if Tilly went there she would be safe and flourish. Parenting doesn't need to be perfect, but it must be 'good enough'.

We returned to Mum's for a cup of tea and a slice of her homemade sponge cake. Then Adrian did a few jobs around the house, including removing leaves from the storm drain outside. We left shortly after six o'clock. It was a cloudy, moonless night, but the roads weren't icy. On the drive home Tilly's phone rang. 'It's Gran,' she said when she saw the caller display. I glanced at her in the rear-view mirror as she put the phone to her ear. She listened for a few moments and then said, 'We're in the car. She's driving. OK, I'll tell her.'

'Everything OK?' I asked as she finished.

'Gran wants you to phone her once we're home.'

'What's it about?' I asked, puzzled.

'She wouldn't tell me.'

I could see Tilly was worried, as I was, and my immediate thought was that Dave had got to Heather and she'd either returned home or he'd beaten her. Nancy would want to tell me first and then break the news to Tilly.

'I'm sure it's nothing much,' Lucy said from the back seat, trying to reassure Tilly.

'How would you know?' Tilly said under her breath.

Thankfully Lucy didn't retaliate.

I remained concerned though, and as soon as we were home I went to my bedroom and, closing the door, made the call. Nancy answered straight away. 'It's Cathy. Is everything all right?'

'We've had a shock,' she said. 'I didn't want to tell Tilly in case she did anything silly. I knew you were out all day, which is why I didn't phone earlier.' My heart began beating furiously as I thought my worst fears were about to be realized.

'Whatever's happened?' I asked, sitting on the bed.

'Dave came here during the night. He brought all Heather's belongings in plastic bin liners and left them in the front garden. We didn't see him. Babs saw the bags first thing this morning and knocked on our door. Heather was hysterical when she saw them and knew Dave had been just outside her bedroom window. He must have been very quiet because we didn't hear a thing. Heather is still badly shaken and worried he'll come back. I telephoned the police, but he hasn't done anything illegal so they can't arrest him. If he threatens Heather or keeps coming back, they'll speak to him.'

'Oh, dear,' I said, although I was actually quite relieved. I'd been expecting far worse than this. 'He did similar with Tilly's belongings, bagged them all up,' I said. 'Hopefully that will be an end to it. Did he send all Heather's belongings?'

'Yes, everything, even her rubbish. And surprisingly the mobile phone Tilly gave her. We've unpacked some of the bags and Tilly can help us with the rest tomorrow. Heather is still pretty upset, so I'd better tell Tilly myself.'

'Unless you want me to?' I suggested.

'Yes, please, if you wouldn't mind. I'm exhausted and I didn't want Heather speaking to Tilly and getting hysterical again and then upsetting her.'

'Don't worry, I'll tell Tilly and reassure her.'

'Thank you. Give her my love and say we'll see her after school tomorrow. Will she be coming by bus?'

'In view of this, I think I might collect her from school and bring her to you, at least for tomorrow.'

'Thanks, love.'

We said goodbye, and I opened my bedroom door to find Tilly. She was waiting outside, listening. She would have heard my side of the conversation only.

'They are both all right,' I said. I then told her what Nancy had told me, adding that I didn't think Dave would go to the bungalow again, as he'd taken all her mother's belongings. But to be on the safe side I would collect her after school and take her to her gran's for contact, then collect her at five o'clock.

'Why five and not six?' she asked.

'That's the time of contact during the school week,' I said. 'And by the way, Dave returned the mobile phone you gave your mum, so you can show her how to use it.'

'That was nice of him,' she said sarcastically.

'Well, at least she got it back.'

However, later that night, as I was lying in bed starting to drift off to sleep – that twilight zone when the day's events are being processed from a distance – I suddenly had the most horrendous thought. I was fully awake in a second. I sat bolt upright and switched on my bedside light so I could think more clearly. Dave had returned Heather's phone with the rest of her belongings. I had never for one moment thought it was an altruistic act, but his way of keeping control and sending the message that he was removing Heather from his life as he had done Tilly. But what if there was a more sinister reason? Could he have placed a tracker on Heather's phone as he had Tilly's? Surely not. I was being fanciful, overthinking, I was tired, my imagination was running wild. Or was it?

If I'd had a partner beside me in the bed, I would have discussed it with them, but it was just me and my speculation. It was the middle of the night, a time when problems can seem bigger than they are. But on the other hand, fostering had taught me that incredible and nasty things did happen and some people can be very devious. If Dave had placed tracking software on Heather's phone, then as soon as she switched it on he would know exactly where she was every minute of the day. At present she was at her mother's, but supposing she ventured outside, which she would do one day? He'd know where she was. Was she safe?

I tossed and turned for most of the night until I eventually decided what I was going to do. I was up and dressed early, tired from little sleep, and even more concerned for Heather's safety. I heard Tilly get up and then, once she came downstairs, dressed in her school uniform, and was eating her breakfast, I joined her at the table. Adrian and Lucy had already left for work and Paula was in the bathroom.

'I'm going to take you to school this morning as well as to contact,' I said. 'I'd feel happier doing that. But there's something I want you to do when you get to your gran's.'

'I know, you said yesterday, help Mum unpack.'

'Yes, but there is something else. I need you to do it without telling your mum or gran. It might be nothing and I don't want to worry them unnecessarily.' Tilly had stopped eating now and was staring at me.

'You're scaring me,' she said.

'I didn't mean to frighten you. As I said it might be nothing. But you know that tracking software Dave put on your phone?' She nodded. 'I want you to check he hasn't put it on your mother's phone.' She dropped her spoon with a clatter and her eyes blazed with anger.

'The bastard! I bet he has! That's just the sort of thing he'd do!'

'No, listen, we don't know he has, but I think you should check. Would you recognize it again if it was on her phone?'

'Yes, I still check mine sometimes.'

'Good. But please do it away from your mum and gran. There is no point in worrying them unnecessarily.'

But Tilly was already convinced Dave was guilty. 'The bastard!' she said again. 'Shall I go to Gran's now and check?'

'No. You're going to school. Finish your breakfast, please, and I'll take you.'

* * *

As I drove Tilly to school, she talked about the tracking on her mother's phone non-stop, animated and wound up. I realized I shouldn't have told her until that afternoon when I'd collected her and we were on the way to her gran's. But it was a bit late now and all I could do was try to calm her down before she went into school. I pointed out that I could be wrong and there might not be a tracker.

'I bet there is,' she persisted. 'He's always been a control freak.'

She'd texted Abby from the car to say she was on her way, and when we arrived she was waiting outside the school gates. She waved as I pulled up and dropped off Tilly. 'Try to concentrate on your lessons,' I told Tilly as she got out. 'See you later.'

I watched the two of them go in through the main gates and then I drove home. I guessed Tilly would tell Abby. Top of my list of things to do was to phone Isa. At 9.15 I called her office. She was at her desk. I brought her up to date, including Tilly's visit to see her gran and mother on Saturday, Heather's belongings left in the front garden overnight, my suspicion about Heather's phone and that Tilly was going to check it for tracking software that afternoon.

'Definitely worth checking,' Isa said. 'Well done. I don't think I would have made that connection.'

I was pleased she agreed, and I felt vindicated. I confirmed the contact arrangements for the week, and said I had taken Tilly to school and would collect her this afternoon and take her to her gran's. Isa asked me to do the same for the whole week, her feeling being that a week was a reasonable time to let the situation calm down, and that if Dave hadn't tried to contact Tilly by the end of the week then he probably wouldn't. I could continue to take and collect Tilly indefinitely if necessary, as I do for younger children, but Tilly was a young adult who liked the freedom of making her own travel arrangements. She often saw friends on the bus and they chatted, shared video clips, music and photos on their phones as young people do. Isa finished by asking me to let her know what, if anything, Tilly found on her mother's phone.

I had plenty to do that day, but of course the matter of Heather's phone played on my mind. It was possible she'd already turned it on and could be planning to go out, perhaps for a short walk. It was a cold but bright day, and she might feel like a breath of fresh air. I was so worried that at midday I telephoned Nancy and, trying to keep the anxiety from my voice, said, 'Hi, it's Cathy. I was just wondering how you and Heather were?'

'That's very sweet of you, love. Thank you. We're taking it easy after the weekend. We've been doing a bit more unpacking, gradual like.'

'So you're both OK?'

'Mustn't grumble. I've got my last chemo tomorrow. I've asked Heather to come with me. We'll get a cab there and back. It will be nice to have her company.'

'That's great. But you haven't any plans to go out today?'

'No. We're seeing Tilly later.'

'Yes, I'll drop her off straight after school. Well, enjoy the rest of your day.'

'Thanks, love, and you.'

I was relieved, and the fact that Heather was going to go with her mother to the hospital showed she was already gaining confidence. At the first meeting I'd had with her and Dave, she hadn't been able to go in a cab when it had been suggested as a way of her going to contact. Dave had claimed she was suffering from agoraphobia, although Tilly had said it was his fault her mother never went out. It seemed she was right.

That afternoon I arrived in plenty of time to collect Tilly from school. I waited in the car a little way from the gates for school to finish. She came out with Abby, who headed off in the opposite direction.

'I told my friends what Dave's done and everyone says he should be arrested!' Tilly said passionately as she got into the car. Clearly the drama had continued all day and I doubted Tilly had learnt much in lessons.

'We don't know for certain Dave has put a tracker on your mother's phone,' I reminded her. 'I hope he doesn't get wind of all this gossip.'

'Don't care,' she said belligerently. 'I hate him.' But of course, as an adult, I knew you couldn't go around accusing people without proof.

Tilly spent the car journey taking calls and answering texts from her friends, giving them updates on our progress to her gran's. I felt as if I was in an action movie. As we approached the bungalow I said, 'Let me know as soon as you've had a chance to check the phone. But please don't tell your mother and gran until we're sure. If Dave hasn't put a tracker on her phone then you'll have to tell your friends we were wrong.'

'I bet he has,' she insisted. She sent one last text and got out.

Nancy opened the front door and gave a little wave, which I returned, then I headed for home. I guessed Tilly would check her mother's phone as soon as possible, so I was expecting my phone to go off at any moment. However, it didn't ring until I'd parked outside my house. Cutting the engine, I snatched it up. It was Tilly.

'Yes?' I said.

'You were right! The bastard has put tracking software on Mum's phone, the same one he put on mine. I've removed it and I've told Mum and Gran what he's done. Gran's going to call the police, but she wants to speak to you first.'

'Put her on,' I said, my pulse racing. So I had been right.

I stayed in the car as Nancy came on the phone. 'Cathy, am I understanding this right? Dave knows where Heather is through her phone?'

'He would have been able to, yes, but Tilly has removed the software so it's safe.'

'How is that possible?' Nancy asked, slightly breathless. 'I don't understand. It's beyond me.'

'And me,' I admitted. 'But it is possible. Dave did the same to Tilly's phone.'

'She told me. What a dreadful world we live in. I'll report it to the police.'

'You can, but I'm not sure it's illegal.'

'You're kidding me?'

'No, I'm not. From what I know, it's a very grey area.'

I then explained what I knew of the law in the area.

CHAPTER SIXTEEN

ACCUSED

I remained in the car to telephone Isa. She was expecting my call. I told her Tilly had found a tracker on her mother's phone – the same software she'd found on hers – and that she'd removed it. Isa had already discussed with her manager, Nikki Bets, about the legality of what Dave was doing and it did indeed appear to be a grey area. While it is illegal to track another person's phone without their permission per se (unless you are law enforcement), it's not illegal for a parent to track their child's or loved one's phone. If Heather wanted to take it further, she'd have to sue Dave and try to prove that tracking her had caused her mental anguish or material loss. Dave would doubtless claim he had done it in her best interest, given her emotional fragility. Not that I could see Heather ever taking it to court. She wasn't up to it.

'So,' Isa concluded, 'Nancy can report it to the police, but I doubt they're going to take it any further.'

She was right.

When I collected Tilly from contact she opened the door, clearly annoyed. 'The police aren't going to do anything! And Mum is refusing to use her phone because she doesn't think it's safe. Can you tell her?'

I went in. Nancy was in her usual armchair in the living

room and Heather was sitting on the sofa, looking very anxious. Her phone was on the coffee table.

'I really don't know what to think of the police nowadays,' Nancy said. 'It didn't used to be like this.'

'Cathy, tell Mum her phone is safe now,' Tilly said forcefully, picking up the phone.

Nancy and Heather looked at me. 'It's safe for you to use,' I said. 'Tilly has taken off the software. It's like any mobile phone now.'

'How can we be sure?' Nancy asked. 'I mean, you can't tell by looking at it or if you use it.'

'Tilly knows what she's doing,' I said. 'She sorted out her own phone and it's been fine since.' But I could see from their expressions they both still had doubts. 'If it puts your minds at rest, I could take the phone to a shop to have it checked,' I suggested.

'And they are experts?' Nancy asked sceptically. 'They will know for certain if it's safe to use?'

'Yes,' I said.

'Please do so then and let me know what I owe you.'

'I'll take it in tomorrow,' I replied.

'Thank you,' Heather said quietly.

'I don't know why she can't just use the landline like I do,' Nancy said.

Tilly sighed but didn't comment. We said goodbye and let ourselves out.

'I don't know why they didn't trust me to do it,' Tilly grumbled as we returned to my car. 'I know what I'm doing. Mum is paranoid about Dave finding her.'

'With good reason,' I said. 'I know you've made her phone safe, but it won't hurt to have it checked if it puts their minds at rest.'

We got into the car and Tilly handed me the phone. I put it in my bag, ready to take to the shop the following day. She then spent the entire journey texting friends, and would have spent all evening on her phone if I hadn't intervened.

'Schoolwork,' I said later, going into her room. 'You were doing well before half term. Don't let it slip.'

'I can't concentrate with all this going on,' she bemoaned.

'I know it's difficult. Would it help if I looked after your phone for an hour or so?'

'I'll do it,' she said tartly.

'Good. You don't want to let Dave's actions ruin your chances of success, do you?'

'No, of course not!'

The following day, after I'd dropped off Tilly at school, I drove straight to the phone shop. It was in a small parade of shops on the edge of town and was owned by two brothers who seemed to know everything there was to know about mobile phones, laptops, tablets and other devices. Previously they'd repaired our phones and replaced cracked screens. They also advertised they unblocked phones.

I went in and put Heather's phone on the counter. The brother who served me didn't look at all surprised when I said I wanted the phone checked for tracking software and spyware. I waited as he took it to the workbench at the back of the shop and plugged it in. A few minutes later he pronounced it clean. 'It's hardly been used,' he said.

'No, that's right.'

I paid cash. It was very reasonable, and I returned to my car. I sent a text to Tilly so she would read it in her lunch break when they were allowed to switch on their phones: *Your mum's phone is clear. Just had it checked. x*

Later she texted back: *Thanks. I'll take it with me tomorrow.*

But as one drama ended, the next began. The following day, when I collected Tilly from her gran's, she came out in a bad mood. 'That bloody social worker!' she cursed, slamming the front door shut behind her. 'She's been to see Gran today and told her I couldn't come and live here!'

'What, never ever?' I asked, pretty sure Isa hadn't said it with such finality.

She shrugged. 'She said I was doing well with you.'

'Which you are.'

'She told Gran that Mum needed a lot of support at present, and she needed time to recover her health.'

'Which is true,' I said, unlocking the car.

'I know, but I can help them if I live here.'

'You help them a lot already. I think Isa is worried it could prove too much for you if you were here all the time.'

She huffed as she got into the car. 'She said we could discuss it again in a month or so.'

'That sounds like a good idea.'

'I don't see why I can't live there now,' Tilly moaned, and put in her earphones.

February slipped into March. Lucy had her next scan and learnt she was expecting a girl. The baby was developing well, and we were all delighted. She gave me another scan photo, which I propped up beside the first. I could see how much the baby had grown. Another four and a half months and I would see my first grandchild in person.

It was the middle of March before Lucy and Darren finally signed the lease on their flat and were given the keys. Adrian, Paula and I helped Lucy move in, taking the bags and boxes she'd packed from her bedroom downstairs and into our cars. There was still quite a bit left in her room. As well as the furniture, there were ornaments, soft toys and books on her shelves, and clothes and various odds and ends in the chest of drawers. All of this could stay where it was for as long as she wished. I was in no hurry to clear out her room.

Adrian and I drove in convoy to their new flat, Lucy in my car and Paula in Adrian's. Tilly was at her grandmother's. Darren was already at the flat. His parents were there too, so we finally met – not for the meal I'd originally suggested but carrying boxes of our children's belongs from our cars into their flat. His parents are called Tod and Tina, a nice couple I immediately warmed to, and who seemed as compatible as their names suggested.

Once we'd finished unloading the cars, we went into the flat for a glass of water; their new cups and kettle had yet to be unpacked. We offered to stay and help unpack, but it was clear Lucy and Darren wanted time alone, so the rest of us left, saying we hoped we'd see each other again before long. Like me, Darren's parents had given Lucy and Darren some money towards the cost of furnishing their flat.

Nothing further had been heard from Dave so Tilly began using the bus again for school and contact. Each time she visited her mother she gave her a lesson on how to use her mobile phone as well as surreptitiously checking that no more spyware had appeared. Heather was still wary about using her phone and kept it switched off most of the time. That meant Tilly couldn't text her mother and had to phone her grandmother's landline to speak to them. Tilly lost patience with her mother over this and other small things. I pointed out that it would be a long time before she recovered from all the years of abuse, control and belittlement she'd suffered.

There were no longer any physical scars, but the emotional ones would run deep.

Nancy's torn ligament healed and the walking aid she'd been using was returned to the hospital. She had her last dose of chemo and would be scanned again in six weeks, but at present she was cancer free. It was fantastic news. Tilly continued to see them both after school on Mondays, Wednesdays and Fridays and one afternoon over the weekend. She telephoned them in between more or less when she liked.

By the end of March our lives had settled down. Spring flowers were blooming in the parks and front gardens and birds were nest building. I was still without a supervising social worker and sending my reports to the team manager, Jaclyn Pearson. Isa paid us another of her six-weekly visits and Tilly badgered her again about moving in with her gran and mother, although she admitted she was happy living with us. Isa said it could be reviewed in the future, but she didn't think it was right for her just yet. It's usually considered the next best option for a child or young person to be brought up by a relative if the parents can't, but I could see the reasons for Isa's decision. Nancy was doing well, but it would be some time before she regained full health and Heather needed a lot of support and would only leave home in a cab with her mother beside her. Tilly was settled with us and doing much better at school.

However, realistically, at Tilly's age if she really wanted to live with her mother and gran, Isa would have a hard time stopping her. She'd simply get on a bus and go. At present she was abiding by the contact arrangements, although that could change. Isa said they could review the situation again in a month. Tilly asked if she could stay at her gran's at the weekend and Isa agreed to every other weekend once the dining room was changed into a bedroom.

That was done very quickly. The three of them worked non-stop and in the middle of April Tilly spent her first weekend at her gran's, taking an overnight bag and laptop with her so she could do her homework. She went there straight from school on Friday and returned Sunday evening, moaning it was disruptive to keep having to return to me and why couldn't she live there now there was a bedroom? I told her to discuss it with Isa.

Also around this time Lucy's baby bump really began to show. The sickness had left her and she looked very well, and had also put on some weight. I saw her at the weekends and she stopped by during the week, sometimes when Darren was visiting his family. She didn't take any more things from her room and I felt she probably liked the idea of retaining her space with me, which was fine.

I missed her dreadfully, of course I did. Calling, 'Hi, Mum,' as she let herself in after a day at work so I knew straight away from her tone what sort of day she'd had. Then coming to find me in the kitchen and kissing me before she did anything else. It was her priority. She was no longer at the dinner table with us, teasing Adrian. He missed her too, although he didn't say much. Paula missed their sisterly chats. 'Why did she have to get herself pregnant and move out?' she once said. Naturally Paula was looking forward to being an aunty, as I was looking forward to being a grandmother, but it didn't stop us missing Lucy. She was missing us too and often texted our WhatsApp group, *Hi guys, miss & love you loads*. We replied, *Miss & love you too. Lots!*

I asked Lucy once if Bonnie, her birth mother, had been in touch again. She hadn't, not after her initial flurry of interest when Lucy had first told her. This was typical of Bonnie and I thought the same was likely to happen after the birth of the baby. She'd be all over her granddaughter for a few hours and then nothing. Bonnie wasn't a bad person, but she lacked responsibility and shied away from commitment – two qualities essential for good parenting.

School broke up for the Easter holiday. Tilly and I received invitations and review forms for her second review, which would be held at the council offices. Tilly told me her mother and gran had also received invitations. Her mother had said she didn't think she would be up to attending the review, which annoyed Tilly.

'Your mother is struggling at present and isn't going out much,' I said.

'Gran said they could go by cab,' Tilly replied.

'Or we could collect them if it helps?' I offered.

'I'll ask them,' she said, and went off to phone her gran.

She reappeared five minutes later, disgruntled. 'Mum still isn't sure if she'll go. Gran said not to trouble you for a lift. If they go, they'll get a cab.'

'All right, love. The offer's there.'

It was important to Tilly that her family attended her review, as it is for most children in care. It shows they are taking an active interest in their child's welfare and making their views heard. It would also be seen as important by the social services, especially if Nancy and Heather were making a case for Tilly going to live with them. That wouldn't be decided at the review, but their presence would give weight to their commitment to looking after Tilly long term.

* * *

A week later we assembled in the council offices for the review, still not knowing if Heather and Nancy would be attending. Tilly was assuming they wouldn't be from what her mother had said. Joanna Hargreaves was the Independent Reviewing Officer again – it's usual to have the same IRO for continuity. Isa was present with her manager, Nikki Bets. Jaclyn Pearson attended in place of my supervising social worker. Faith Jenkins, deputy head, wasn't present as it was the school holiday, so she'd sent a report. At two o'clock, the time the review was scheduled to start, the door opened and Nancy came in, followed by Heather. Tilly leapt from her chair and ran to hug them. I was pleased they'd made it.

'I'm sorry we're late,' Nancy said, out of breath, and sitting in the nearest chair. She was wearing a smart blue coat with a matching hat that covered her hair loss. Heather was dressed smartly too, in a light grey coat and sat next to her mother, timid, anxious and self-conscious.

'Welcome,' the IRO said with a smile, and typed a note of their presence. 'Are we expecting anyone else?' she asked Isa.

'No,' she confirmed.

'Let's begin then. It's usual so start with introductions. I'm Joanna Hargreaves, the Independent Reviewing Officer. I shall be chairing and minuting this meeting.' We took it in turns to give our names and roles. Heather spoke so quietly she was barely audible.

With the introductions over, I was now expecting the IRO to ask Tilly or me to speak first as is usual at these reviews. Instead, she took a moment and looked at us all, her expression serious. She also appeared to be uncomfortable about what she was about to say, and I wondered what on earth was the matter.

'Before we hear from everyone,' she said, 'I need to make you aware of a complaint I've received.' All eyes were on her. A complaint? I felt my pulse quicken.

'The complaint is from Mr David Mitchel, Tilly's stepfather. He telephoned me, very agitated, a few weeks ago, claiming that Tilly and her foster carer had broken into his property. He's threatening to involve the police.'

My stomach churned and my mouth went dry. Everyone was looking at me for an explanation. 'When was this supposed to have happened?' I asked, my voice unsteady. I had a nasty feeling I knew what he was referring to.

CHAPTER SEVENTEEN

'YOU'LL HATE ME'

The IRO told me the date of the incident. 'I'll check my log notes,' I said, my voice uneven. Thankfully I'd brought them with me.

The room was silent and Tilly was watching me carefully as I took my log book from my bag and turned to the correct page. As I thought, it was the day Heather had gone missing. I felt my pulse start to race.

'We didn't break into Mr Mitchel's property,' I said, addressing the IRO. 'We let ourselves in through the side gate and went into the back garden for a few minutes. That was all. Tilly's mother was living there then, and Tilly had been due to see her that afternoon, but she couldn't reach her. She repeatedly phoned her, but she didn't answer. We knew that Heather rarely went out and that she was expecting Tilly, so we were both very worried. Eventually I drove to the house and we tried the front doorbell. No one answered, so we went down the sideway to see if the back door was unlocked. It wasn't. We looked through the windows and knocked on the door, but we didn't break in. There was no sign of Heather. I was about to telephone the police when Nancy called to say Heather was with her, having left Mr Mitchel. We were surprised. It had never occurred to us she might be there. We left the property straight away and closed the side gate behind us. We didn't do any damage and we certainly didn't break into the house.'

'I suppose Mr Mitchel is viewing you being on his property as breaking in,' the IRO said as she typed. 'What happened then?'

'I drove us straight to Nancy's home where Heather was.'

Nancy nodded.

'The house he is referring to is the one where Tilly lived until she came into care?' the IRO asked.

'Yes,' Tilly and I said together.

'I'll vouch for them,' Nancy said. 'What Cathy has said is true. Heather fled that brute and came to live with me.'

I looked at Heather, who'd gone very pale.

'I'll explain the circumstances to Mr Mitchel,' the IRO said calmly. 'Thank you.'

'How did he know we'd been there?' Tilly asked. I could guess.

'When he arrived home he found the side gate wasn't bolted,' the IRO said. 'He asked some neighbours if they'd seen anything suspicious. Someone living on the opposite side of the road said they'd seen his daughter with a woman, and that Tilly had climbed over the side gate and let them in.'

'Arsehole,' Tilly hissed.

'There was no damage done,' I said again. 'We acted in good faith, because we were so concerned for Heather.'

'I understand,' the IRO said with a reassuring smile. 'If he does take it further you will have to tell the police what you've told me. I'll speak to Mr Mitchel and hopefully put an end to it. He was very angry when he telephoned, and then followed it with a written complaint, which I've had to act on. I'll give him an apology and assure him it won't happen again.'

'I'm not apologizing!' Tilly snapped.

'Thank you,' I said.

I looked again at Heather, who was clearly shaken by all this, as indeed was I. Dave was trying to intimidate me with his threats, just as he had intimated Heather all those years. This was him taking revenge. Tilly and Heather had escaped his clutches and he was determined to retain as much control as possible in any way he could.

The IRO continued with the review and Tilly was asked to speak, but she was still angry. She said in a tight voice that she liked me and my family but wanted to live with her mother and gran. She then answered all the IRO's questions with curt monosyllables: Yes. No. Don't know. Fine.

I was asked to speak next and I tried to concentrate on what I needed to say, but it was difficult to put aside thoughts of Dave and the trouble he was trying to cause. I said that Tilly continued to do well in all aspects of her life at home and school. That she had a good circle of friends and a special friend, Abby. I said she was in good health and her dental and optician check-ups were up to date. That she was eating and sleeping well and getting home on time. I confirmed I had given her a front door key – mentioned at the first review. And she hadn't had any accidents or injuries apart from a small cut to her finger from a splinter, which had now healed.

The IRO asked me a few questions about contact and how that was going, and then asked Isa to give her report. It passed in a blur – I was only half listening, worrying that Dave Mitchel would take his complaint to the police, and what he was thinking of doing next. I doubted he would give up. I heard Isa say that the care plan for Tilly was the same, although consideration was being given to the idea of her going to live with her gran and mother in the future – when Nancy's health recovered and Heather felt more secure. She said she'd visited Nancy and Heather and had agreed to Tilly staying there every other weekend. She covered her visits to my house and had asked Tilly again if she would like to see a therapist at CAMHS (Child and Adolescent Mental Health Service), but she didn't.

The IRO asked her about the tracker on Tilly's phone, which had been brought up at the last review. Isa said her phone was clear but that Mr Mitchel had done similar to Heather's phone.

'He's certainly not a man to give up easily,' the IRO remarked. She'd met him at the start of the previous review.

Once Isa had given her report, the IRO then paraphrased the school report the deputy head had sent. In essence it said that Tilly was a pleasant student and was making steady progress in all subjects but couldn't afford to slacken, as it was an important year for her.

Jaclyn Pearson, in place of my supervising social worker, went next. She said that although she hadn't had a chance to visit me at home, she'd read the reports from my previous supervising social worker and had also spoken to Isa. She was satisfied that Tilly was receiving a good standard of care. She said she was sure I had acted in good faith when I'd gone to Mr Mitchel's property, and thanked me for all I was doing.

Nancy and Heather were asked if they would like to speak. Heather said very quietly, 'I would like Tilly to live with us.' Then looked at her mother to say more.

Nancy said in a much firmer, louder voice, 'Isa has looked around my bungalow and seen Tilly's bedroom and is satisfied it is suitable. We are Tilly's family and she should be with us permanently. I know I'm not in perfect health, but I am recovering. I intend to beat this cancer, just as I will beat Dave Mitchel if he comes anywhere near us.' We all smiled.

'Well said, Gran!' Tilly said and patted her arm affectionately.

'Thank you,' the IRO said and finished typing.

She thanked Tilly and me for sending in our review forms and, with no further reports, she set the date for the next review in three months' time and closed the meeting. Isa and her manager immediately stood, saying they had to dash to another meeting. The IRO also stood and began packing away her laptop and paperwork as Nancy said, 'That Dave Mitchel is a nasty piece of work. You can't believe anything he says.'

Clearly the IRO couldn't discuss this now the review was over, so she said diplomatically, 'Thank you. I've noted your concerns. I'll circulate the minutes as soon as they are ready.' With a polite but formal smile, she tucked her laptop into her briefcase and, saying goodbye, left the room.

'Well, that was a waste of time,' Nancy said, getting to her feet. 'Where can I call for a cab?'

'I can give you a lift if you wish?' I offered.

'Yes, please, dear. I'm exhausted.'

'You know, Mum, if you had your phone with you, you could call a cab,' Tilly said, pointing out one of the advantages of having a mobile.

'I'm happy to take you home,' I said. 'But mobiles are useful.' I knew Tilly had reassured her mother plenty of times that there was no tracker on her phone, but Dave's hold on her ran deep. It had crossed my mind that perhaps a new phone might be the answer and put Heather's mind at rest. But that was really up to them.

We made our way downstairs and handed in our ID badges at reception. Nancy was out of breath and I suggested they waited in reception where there were some seats, while I fetched the car. There was a drop-off collection point just outside. The three of them stayed while I fetched the car. Tilly helped Nancy into the front passenger seat and then she and Heather sat in the back. The conversation soon turned to Dave making trouble. Tilly and Nancy had plenty to say, while Heather remained very quiet. I glanced at her in the rear-view mirror. Her expression said it all. She was petrified. Years of bullying and coercive control had taught her that Dave was a threat even from a distance. The mere mention of his name frightened her.

I drew up and parked outside their bungalow. Getting out, I went round to the passenger door and helped Nancy out as Heather and Tilly got out of the rear. I saw Heather looking anxiously up and down the street, presumably looking for any sign of Dave.

'I'll stay and then catch the bus back,' Tilly said, wanting to spend more time with her gran and mother.

'It's not really contact today,' I pointed out.

'It's OK, I'll just stay for a couple of hours,' Tilly persisted.

'No, you go with Cathy as you are supposed to,' Nancy said. 'We're seeing you again tomorrow.' Which Tilly accepted. It's so much easier if the child's family can work with the foster carer as Nancy and Heather were doing.

Tilly kissed her gran and mother goodbye. We waited until they were inside before I pulled away. Tilly telephoned Abby straight away and told her about the review, Dave's complaint and what an 'arsehole' he was. I couldn't hear what Abby was saying, but clearly she was sympathetic to Tilly.

'I'll throw a brick through his window!' Tilly said at one point.

'No, you won't!' I said. 'That would be playing right into his hands. We don't want any more trouble.'

'Only joking,' she said. But I wasn't so sure.

Tilly made the most of the Easter holidays, and on the days she wasn't seeing her mother and gran she went out with Abby, and sometimes with other friends too. When I foster younger children I take them on outings during school holidays and arrange activities at home, but it was different with teenagers. I asked Tilly if there was anywhere she'd like to go and suggested we could take Abby as well. But she wasn't really interested and said she was trying to persuade her mother to go on a shopping trip but so far without success. Heather didn't need any more clothes now Dave had sent them all, but it was the idea of a mother-and-daughter outing that Tilly liked. She was looking forward to a time when they could do things together like Abby did with her mother.

School returned for the summer term and we fell into our weekday routine. Paula, who was in her final year at college, had exams looming and was studying hard. She and Adrian were due to see their father so met him for lunch. Life settled down again. You often find in fostering there are peaks and troughs of activity, but generally after the first few months things usually get a bit easier as the child or young person adjusts to being in care. Usually, but not always. Sometimes the challenges continue.

Tilly was now spending every other weekend with her mother and gran and had left clothes and toiletries there. She was sure it was only a matter of time before she lived there permanently. I thought so too. Isa had indicated it was likely to be appropriate once Nancy was in better health and Heather was stronger and in a better position to parent Tilly.

By the middle of May, when I hadn't heard any more about 'breaking into' Dave's house, I thought that was probably the end of it and he hadn't involved the police as he'd threatened. Isa, her manager, Tilly and her gran thought so too. Only Heather – still living in fear of him – felt he would want to 'get his own back', one way or another.

'Mum would think that,' Tilly said to me. 'She's scared of him. But I bet he's got another woman by now.'

Heaven help her if so, I thought. Little did she know what lay in store, for I doubted Dave had changed. He was a presentable man who dressed smartly and could appear charming when he wanted to, before he turned. From what I knew of his courting Heather, it had been quick, but he'd said and done all the right things. Until he had her in his clutches and then all that had changed.

On another matter, Tilly had told me her gran had made a will, leaving her bungalow to Heather so she and Tilly would always have somewhere to live. Being told this had upset Tilly, but I explained that making a will was sensible and that I'd made one. I said I was sure it wouldn't be needed for many years to come and her gran would make a full recovery. Tilly also told me her gran was trying to persuade her mother to see a solicitor to start divorce proceedings and see if she was entitled to any money. Heather had no income and Nancy was supporting her, which couldn't go on forever. I assumed that, once Heather was feeling better, she'd register at the job centre and look for work. Not only to give her an income, but to help rebuild her confidence and self-esteem.

* * *

On Thursday of the third week in May, Tilly was late home from school. Four-thirty – the time she was usually home – came and went. When it got to five o'clock I texted her. *Everything OK?*

She didn't reply for another half an hour. Her text read: *Been talking to Abby. Coming back now.* Which seemed slightly odd, as she usually let me know straight away if she was going to be late.

It was after six o'clock when Tilly finally arrived home. I wasn't pleased and I was about to serve dinner. I heard her let herself in the front door and called, 'In here. We're about to eat.'

'I'm not hungry,' she replied, and went straight upstairs to her room. That wasn't like Tilly.

I left Adrian and Paula eating and went up to her bedroom. The door was closed so I knocked.

'What is it?' came her terse reply.

'Can I come in?'

There was no reply, so I knocked again and went in. Tilly was propped up on her bed, phone on her lap. I assumed she'd been texting.

'Are you all right, love?' I asked.

'Why shouldn't I be?' she snapped, glaring at me.

'It's not like you to be late home and then not want your dinner.'

'Can you just leave me alone, please?' she said bluntly.

I hesitated. 'Are you sure?'

'Yes.'

'All right. I'll be downstairs if you want me.'

I left, drawing the door to behind me. Perhaps she just needed time alone. If she didn't come down soon, I would come up and check on her again. It crossed my mind that perhaps she'd had an argument with Abby. They'd been seeing a lot of each other and best friends do fall out. But why not tell me?

'What's the matter with Tilly?' Paula asked as I joined them at the table.

'She won't say. I'll talk to her again later.'

We continued our meal but without our usual bright chatter, for we were all aware that something was the matter with Tilly.

She didn't appear, so once I'd finished, I plated up her dinner and I went to her room. Twenty minutes had passed, long enough for a young person to be alone fretting about something. I knocked on her door and went in. She'd been crying.

'What is it, love?' I asked. I went over and perched on the edge of the bed. 'Tell me?'

'I can't,' she said, wiping her eyes. 'You'll hate me.'

'No, I won't. I will help you to sort it out.' But a cold chill ran down my spine. What had she done to make me think I would hate her? It must be something bad. 'Tilly, you need to tell me what's happened, love, so I can help you.'

She shook her head and looked away, still holding her phone, although the screen was blank.

'Have you been back to Dave's house and done damage?' I asked. I wondered if she had thrown a brick through his window as she'd threatened.

She shook her head.

'Is there a problem at school?' I tried.

'No.'

'Have you fallen out with Abby?'

She shook her head again.

'Tilly, you need to tell me so I can help you.' I was really worried now. This wasn't the Tilly I knew. 'Nothing is so bad it can't be sorted out.' But I was starting to doubt my own words. 'What is it, Tilly? What's happened?' I asked, trying to keep the anxiety from my voice.

Touching her phone screen to bring it to life she held it towards me. I looked at a photo. It was a picture of Tilly in sexy underwear, matching bra and skimpy pants. It was the type of selfie a teenager might take. No harm done unless you'd sent it to someone who'd then circulated it. I assumed that is what had happened.

'Did you send it to someone?' I asked.

'No. It was sent to me.'

'By whom?' I asked, puzzled.

'I don't know.' And she began to cry again.

CHAPTER EIGHTEEN

THE PHOTOGRAPH

'Tilly, it was very wrong of the person to circulate your photograph,' I said passing her a tissue. 'Try to remember who you sent it to you and I'll report them.' I knew the police took this type of crime very seriously, as it can ruin young lives. Revenge porn, as it's known, is when someone discloses a private sexual photograph or film without the person's consent and with the intent of causing them distress. It is an offence, punishable with a fine or imprisonment.

'But I don't think I sent it to anyone,' Tilly said, wiping her yes. 'I don't even remember taking it.'

'It's OK. I expect you've forgotten. You've got a lot of selfies on your phone.' I knew, because she'd shown me some, although not of her in underwear. 'Try not to worry. We'll get to the bottom of this. I'm pleased you've been able to tell me.' I gave her a hug.

'I'm sure I didn't take it,' she said. 'I've been through all the photos on my phone and I can't find it there.'

'Perhaps you deleted it,' I suggested.

'Maybe,' she conceded.

'Or perhaps it wasn't a selfie and someone else took it?' I said. 'Abby, maybe?'

'I don't think so.' She sniffed and blew her nose.

'You look a bit younger in the photo so I'm guessing it was taken last year. From the background it looks as though it was taken in a bedroom. Was it your bedroom at home?'

'Yes.'

'Perhaps you and Abby were doing a photoshoot?' I said, trying to lighten her mood. They wouldn't be the first young people dreaming of careers in modelling to take photos of each other in sexy underwear.

'I don't think so,' Tilly said. 'Abby hasn't got a copy on her phone. She looked.'

'Who else has received the photo?' I asked.

'No one as far as I know. Just me.' So it didn't appear to be as bad as I first thought.

'And you don't recognize the phone number of the person who sent you the photo?' I asked.

'No. I texted and asked who it was, but they didn't reply, which freaked me out. Why would they send it to me?'

'I don't know, love. Someone's idea of a laugh, I expect. If you remember who you sent the photo to, tell me. And if anyone else receives a copy, tell me straight away and I'll report it. I'll also let Isa and the school know.'

'Last term a girl in the year above me finished with her boyfriend and the next morning a photo of her topless was on everyone's phone.'

'I know that sort of thing can happen. Could it be from an ex-boyfriend of yours?' I asked. Tilly would have been around thirteen at the time the photo was taken, so rather young to have been in an intimate relationship, but I couldn't afford to be judgemental or rule it out. I just wanted to get to the truth.

'I haven't had a proper boyfriend,' Tilly said, which is what I'd thought. 'Shall I phone the number and see who it is?'

'No. I will,' I said. 'You come down and have some dinner and I'll phone.'

'I'm not hungry. Can you phone now?' She was clearly very worried.

'Come on then. My phone is downstairs.'

Adrian was in the hall putting on his shoes as we came down. 'I'm going to Kirsty's for a while. Everything OK?'

'Yes, love. Give Kirsty my love,' I said.

'Will do.'

I took my phone from my handbag. I hesitated as to whether I should block my number but decided I wouldn't as I wanted a reply. Tilly read the sender's number from her phone and I keyed it in. My call went straight through to voicemail with a generic recorded voice telling me to leave a message after the tone. 'I'm Tilly's foster carer,' I said, my voice firm and dispassionate. 'You have sent her a photograph and I would like an explanation. If she or anyone else receives any further photos of her, I will be reporting it to the police. Please phone as soon as you listen to this message.'

'Do you think he will phone you?' Tilly asked as I ended the call.

'Probably not, and it might not be a male. But hopefully the mention of the police will deter them if they were planning to send any more.'

'Thank you.'

'It's OK. Now, come and have some dinner. Have you got any homework?'

'Loads,' she sighed.

'Have your dinner and then do your homework. If the person returns my call, I'll let you know.'

I wasn't really expecting them to. My guess was that it was a student at Tilly's school playing a prank. Hopefully my call with the mention of the police would have scared them off any more silliness.

I sat with Tilly while she ate a little of her dinner, but she hadn't any appetite. She then went to her bedroom to do her homework. I went to the computer in the front room and emailed Isa. I told her about the photo, that Tilly didn't know who could have sent it, but as far as we knew it hadn't been sent to anyone else. I told her of the voicemail message I'd left on the sender's phone, and also that I would call Faith Jenkins, the deputy head, tomorrow and let her know what had happened. I wasn't expecting a reply from Isa – it was out of hours – but she would read my email when she logged into her work account in the morning.

The evening passed, I kept my phone near me, but I didn't receive a call from the person who'd sent the photo. I reassured Tilly I thought that was probably the end of it, but she had a restless night. The following morning, as soon as she heard me moving around, she came to find me, still in her nightwear, and asked if I'd had a reply. I told her I hadn't and reassured her again I was pretty certain that was the last of it, but if she received any messages from the person while she was at school, she must tell Miss Jenkins and me immediately. I was dealing with this as I would have done if it had happened to one of my own children, as foster carers are expected to. When making decisions about the looked-after child the litmus test is: what would I do if they were my child?

Tilly didn't want any breakfast. She was clearly still very worried and had already been in touch with Abby and other friends, checking to see if they had received any photos of her. They hadn't. Before she left for school I asked her to text me at lunchtime, when they were allowed to turn on their phones, to let me know she was OK. In fact, she texted just before school started to say that so far no one else had received a photo. I replied I didn't think they would and told her not to worry.

At 9.30 I telephoned Miss Jenkins, the deputy head, and explained what had happened. She was very supportive and said she would remind all the students in assembly that the school didn't tolerate any form of bullying or harassment, whether it was in person, by phone or social media. She said she wouldn't mention Tilly specifically but would give a general warning that if any student was found to be distributing harmful material, they would be dealt with severely and their parents and the police informed. Like me, she thought it was probably another student who'd sent it. 'They can make very poor decisions at this age,' she said. Which I knew.

Isa replied to my email, thanking me for the update and asking to be kept informed. She also said that Tilly had telephoned her while she'd been at her gran's one day last week and asked if she could go there every weekend and she'd agreed. I received an email from Jaclyn Pearson, team manager for supervising social workers, saying they had finally appointed another social worker and she would be in touch with me shortly.

Tilly didn't wait for the lunch break to check her phone again. I received a text from her mid-morning saying she hadn't received any more messages, and Miss Jenkins had spoken to her. She asked if I'd heard anything and I replied I hadn't and I thought that was the end of it now. I received a similar text from her at the end of school. She was going straight to her gran's for contact. I phoned her while she was on the bus and she sounded far more positive. She told me she hadn't heard anything further and Miss Jenkins had seen her again and said she felt sure it was a silly prank and the person responsible was probably very sorry now. I agreed, although it still remained a mystery as to who had taken the photo. My feeling was that Tilly, possibly with a friend, had taken it and sent it to someone for a laugh or a dare. There'd been so much going on in Tilly's life at that time, it was likely she'd forgotten, or perhaps she'd remembered and didn't like to tell me. Tilly was sensible most of the time, but I'd looked after enough teenagers as well as bringing up three of my own to know they could act impulsively without thinking of the consequences.

On Friday Tilly went straight from school to spend the weekend with her gran and mother, and on Saturday Lucy and Darren came for lunch. It was a gloriously warm sunny day, but Lucy, now nearly seven months pregnant, felt the heat. Darren was very attentive and kept offering her cold drinks, even a cold flannel for her forehead. After lunch we sat in the garden in the shade of the tree where Lucy made herself as comfortable as possible, feet up, on a sun lounger.

'I wish our flat had a garden,' she remarked.

'You can use this one whenever you wish,' I said, which she already knew. I hoped I'd be seeing a lot of her and the baby when she was born.

As we talked, Lucy mentioned she was going to work as long as possible before the birth so she could take a full year of maternity leave afterwards. She also said they'd opted for a water birth, assuming there were no complications during labour. Our hospital had recently built two new suites with birthing pools. Giving birth in water can help the woman relax and manage the pain of labour.

'Do you get in with her?' Paula asked Darren.

Adrian thought she was joking until Darren replied, 'Not in these ones. They're not big enough. Only a few hospitals have the very large pools.'

Darren had been attending the antenatal appointments with Lucy and during one visit they'd been shown around the maternity unit. He seemed to know what to expect and was taking it in his stride.

It was a lovely afternoon and we stayed in the garden until the sun set, when Lucy and Darren went home. Paula did some studying, and Adrian went to see Kirsty.

On Sunday, Paula and I visited my mother, who was also feeling the heat. She didn't want to go out to eat so I made us a salad lunch, which we had in her garden. I'd read somewhere that the elderly can't regulate their body temperatures as successfully as younger people. Mum naturally asked after the rest of the family: Adrian, Lucy and Tilly. I told her a bit about what they were all doing, and that they would see her soon. We left shortly after five o'clock so I could be home for when Tilly arrived. Although she had a front door key, I didn't like her to be alone in the house for too long.

As it was, she didn't return until nearly seven o'clock and she was in a huff because she'd discovered she'd left her weekend homework at her gran's.

'It's supposed to be in tomorrow,' she moaned.

'You'll have to explain what's happened, apologize and hand it in on Tuesday,' I said.

'More trouble!'

I was becoming concerned that with all the contact – Monday, Wednesday and Friday after school and now every weekend – Tilly wasn't finding time to do her schoolwork. When I asked her she always assured me she was doing it, and I assumed if there was a problem then the school would contact me.

They did.

A week later, on Monday afternoon, Miss Jenkins telephoned. 'I'm afraid Tilly hasn't handed in her homework again.'

'Again!'

'I'm afraid so. Some of her subject teachers are worried she's slipping behind. I thought you'd want to know.'

'Yes, thank you. I'm sorry, I'll talk to her.' Not only was it important that Tilly did well at school for her own sake, but it reflected badly on me, as I was responsible for her.

When she returned from seeing her mother and gran, I told her straight away what Miss Jenkins had said.

'The old rat bag!' she cursed.

'Tilly, I'm pleased she did call me. She wants you to do well, just as I do. I'm sure your gran and mother do too. It must be difficult for you to shut yourself away over the weekend to do your homework.'

'I don't shut myself away,' she said moodily. 'I do my work on my lap in the living room while they watch television.' Little wonder she was slipping behind. Students need a quiet place to be able to concentrate on their schoolwork.

'Gran says she'll get me a desk when I live there,' Tilly said, still irritated.

'That's nice of her, but in the meantime I think it might be better if you didn't go there after school on Friday, but –'

'No,' she interrupted.

'Listen to me first. You could get all your homework done here on Friday evening, so you would have the weekend free and not have to worry about it.'

She groaned and then said, 'I'll think about it.'

'Good, and I'll see what Isa says.'

I emailed Isa the following day with my suggestion and she replied to say it was fine with her. Thankfully Tilly saw the advantages in this new arrangement and agreed that from now on, she would do her homework on Friday evening at home with me, then go to her gran's on Saturday morning to stay for the weekend.

'I'll be moving in there before long anyway,' she said. Which was quite possible.

On Tuesday my new supervising social worker, Joy Philips, telephoned. She sounded very upbeat and efficient. She'd read Edith's reports on my previous placements and had also brought herself up to date on Tilly. She thanked me for all I was doing for her and for managing without a supervising social worker. I didn't say it had been easy.

She pointed out that my annual review was coming up soon and said she'd email the forms I needed to complete. She then arranged to visit me on Thursday afternoon when she would complete the foster-carer health and safety check. This is done annually at the same time as the carer's review. It involves checking the carer's fire-safety plan and safer-caring policy, as well as going round the house and checking things like carbon monoxide and smoke alarms, window-safety catches, bolts on doors and plug-socket covers. The list seemed to grow each year. She would also want to see my house and car insurance, and the car's MOT, electrical and gas safety check certificates, home and contents insurance, and pet assessment. She was likely to be with me for over two hours, if not longer, and that was in addition to the review forms I would have to complete online. Foster carers often silently groan when they are faced with their annual review. The form filling can be quite daunting when we are short of time and all we want to do is get on with looking after the child. But of course, ultimately, it's for the good of the child to make sure they are receiving the best standard of care possible.

As it turned out, my grumbles about my annual review were soon overridden by a much greater worry. On Wednesday Tilly went to see her mother and gran after school as usual, but at five o'clock, the time she was supposed to leave to catch the bus home, Nancy called my landline.

'Can you come and collect Tilly?' she said, out of breath and anxious. 'She's in no fit state to catch the bus.'

'Why? What's happened?' I asked, immediately concerned.

'I don't really understand these things, but it's something to do with a photograph Tilly found on her mother's phone.' My heart began to race.

'What photo?'

'I haven't seen it, but it's a picture of Tilly. I don't understand what all the fuss is about, but Tilly has gone on at her mother something awful and got herself in a right state. They've both been in tears.'

'I'll come straight over.'

'Thank you.'

Grabbing my bag and keys, I flew out of the front door. A photo on Heather's phone? Was it the same photo Tilly had been sent? But why was Tilly angry with her mother? Could Heather have been the one who'd sent it? But she hardly used her phone, and why would she send the photo to Tilly without an explanation? It didn't make sense.

I got caught up in the rush-hour traffic and it was half an hour before I drew up outside Nancy's bungalow. I walked quickly up the front path and rang the bell. Tilly opened the door. 'What's happened?' I asked. She looked annoyed but wasn't crying. I guessed they'd all had time to calm down.

'Mum was sent that photo too but didn't tell me,' Tilly said.

'Come in and close the door!' Nancy called from the living. 'I don't want the whole street hearing our business.'

'Is it the same photo?' I asked Tilly as I went in, lowering my voice.

'Yes. It was sent from the same number, and at the same time, but Mum didn't see it for some days because she didn't switch on her phone, and then she didn't tell me!'

I followed Tilly into the living room where Nancy was in her usual armchair and Heather was sitting on the sofa. You could cut the atmosphere with a knife.

'I really didn't need all this upset,' Nancy said with a heartfelt sigh.

'I've told you, Mum, it's not my fault,' Heather said. It's got nothing to do with me. I didn't even know it was on my phone.'

'Because you never use it!' Tilly snapped.

'Heather, do you have any idea who might have sent the photo?' I asked. 'It is important.'

'No,' she said. 'I've already told Tilly that.'

I looked at her carefully. Something in her manner said she knew a lot more than she was saying.

CHAPTER NINETEEN

A MESSAGE

'Even when Mum found the photo, she didn't tell me!' Tilly said, with rising anger.

'Because I knew you'd be angry with me, and I was right,' Heather returned, trembling with emotion.

'Tilly is angry because you *didn't* tell her,' I pointed out. 'The fact that you have received a copy of the photo changes things.'

'Will someone please tell me what's going on?' Nancy asked with another heartfelt sigh.

'I've tried to explain to you, Gran,' Tilly said. 'Someone sent a photo of me in my underwear to Mum and me.'

'Yes, I know, but why?'

'That's what we'd like to know,' I said.

'Who took the photo?' Nancy asked.

'I suppose I did,' Tilly said, 'when I was living with Mum, but I don't remember taking it.'

'So what's the problem?' Nancy asked.

Tilly looked at me, clearly frustrated, but Nancy was of a different generation. She would have taken photographs on a camera, had them printed at the chemist and then mounted them in an album. There'd been no malicious and anonymous circulating of images online.

'Gran, I need to know who sent them and why,' Tilly said firmly, putting it as simply as possible.

'You don't have any clue?' I asked Heather again.

She shook her head but didn't make eye contact.

There was no point in pressing her further. It was clear that if she was harbouring any suspicion as to who was responsible, she wasn't going to say now. They'd all exchanged angry words and Tilly had probably said more than she should have, but she had my sympathy. Nancy could be forgiven for not appreciating the seriousness of what had happened, but I felt Heather could have shown more empathy. Tilly was her daughter.

'I'm tired,' Nancy said.

'We'll go,' I replied. Then to Heather, 'If you do remember anything, can you let Tilly or me know straight away, please?'

'Yes.'

'OK, let's go then.'

Tilly said a subdued goodbye to her mother and gran without her usual warmth, and we left the two of them sitting in awkward silence.

'Are you all right?' I asked her as we went down the front garden path.

'Gran says she can't cope with all this upset. I think she means she can't cope with me.'

'I'm sure she doesn't mean that,' I said. 'She's struggling to understand.' We paused by the car before getting in. 'Your gran is recovering from cancer and chemo. Things are bound to get on top of her. Perhaps you can now see why Isa wanted you to wait before moving in?'

Tilly nodded and we got into the car.

'I remember Gran used to be so strong,' Tilly said, fastening her seatbelt.

'Yes, and she will be again. Give her time and try to keep her stress levels down.' I started the car and pulled away. I was still thinking about something that had occurred to me while we'd been in the living room. 'Tilly, not many people know your mother's mobile number, do they?'

'No. Me, Gran, you, and I think she gave it to the doctor.'

'Dave will have it too,' I pointed out. 'Have you checked her phone for spyware recently?'

'Yes. I looked today. It's clear. That's how I discovered the photo, while I was checking.'

'Is it possible Dave sent the photos?' I said.

'No, I wouldn't have sent it to him.'

'Could he have taken it?' I asked.

'What? No! I would never have posed in my underwear for him! Not in a million years. What do you take me for?'

I paused and chose my words very carefully. 'Tilly, I've been fostering a long time and sadly many of the children and young adults I've looked after have been sexually abused. It's never their fault, but often they have been persuaded, threatened or bribed with gifts, to do sexual things for the abuser. It's called grooming. They are made to feel very guilty, like it's their fault. They are often too scared to tell as they fear they will be punished or are worried what others will think of them. Mostly the abuser is someone they know, sometimes a family member who they loved and trusted. That can make it even more difficult for them to tell.' I paused and glanced at Tilly.

'I know where you're coming from on this,' she said. 'But no, Dave didn't sexually abuse me. And I certainly wouldn't have posed for him in my underwear no matter what he said or gave me.'

'OK, love.'

Was she telling me the truth? I wasn't sure, but I had laid the foundations and opened the door for her to tell me if she did have a terrible secret. It had always concerned me that Dave had given her a lot of gifts – for example, nice clothes, a smart phone and an iPad. She'd been treated specially, spoiled by him, when he'd hardly given his wife anything. Had he been grooming Tilly into posing for the photo, or worse?

I remembered her original comments when she hadn't wanted to show me the photo on her phone – 'You'll hate me,' she'd said. It fitted with the guilt she might have been feeling if Dave had coerced her into posing in her underwear. Tilly despised her stepfather but claimed it was because of the way he treated her mother. Was there another, even more sinister reason? While I wasn't going to let my speculations run away with me, I'd seen enough in all my years of fostering to know that, sadly, this was an option I couldn't rule out.

Tilly was subdued that evening but managed to do a little of her schoolwork before saying she was going to have an early night. The following morning before she left for school I reminded her that my new supervising social worker, Joy, would be here when she returned. Joy had timed her visit so she could meet Tilly. I also wished Paula good luck, as her exams started today.

That morning I did a large food shop, packed it all away and then gave the house a tidy in preparation for Joy's visit that afternoon. I collected together all the information and certificates she would need for my annual review and set them ready with my log book and fostering folder in the living room. Joy arrived promptly at 2.30. Of average height and build, she looked to be in her late forties. She was dressed smart-casual, in light grey trousers and a short-sleeved blouse, and had neatly layered chin-length brown hair.

'Lovely to meet you,' she said with a smile. Coming in, she shook my hand. 'I'm sorry you have been left so long without a supervising social worker.'

'It's OK. It wasn't your fault,' I said.

'No, but it's poor practice.' Which was true.

I showed her through to the living room where the patio doors were slightly open on another lovely June day. Sammy was sitting on the patio in the shade. Joy admired the garden and then accepted a coffee. She came with me into the kitchen while I made it, telling me a bit about herself and her work history, first in child protection and now in fostering. We took our drinks into the living room.

'We've got a lot to get through,' Joy said, sitting on the sofa and placing her coffee on the table. She opened a folder and then her laptop. 'Thanks for completing your review forms online. Your DBS [Disclosure and Barring Service – a police check] is still current, but I noticed you're due for a medical this year.'

'Yes, I am.' Foster carers have a medical every two years and they and their families are police-checked every three years. The UK has some of the most stringent vetting and monitoring practices for foster carers in the world.

'I'll email the form you need for the medical,' she said as she typed. 'Now let's talk about Tilly. I'm looking forward to meeting her later. How is she getting on?'

I spent the next twenty minutes or so bringing Joy up to date about Tilly while she asked various questions and made notes on her laptop. I included school, health, friendships, family ties and yesterday's upset when Tilly had found the photo on her mother's phone. I didn't share my speculation about Dave possibly abusing Tilly.

'So you really don't know where the photo came from?' Joy asked, puzzled.

'No. Tilly thinks she might have taken it, but she can't remember sending it to anyone.'

Joy nodded as she typed, and I continued with my update. Joy was very sympathetic to Nancy's ill health and Heather's suffering, but like Isa her first priority was the well-being of Tilly. She felt that being in care offered her the best chance of stability and routine at present. Joy then began the Health and Safety Checklist. We went into all the rooms in the house, and then into the garden as she checked and ticked the boxes and asked me various questions. She even needed to check the padlocks on the shed door and side gate. The garden, like the house, had to be well maintained and safe for children of all ages. It was a ten-page document and took us the best part of an hour. At the end I was asked to sign it.

We returned to the living room with another cup of coffee and Joy asked me about our household routine, what we did in our leisure time and if there had been any changes to the household. I told her Lucy was no longer living with us and the reason why. Paula came home having completed her exams for the day; there were more the following week. I introduced her to Joy, who asked her how she'd done. Paula said she wasn't sure but had tried her best, which is all any of us can do. Joy also asked her how she liked fostering. Paula said, 'Fine. It's interesting. We've been doing it a long time.' Then she excused herself and got a drink before going to her room. I think she was exhausted, and of course fostering was the norm for her.

It was now gone four o'clock and I was expecting Tilly home soon.

'Does Tilly attend any out-of-school activities?' Joy asked me.

'No. She feels that with going to her gran's and schoolwork there isn't time. I've suggested she may like to enrol in one of the summer sport activities at our local leisure centre.' The schools broke up in seven weeks and places filled quickly.

'What did Tilly say?' Joy asked, making a note.

'She wasn't keen. She said she was planning on spending more time with her friends and Gran.'

'Has Isa agreed to the additional contact?'

'Not yet.'

'Have you booked to go away?' Joy asked.

'Just for a long weekend to a holiday village. I booked it a while ago, so I'm hoping Tilly will come with us. It's just Paula and me going, as Lucy won't be coming and Adrian is going away with Kirsty.'

I heard a key go in the front door and Tilly let herself in.

'We're in here,' I called from the living room.

'I'll get a drink and then come in,' she replied.

A couple of minutes later Tilly appeared with a glass of juice. She looked reasonably happy, so I assumed she'd had a good day.

'Lovely to meet you,' Joy said, smiling. 'I'm Cathy's new supervising social worker. How are you?'

'All right,' Tilly said, and sat beside me on the sofa.

Unlike the child's social worker, the foster carer's supervising social worker doesn't have to spend time alone with the child, so I stayed as Joy talked to Tilly. She asked her how she was getting on at school, what she liked to do in her spare time and finally if there was anything she needed.

'More phone credit,' Tilly said, throwing me a knowing look.

'You'll have your allowance on Saturday as usual,' I reminded her. It was reasonable that Tilly learnt to budget her money, just as we all have to.

Joy agreed and asked her how much allowance I gave her and what she liked to spend it on. As we'd been talking Tilly's phone, lying between us on the sofa, had been vibrating with incoming messages, which she'd resisted the urge to check. A few minutes later she asked Joy if she was going to be much longer as she had homework to do. I thought it was probably more about answering all the messages. Joy said she'd finished, thanked her and said she hoped to see her again soon.

Tilly went upstairs to her bedroom as Joy packed away her laptop and folders, thanking me for my time. 'I know how busy you foster carers are,' she said, which I was pleased to hear. I saw her out and then cleared away all my paperwork and the certificates Joy had needed to see. My first impression of her was that she was caring, efficient and level-headed. More like Jill than Edith – my previous supervising social workers.

I went into the kitchen, fed Sammy and began opening and closing various cupboard doors, wondering what we could have for dinner. Suddenly I heard Tilly's raised voice on the phone. 'What? You're kidding me! Cathy said that.'

She sounded very emotional and, wondering what was wrong and what I'd said, I went upstairs to her bedroom. The door was slightly ajar. I knocked and pushed it open. Tilly was standing in the middle of the room, clearly agitated, her phone pressed to her ear. As I entered, she turned to me.

'You were right,' she said. 'It was him. Can you speak to my mother?' She thrust the phone into my hand.

'Heather, it's Cathy,' I said. 'What's the matter?'

'I knew Tilly would be angry,' she said in a small voice. 'Which is why I didn't want to tell her, but Mum said I had to.'

'Tell her what?' I asked, meeting Tilly's gaze.

'When I switched on my phone today a text message came through. It was from the same number that sent the photo. The message said, *You should be ashamed of yourself allowing your daughter to dress like that*.'

'I see,' I said.

'Dave sent it.'

'What makes you say that?'

'It's the type of thing he used to say to me. He was always giving Tilly money for new clothes, but then he'd have a go at me about what she'd bought. Her skirt was too short, her trousers too tight, her top too low so you could see her breasts. He was always accusing me of letting her dress like a tart. I'm sure at some point he actually used those very words that are in the message – *You should be ashamed of yourself allowing your daughter to dress like that*.'

'Have you tried phoning the number or replying to the text?' I asked.

'No. I'm too afraid. I'm sure it's him.'

'Probably best not to respond, but don't delete the message for now.'

'I'm not using my phone ever again,' she said, her voice catching.

'We'll get you a new SIM so he won't know your number.'

'But he knows where I'm living,' she said, all her old fears returning.

'If he does show up there, call the police.'

'I felt so scared getting that text. Just like I used to,' Heather admitted. 'I know he's not actually threatening to kill me or anything, but just receiving it was enough.'

'I understand.' Victims of domestic violence can be threatened or controlled by their abuser with just a look or tone of voice, which might not be obvious to anyone else.

'Do you think we should tell the police about the message?' Heather asked. 'Mum says it'll be a waste of time.'

'It's up to you, but I will tell Tilly's social worker. Heather, can I ask you something? It's a bit personal.'

'Yes.'

'Did Dave ever act inappropriately towards Tilly? You know, in a manner which made you feel uncomfortable?' Tilly was watching me carefully, her eyes widening at my question.

There was silence before Heather said, 'I'm not sure. I'm so confused about everything that happened in my life with him. He always liked Tilly better than me. I could never do anything right, but she was faultless in his eyes. He spoilt her.'

'OK, but as far as you know, did he act inappropriately?'

'I don't think so. Say goodbye to Tilly for me. I'm going to have a lie-down. I don't feel so good.'

'I will. Take care.'

CHAPTER TWENTY

MORE PHOTOGRAPHS

On Saturday I gave Tilly extra money in her allowance so she could buy a new SIM card for her mother's phone. Replacing it was something that should have been done when the tracking software had been discovered. Now Tilly was going to have to explain to her mother and gran that the new SIM carried a new number, which Dave wouldn't know so he wouldn't be able to contact Heather again. I thought Heather would need a lot of convincing.

I emailed an update to Isa, copying in Joy, as I was supposed to. While the text message hadn't been sent to Tilly but her mother, it was relevant to her and part of the wider picture so they needed to know. I also noted it in my log.

Lucy and Darren came for lunch. It was another lovely day and we ate outside. After, when I was in the kitchen putting the finishing touches to the trifle I'd made for dessert, Lucy came in and propped herself against a cupboard with a small sigh.

'You OK, love?' I asked her.

She gave a half-hearted nod. 'Does it hurt a lot when you have a baby?' she asked.

I stopped what I was doing to look at her. 'It's very uncomfortable, but you can have pain relief if you need it. And your body soon forgets the discomfort once you have your baby.'

'I'm really scared,' she admitted.

'Oh, love.' I went to her and hugged her, wrapping her protectively in my arms as I used to when she was a child. 'You'll be fine,' I reassured her, and kissed her cheek. 'Darren will be with you and you can ask for an epidural if the pain becomes too much.'

'I want to try a water birth first and see how it goes,' she said.

'All right, but don't feel you have to prove anything. Ask for pain relief as and when you need it.' For many women, including myself, giving birth is painful, but as soon as your little bundle is placed in your arms it all becomes worthwhile and you forget the pain and all the hours of discomfort.

'Someone I know was in labour for two days,' Lucy said, looking worried. 'She had to have a blood transfusion and a forceps delivery and loads of stitches. She said it was a nightmare and she'd never do it again.'

How insensitive to tell someone who was heavily pregnant that, I thought!

'She obviously had a very bad experience,' I said. 'But for most women the pain is manageable and the birth goes to plan. Some women hardly feel any pain at all.'

'I hope that's me,' Lucy said, with a grimace.

'Is everything else all right?' I asked.

'I guess.'

'Come on, Lucy. What's the matter?' I took her hand in mine. 'You've been quiet all afternoon. Is it just that you're worried about giving birth or is there something else bothering you?' I wondered if her and Darren were having problems.

'I'm really worried I'm not going to be a good mum, and I'll make a mess of it like Bonnie did,' she admitted, and her eyes filled.

'Lucy, that won't happen, love,' I said, hugging her again. 'You'll make a fantastic mother.'

'But how can you be sure? Bonnie was crap.'

'Because I know you and you're my daughter. You are kind, sensible and caring, and you love children. You chose a career working with children. You'll be a wonderful mother and if you do need any help, you've got Darren and all of us. Bonnie didn't have anyone and struggled with a lot of problems. You and she are two very different people with different life experiences. History won't repeat itself. Good parenting isn't inherited, it's learnt, so stop worrying. You are going to be the best mother ever.'

I passed her a tissue and waited as she wiped her eyes, then asked. 'What's brought this on? Have you heard from Bonnie again?'

She shook her head. 'No. I've just been thinking and worrying. Darren said it's probably my hormones. I feel very tearful at times. I get tired and sometimes things seem to get on top of me.'

'That can happen in late pregnancy. Have you mentioned it to the doctor?'

'No, I'll be OK.'

'Do you think you should stop working earlier than you planned so you can rest? We could spend more time together.'

She smiled. 'I'll see how it goes. I've only got another four weeks anyway. Then, after the baby is born, we will spend lots of time together.'

'Good. I'll look forward to that. I'm glad we've had this chat.'

'So am I, Mum.' We hugged some more.

'Are you feeling a bit brighter now?' I asked after a moment.

'I am, thanks. Shall we have that trifle now?'

'Yes, you take it and I'll bring the fresh fruit salad.'

We returned to the garden carrying the bowls of dessert and Lucy seemed happier for our chat. I would keep an eye on her, though, and text or phone her each day and make a point of asking how she felt. I didn't think she was depressed, just a bit up and down, which – as I'd told her – can happen in pregnancy. It was reassuring that she'd confided in Darren and I felt sure he would persuade her to go to the doctor if he felt it was necessary.

On Sunday Adrian and I went to see Mum in his car. Paula was doing some last-minute studying in preparation for her final exams the following week. We ate out and then Adrian did some odd jobs for Mum as I cleaned the kitchen floor. Some of the housework was becoming too much for Mum and I'd talked to her about getting a cleaner. She didn't want one, claiming she could manage, so if I spotted something needed doing then I quietly did it.

Adrian and I returned home just before Tilly, then he went out to see Kirsty. Tilly said she'd had a nice weekend and that she, her mother and gran had walked to their local park. This was a first as far as I knew. Due to Nancy's ill health and Heather's ongoing concerns about Dave, the three of them hadn't gone that far before. It was an achievement and gave hope for the future. Tilly said she'd replaced the SIM in her mother's phone and had reassured her it was safe. She'd left it fully charged and switched on.

* * *

On Monday, after I'd seen everyone off, I booked an appointment online at my doctor's for the medical I needed for my review, then did some housework and two loads of washing, which I hung on the line to dry. Shortly after one o'clock I took a sandwich lunch through to the front room and switched on the computer, ready to do some admin work. I was just about to start when the landline rang. I answered it at my desk. My heart fell as I heard Miss Jenkins's voice. I knew it had to be bad news for the deputy head to phone halfway through Monday.

'I've got Tilly with me in my office,' she said. 'She's very distraught. When she switched on her phone at lunchtime some indecent images came through. She says they are of her, although her face isn't visible. She's claiming they are from her stepfather.'

'They can't be,' I said. 'He doesn't have her phone number. When we converted her phone to pay as you go she had a new SIM, which gave her a new number. Unless he's obtained it from someone or Tilly has given it to him, which I doubt.'

'I'm not convinced the images are of Tilly or that her stepfather sent them,' Miss Jenkins said. 'Tilly was hysterical. But they are indecent and sending them is an offence. After everything I've said to the students! I've notified the police and also Tilly's social worker, but she's in court. Tilly's in no fit state to return to lessons this afternoon so can you come and collect her, please?'

'Yes, of course, I'll leave straight away.'

'Thank you. I've returned Tilly's phone to her, but don't let her delete the images as the police will want to see them.'

'All right.'

I got into my car and drove as fast as the speed limit allowed to Tilly's school, all manner of thoughts flashing through my mind. Tilly was waiting in reception when I arrived, as the deputy head's room was being used for a meeting. She looked pale and shaken but relieved to see me. 'Miss doesn't believe me,' she said as I signed us out. 'It *is* me in the photos and Dave *did* send them.'

'How can you be sure?' I asked as we left the building.

'The phone number is the same one that sent the other photo and text to Mum. She's sure it's him.' But it was still supposition. We crossed the playground and let ourselves out of the main gate.

'The police will get to the bottom of it,' I said, unlocking the car doors. 'Do we know when they are visiting us?'

'No. But it is me,' Tilly persisted. We got into the car. 'Look,' she said, tilting her phone towards me so I could see the screen. She swiped through three images. They were different shots of a naked female, who looked about the same age, colouring and build as Tilly. They weren't posed photographs as the previous one she'd received had been, but more casual shots. The subject was always turned away, so it was impossible to identify the girl, but they were indecent. In two of them the subject had been caught bending over, exposing her bottom and genitalia. The background seemed to have been Photoshopped as it was a country scene.

'That's my mole, there,' Tilly said, pointing to the mark visible on the third photo.

Just above the subject's left buttock was a mole. I'd never seen Tilly naked, but she would know if she had a mole or not. Yet how many thousands of other young women had moles in a similar place? I could understand why Tilly was so upset, and if they weren't of her, why had they been sent to her?

'OK, love,' I said. She put away her phone and I started the engine and began the drive home.

'I think Dave took them in my bedroom,' Tilly said after a moment.

'Without you knowing?' I asked sceptically.

'Yes. I didn't let him take them!' she said, her upset and anger flaring again.

'I know, love. I'm not suggesting you did, but how could he have taken them without you knowing?' Yet as I said it, I realized there was a way. 'Through your phone,' I added.

Tilly looked at me.

'Spyware can be bought online that allows the user to look through the lens of a camera, laptop or tablet.'

'Yes! That's what's happened. It must be!' she cried.

'No, Tilly calm down. I could be wrong.'

'I'm sure you're right,' she insisted. 'We'll tell the police. I know those photos are of me. I didn't take them and neither did Abby, and I certainly didn't pose for him. I bet he took that other one too, and what else has he taken that I don't know about?' She stared at me, horrified. 'The bastard! I'll fucking kill him!'

'Tilly, we're jumping to conclusions. We'll tell the police and they can investigate. Your friend who found the tracking software on your phone that time on the bus, he didn't say he'd found spyware too, did he?'

'No, he would have said. Perhaps Dave removed it before I left home.'

'It's possible, or maybe there is another explanation we haven't thought of yet,' I suggested. I pride myself on being level-headed and I was really struggling to believe someone, possibly Dave, had placed spyware on Tilly's phone and taken indecent images of her. It was like a scene from a spy movie.

Yet tracking software had been found on Tilly's phone, so was it really such a huge leap to believe Dave had done this too? Assuming it was him, which had yet to be proved.

'I hope the police come soon,' Tilly said as I drove. 'I'm seeing Gran and Mum this afternoon.'

'You might have to give that a miss today,' I said. 'You'll need to stay in until the police have been. They might not arrive until this evening or tonight.' I'd had to wait in for the police before with other young people I'd fostered. They arrived when they could. I doubted this would be a priority, given all the other, more serious crimes and incidents they'd probably be responding to.

I was wrong.

As I pulled into our road and our house came into view, we could see a police car parked outside. 'They're here!' Tilly cried.

'Yes.'

I drew up and parked. A policewoman was at our front door.

'Hello,' I said, getting out. 'Have you come to see Tilly?'

'Yes. I'm Police Constable Macie Byrne.'

'I'm Cathy Glass, Tilly's foster carer.'

She said hello to Tilly. I let us in, and we went through to the living room.

'I'll need to take some details,' PC Byrne said. 'Are you able to stay with us?' she asked me.

'Yes.' All minors should have an appropriate adult with them when they are interviewed by the police.

We sat down and PC Byrne took out a notepad and pen and asked Tilly for her full name, date of birth, mobile-phone number and address. She gave her the details, this address and also her gran's, explaining she stayed there at weekends.

'She used to live with her mother and her stepfather, Dave, at his house,' I added. 'He still lives there.' I gave her that address too.

'But this is where I can reach Tilly if necessary?' she asked, meaning my home.

'Yes,' I confirmed.

'Your teacher telephoned us and said you'd received some indecent images on your phone?' she said to Tilly.

'She's not my teacher. She's the deputy head,' Tilly corrected.

'Can I have a look at your phone, please?'

Tilly stood, went over and showed her the images on her phone, pointing out the mole that she felt confirmed the photos were of her.

'It's not nice for a young girl to receive these,' PC Byrne said, and noted the number they had come from.

'And there is this one,' Tilly said, showing her the previous one of her posing in sexy underwear. 'I convinced myself I'd taken it and had forgotten, but I knew I hadn't really.'

'Do you know who sent them?'

'Dave, my stepfather,' Tilly said decisively, and returned to sit next to me. 'I used to live with him and Mum.' She then explained the situation that had led to her coming into care: the dreadful arguments that had become physical, the abusive way Dave had treated her mother until she couldn't stand it any more.

'But why do you think your stepfather is responsible?' the PC asked.

'I know it's him. He's weird, and he's angry because Mum and I escaped him. He sent us both the photo of me in my underwear. Who else would do that? Mum doesn't know anyone apart from him, me and Gran. He saw to that.'

As PC Byrne finished writing, I said, 'The other thing you need to know is that tracking software was found on Tilly's phone. It was removed and we changed her number, so I'm not sure how Dave would have got hold of it, if it is him.'

'Presumably you gave your new number to your friends?' PC Byrne asked Tilly. 'Could one of them be responsible?'

'No! Why doesn't anyone believe me!' Tilly cried.

'We do,' the PC said. 'But you have to understand, I need evidence your stepfather is responsible. I appreciate that all the photos have come from the same number, but couldn't it be someone at school misguidedly thinking they're having a bit of fun?'

'I've never had a boyfriend and even if I had I wouldn't let him take photos of me like that. They're disgusting.'

PC Byrne nodded sympathetically, although I suspected she'd probably seen far worse indecent images in her job. Some of those circulating online are unbelievably shocking and depraved.

'And you're convinced they are of you?' she asked Tilly. 'You can't really tell, as your face isn't visible.'

'Yes, I'll show you my mole.' Tilly jumped up from the sofa and pulled down the waistband of her trousers just far enough to reveal a small mole above her left buttock.

'All right, thank you,' the PC said, throwing me a small smile.

'Will you arrest him?' Tilly asked, sitting down again.

'We'll certainly speak to your stepfather and see what he has to say.'

'He'll lie. He always does,' Tilly snapped.

'We're used to that,' the PC reassured her. 'Can I take your phone?' she asked.

Tilly's face fell. 'I need it. I use it all the time. I can't manage without it,' she exclaimed.

'I won't take it now then, but we might need it in the future.'

Had Tilly been accused of taking or sending indecent images, as had happened with one teenager I'd fostered (see my book *Finding Stevie*), the police officer would have taken her phone as evidence against her. But Tilly was the innocent party in this, and she knew not to delete the images.

'I'll be in touch,' PC Byrne said, and stood. 'Here is my card if you think of anything else.' She handed it to me.

I thanked her and saw her out. Tilly was still wound up and I calmed her down. There was time for her to visit her gran and mother, so she went upstairs to change out of her school uniform, then left to catch the bus.

Five minutes later Paula arrived home, made herself a drink and a snack and went to her room to study. She had her last exam the next day.

Ten minutes later Isa telephoned from her mobile, having just come out of court. I could hear the rumble of traffic in the background as I brought her up to date. 'Thank you,' she said. 'I'll speak to the police officer tomorrow.'

Twenty minutes after her call, as I was updating my log, Tilly telephoned, distraught. 'He sent those photos to Mum too, with a nasty text message saying I was a slut just like her. The bastard! Mum's in pieces. Can you tell that police officer? I haven't got her number.'

'Yes, I will. Were they sent from the same phone?'

'Yes.'

This seemed to add weight to the assumption that Dave had sent them. 'Does your gran know?'

'No. I haven't shown her. I'd be too embarrassed.'

'OK. She doesn't need another upset now.'

'I'll phone PC Byrne, and obviously don't let your mother delete the photos or the message.'

'No, I won't. I've got her phone.'

'Good. And Tilly, none of this is your fault. I want you to remember that.'

There was a small pause before she replied. 'Thank you. I've been feeling it was.'

'No. Absolutely not. I don't know what's going on, but it's certainly not your fault, love.'

CHAPTER TWENTY-ONE

HIDING SOMETHING

With my heart pounding from stress, I took the business card PC Byrne had given me from my fostering folder and called her mobile number. To my relief, she answered. 'It's Cathy Glass, Tilly's foster carer. You were here about an hour ago.'

'Yes, hello.'

'Tilly has just telephoned me from her grandmother's home. She's very upset. Her mother has received the same photos you saw with a nasty text message.'

'From the same number?'

'Yes.'

'I'll try to get there and talk to them before the end of my shift, otherwise it may be tomorrow. Do I have their address?'

'Yes. Tilly gave it to you.'

'Thank you. I'll be in touch.'

PC Byrne's calm and business-like manner was in contrast to how I was feeling. I immediately telephoned Tilly.

'Have you spoken to her?' she asked straight away.

'Yes. She's hoping to visit you this afternoon. But if she doesn't arrive by the time you are due to leave, come home anyway.'

'Wouldn't it be better if I stayed here tonight?' she asked.

'No, I want you to come home.' Apart from the fact that Isa hadn't approved the overnight stay, I felt that with so much upset going on we needed the stability of a routine. 'What reason will you give your gran for the police visit?' I asked Tilly.

'I told her Dave has been sending Mum and me nasty messages and we'd reported it to the police.'

'Yes. That works.'

I was on tenterhooks as I made dinner, wondering what was happening with Tilly and if PC Byrne was there. When Tilly didn't arrive home at 5.30 – the time she was usually back from contact – I called her mobile. It went through to voicemail. I left a message asking her to call me. Concerned, I phoned Nancy's landline and after a couple of rings she answered.

'It's Cathy, Tilly's carer,' I said. 'Tilly's not back yet. What time did she leave?'

'She's still here. We have a police officer with us now.'

'All right. I won't keep you then. If Tilly wants a lift home, tell her to phone me.'

It was after six o'clock when Tilly finally telephoned me, from the bus, and she was highly excitable. 'The police are going to interview Dave,' she said. 'Mum told the police officer she knew it was him. She's taken Mum's phone, but that doesn't matter because she never uses it. I hope he's locked up for ever.'

'And how is your gran?' I asked, concerned about the effect all this was having on her health.

'We didn't show her the photos. She said she was reassured the police were involved and Heather should have reported Dave years ago. Gran thinks this is more about the way he treated Mum than the photos.'

'OK.'

'Got to go now, Abby's calling. See you later.' The call ended.

Tilly was still high on adrenalin when she arrived home and it continued during dinner. She talked non-stop about what had happened at her gran's, how Dave was sly and devious but she thought the police would see through him. That she, her mum and gran hoped he would be put in prison for a very long time. She said she was now thinking of a career as a police officer so she could help women like her mother and her. I thought PC Byrne had made quite an impression.

'It's a good career,' Adrian remarked. 'You're never short of work.'

'But you'll need qualifications, so best do some studying,' I added.

After dinner Tilly went to her bedroom, ostensibly to do some homework, although from what I could hear she spent most of the evening on her phone, updating her friends. The high drama continued with each new call as they hypothesized, surmised and guessed the outcome of the police interviewing Dave. Eventually at 9.30, when there was still no sign of the chatter abating, I told her nicely to switch off her phone. A blissful silence descended on the house. Exhausted, I had an early night.

Tilly found the next day and the day after something of an anti-climax, as nothing appeared to be happening.

'The police will need time to investigate,' I said. 'Weeks, possibly months.' I'm not sure what she was expecting, but I doubted PC Byrne seeing her stepfather would result in the swift summary justice Tilly was hoping for. 'And we don't know for certain that phone number belongs to Dave,' I pointed out. 'It could be someone else sending those photos.' Which wasn't what Tilly wanted to hear, not at all, but at present it was still a possibility.

'Mum and Gran think he's guilty,' she said. 'So do I.'

'And he may be, but the police will need to be able to prove it,' I said. I'd come across cases of child abuse where the abuser was almost certainly guilty, but there hadn't been enough evidence to take it to court.

As the week passed Tilly gradually settled down again. Paula had taken her final exam and she spent more time with me, which was nice. She was also applying to companies offering trainee positions for those with qualifications in business studies. All the application forms were online in the first instance.

On Thursday evening, when Tilly didn't have contact, she and Paula went to our local park, which had tennis courts. They played tennis for an hour or so, then had an ice cream at the park café. On Friday Tilly went to Abby's home after school for supper and I collected her at nine o'clock. On Saturday she left as usual to go to her gran's. I wasn't expecting to hear from her again until she returned on Sunday. But that afternoon while I was doing some gardening, and Paula and Adrian were both out, Tilly called my mobile, which I had with me in the garden.

'Dave has been arrested!' she cried ecstatically. 'PC Byrne has just been here to tell Mum. She'd forgotten I stay here at the weekends and was going to see me at your place, but she doesn't have to now! They found other photos of me, the creep, so it *was* him all along. She says I may have to do a taped interview at the police station and she'll contact Isa next week.'

'So Dave has definitely been arrested?' I asked.

'Yes. That's what she said. If you don't believe me, ask Gran.'

I didn't have a chance to say I believed her, because Nancy was put on the phone.

'It's true,' she said. 'Dave has been arrested. I can't tell you how relieved we all are. Hopefully we can get on with our lives now. Heather will feel safer with him inside.'

Although I knew it was highly likely Dave would be released on bail. 'How is Heather?' I asked.

'Not saying much. Still in a state of shock. I mean, we knew he was nasty, but from what I understand these messages he's been sending are vile.'

'Yes.' I heard their doorbell ring in the bungalow and Tilly's voice call, 'I'll get it, Gran.'

'That'll be my neighbour, Babs,' Nancy said. 'She phoned just after the police car left to make sure we were all right. I told her to come round.'

'I'll leave you to it then,' I said. 'Enjoy the rest of your weekend.'

'We will.'

They were pleased, and so of course was I. They hadn't given any details of the charges or how and when Dave had taken the photographs, but I assumed it was through spyware either on Tilly's phone, laptop or tablet, all of which had webcams. Because the software to achieve this is relatively easy to purchase and use, I've always covered the webcams on our devices with a piece of sticking plaster that can be removed for Skype or FaceTime. The best anti-malware protection won't necessarily detect it if someone is spying on you through the webcam. So great is the problem now that you can buy stylish branded webcam covers, but Adrian,

Paula and Lucy still use a sticking plaster to cover the lens on their laptops.

I picked up the gardening trowel and continued weeding, my thoughts buzzing with this new development. There still remained the question of how Dave had obtained Tilly's new phone number, but I assumed that would come out in time. Tilly had said the police had found more photographs of her but hadn't given any details. The poor child. At present she was relieved and delighted Dave had been caught, but when the dust had settled and she'd had time to reflect on what he'd been doing, she would be devastated and feel violated. I thought she would need a lot of support to get through it and possibly therapy.

Although Dave hadn't physically sexually assaulted her (as far as we knew), secretly taking intimate photographs of her was not only illegal but a dreadful assault on her privacy and dignity. Goodness only knew what perverted pleasure he'd found in sending them to Tilly and her mother. If he hadn't sent them, he might never have been caught. I would do all I could to help Tilly, and I felt sure Isa would suggest she see a counsellor at CAMHS.

On Sunday Paula and I went to see my mother. As usual we left in time to arrive back home just before Tilly. However, she was already in.

'You're home early,' I said. 'Is everything all right?'

'I guess,' she said but looked downcast. 'I wanted some time alone.'

'Anything you want to share?' I asked as Paula went up to her room.

Tilly shrugged. 'Mum was getting on my nerves and Gran was tired, so I left.'

'I expect they are both very worried,' I said.

'It's not that. The police want Mum to go to the police station and make a statement, but she says she doesn't feel up to it, and we should all move on.'

I was surprised by this. At some point they would hope-fully all 'move on', but they hadn't reached that point yet, not by a long way. Tilly needed to see justice first, and if her mother giving a statement helped to achieve this then she needed to do it.

'I guess it's come as a huge shock to your mum, realizing she's been living with a paedophile all these years,' I said, and shuddered at the thought.

'Gran told her she needed to stand by me and do whatever was necessary. Gran said she would go with Mum to the police station and make a statement herself if it helped. Mum thought Gran was blaming her for not protecting me better, but it wasn't like that in my house. Mum didn't protect me, I protected her.'

'Yes, I know. Hopefully your mother will feel a bit better in a few days. She was starting to do all right before this. What about your video evidence? Do we know the date for that yet?'

'No. PC Byrne said she'd speak to Isa about it next week.'

'OK.'

Tilly watched some television in the living room with me that evening, only occasionally checking her phone. She was quiet and looked pensive and a little sad. I thought the high drama of the day before had gone and reality was setting in. I asked her a few times if she was all right and if she wanted to talk, but she didn't. I think she just wanted some company.

Lucy telephoned during the evening for a chat and I took the call in another room. She said she was stopping work the following week, a little earlier than planned, as she was really struggling. I told her I thought that was sensible and if she needed any help financially or otherwise to let me know. She also said she and Darren were trying to think of a name for the baby but hadn't decided on one yet. However, they were going to join their surnames together for their child as some of their friends had done.

'A double-barrelled surname, that's posh,' I said.

'Not really. It just seems to make sense.' I knew the practice had been common in many other countries for generations, and it was gaining popularity in the UK as women were no longer taking the man's name so often when they married.

We chatted for a while longer and then I returned to the living room. Paula joined Tilly and me and the three of us watched a film together.

On Monday Tilly didn't want to go to school. My first thought was that some of her fellow students had received the photographs, but she assured me that wasn't so and she was just exhausted from a broken night's sleep and wouldn't be able to concentrate on her lessons. While I could appreciate the effect all this must be having on her, I didn't want her to start missing school and falling behind again. Also, being at school would give her something else to think about.

'I'll take you in the car,' I offered. 'You're seeing your gran and mother after school.' Which she usually looked forward to.

She turned over in bed and tried to ignore me, but eventually, after a lot of cajoling, she got up. Once showered and dressed, she said she felt better and was OK to catch the bus to school.

'Phone or text me at lunchtime to let me know how you

are,' I told her as I saw her off at the door. 'And remember, Miss Jenkins is there for you too.'

She left with a small nod and, putting in her earbuds, headed off towards the bus stop.

I texted her at lunchtime: *How's it going?*

She replied with a thumbs-up emoji, so I assumed she was all right. I sent her a similar text message at the end of school and she responded with another thumbs-up emoji. I thought about calling her but decided against it. I didn't want her to feel I was being overly protective or checking up on her. I sometimes find it difficult to get the balance right – knowing when to give a young person space to work through their problems, thoughts and feelings, and when to step in with help, support and advice.

When Tilly arrived home from seeing her gran and mother, I naturally asked her how they were. She said her gran had gone to the hospital that morning for a follow-up appointment and the scan had showed there was no sign of cancer, which was wonderful news.

'And your mother?' I asked.

She shrugged. 'Don't know. She was in her bedroom all the time I was there. Gran said she was having a lie-down as she had a headache, so I didn't really see her. I called goodbye as I left, but she must have been asleep as she didn't answer.'

I guessed the strain was taking its toll on Heather, but I knew it would get worse before it got better. Evidence would need to be collected by the police as they put together a case against Dave. Only once it had been to court, assuming there was enough evidence to take it to court, and justice had been done, would Tilly, her mother and gran be able to recover.

* * *

I was expecting to hear from Isa, but it was late Wednesday afternoon before she telephoned, having spoken to PC Byrne. Tilly was at her gran's for contact. 'You're aware Tilly's step-father was arrested last week?' Isa began.

'Yes. The police officer visited Nancy and Heather at the weekend when Tilly was there and told them. I understand the police found more photographs of Tilly?'

'A lot more,' she sighed. 'I need to see Tilly. I'll come tomorrow after school. About four-thirty.'

When Tilly returned home from contact I told her Isa would be visiting us the following afternoon. I also asked her how her mother was.

'The same,' she said, annoyed. 'She was up when I got there, but then went to her room. I didn't see her again. Gran said they'd had words but wouldn't tell me what. I think there's something going on I don't know about.'

'Like what?' I asked.

'I've just said I don't know,' Tilly snapped irritably. 'But they're hiding something, I'm sure. Gran's behaving oddly too.'

'We'll ask Isa when she comes tomorrow,' I said. 'Perhaps she knows something.'

She did, and it was devastating news.

CHAPTER TWENTY-TWO

A TERRIBLE SECRET

'There is no easy way to tell you this,' Isa began, looking very serious. We were in the living room and Isa had a pen and notepad on her lap. 'But you need to know your step-father has been spying on you.'

'I guessed that!' Tilly cried agitatedly. 'Through the lens on my phone.'

'Partly, but there's more to it, I'm afraid,' Isa replied.

Tilly was about to jump in with another comment when I touched her arm. 'Let's hear what Isa has to tell us first,' I said.

Isa nodded, took a breath and looked at Tilly as she spoke. 'Your stepfather has been taking indecent photographs and videos of you for many years.'

'Videos?' Tilly gasped.

'Yes. The police searched his house and took away a lot of material. It goes back some years. They think to when you were aged nine and ten.'

'What!' I cried in disbelief.

Isa nodded solemnly.

'He couldn't have,' Tilly said. 'I didn't have a phone then! How could he have taken photos and videos of me?'

'He used two covert cameras – spy cameras – and secreted one in your bedroom and the other in the bathroom.'

Tilly went ashen, stunned into silence, while I felt physically sick.

'I'm sorry, but you need to know this,' Isa said to Tilly. 'The police will refer to it when you make your statement.'

'He's been watching and filming Tilly since she was nine or ten years of age?' I said, struggling to take it in.

'I'm afraid so,' Isa replied sombrely.

'While I was in the bath and going to the toilet?' Tilly asked, horrified.

'I don't know all the details. The police are still going through the material,' Isa said.

'The fucking pervert!' Tilly cried, tears springing to her eyes.

'He is,' I agreed, and gently touched her arm. 'A paedophile. Did he circulate any of the pictures on the Internet?' I asked.

'There is no evidence of that so far,' Isa replied. 'It seems it was for his own use.'

'I suppose that's a small mercy,' I said. 'So as far as the police know, he only sent those photos to Tilly and her mother?'

'It would seem so.'

'Why?' I asked. 'If he hadn't done that, he might never have been caught.'

Isa shook her head with incomprehension. 'Who knows what was going through his mind? Perhaps it was about control and having the last word or embarrassing them, I don't know.'

'How did the police know to search his house?' I asked. Tilly was still sitting beside me in stunned silence. I was shocked, but I had many questions.

'When police forensics examined Heather's phone they discovered the photos were more likely to have been taken using a camera than a phone. I don't know how they knew, but you can tell if you know what you're looking for. So they applied for a search warrant and found the cameras. They were still in place. Dave has been seeing another woman, a single parent with two young girls. It seems likely they were going to be moving in soon.'

My stomach clenched. 'So he planned on doing the same to them?' I said, appalled.

'Yes, it would appear so. Some of their belongings were already at the house. I think they'd stayed overnight.'

I too fell quiet, and nausea rose as the full horror of what Dave had been doing hit me.

'I know this is very difficult for you,' Isa said to Tilly. 'But I need to ask you, did Dave every try to touch you sexually?'

'Not exactly,' Tilly said. 'But he was very touchy-feely all the time. I didn't like it. He would rub my neck as he passed, run his finger down my back and stand very close. He never did that to Mum. I felt uncomfortable and moved away.'

Isa nodded and made a note. 'The police are likely to ask you too. Did he ever come into your bedroom or the bathroom while you were in there?'

'No, but then if he was secretly filming me, he wouldn't have to! He could see me anyway. Fucking pervert. Where were the cameras hidden? I didn't see them.'

'You wouldn't. They were very small. I'm not sure where exactly they were located, but they were small enough to be hidden inside a clock or lamp. The police have all the details.' She paused and appeared to be choosing her next words very carefully. 'Tilly, there is something else you need to know.' I could tell from her expression it was serious and likely to cause Tilly pain. But what? Hadn't we heard the worst?

'It would seem your mother may have had some idea of what Dave was doing,' Isa said. Oh no, I thought, and swallowed hard. 'She has been interviewed by the police and will give a statement soon. I understand she's saying she suspected Dave might be up to something but didn't know what. I don't know if she will be prosecuted, but you should be aware it's a possibility.'

'She knew?' Tilly said in horror.

'Apparently your stepfather has implicated her.'

I took her hand and held it in mine. She was trembling.

'Is Nancy aware of all this?' I asked Isa.

'Yes, she is now.'

'Tilly thought there was an atmosphere when she was there. Heather has been keeping out of her way and yesterday she spent most of the time in her bedroom.'

Isa nodded. 'Tilly,' she said gently. 'I know this has all come as a huge shock. Is there anything you want to add or ask me?'

'I'm not going to live with Mum,' Tilly said, her voice breaking.

'There are no plans for you to do so, but we need to think about contact.'

'I'll want to see Gran, but not Mum,' Tilly said. 'I knew Gran was worried about something. I bet Mum told her not to tell me.'

'I've spoken to Nancy and she asked me to tell you, as she would have found it very difficult,' Isa explained.

'Tell Mum she needs to keep out of my way when I see Gran,' Tilly said vehemently.

'I can suggest it, but I can't force your mother to keep away from you; she lives with your gran.'

'Perhaps we should give contact a miss this weekend?' I suggested.

'What do you think, Tilly? Would that help?'

'I want to see Gran, but not Mum,' Tilly said again.

Isa looked at me, unsure of what to say for the best.

'What if Tilly went there just for the day?' I suggested. 'It might be easier. It would be impractical for Heather not to come into contact with Tilly for a whole weekend. She's living there and it's only a small bungalow.'

'Or should I set up contact at the Family Centre?' Isa asked Tilly. 'It wouldn't be at the weekend but after school for an hour or so.'

'No. I want to see my gran more than that, and I like going to her home. It's nice, and she's my family. I help her do things. I'll go for the day.'

'Saturday or Sunday?' Isa asked, making a note.

'Saturday,' Tilly said. 'And I want to keep going on Monday and Wednesday after school.'

'Yes, all right,' Isa agreed. 'We'll see how it goes. I'll tell your gran and mother. Also, your video interview is likely to be next week. I'll let you or Cathy know when I have a date and time. Try not to worry. I'll take you to the police station and stay with you.'

'Will I have to go to court?' Tilly asked anxiously.

'Sometimes the video evidence is enough. But if Dave pleads not guilty then it's likely his barrister will want to cross-examine you. You should be able to do that via a video link from another room in court, so you won't have to see him.'

'Is he likely to plead not guilty with all that evidence?' I asked.

'At present he is. He's denying everything.'

'How is that possible? When the police took away photos and videos?' I asked incredulously.

'He's entitled to plea whichever way he likes, that's not to say he will be believed. It will be for the jury to decide after they hear all the evidence,' Isa said.

Tilly looked even more worried. Going to court was another big ordeal for a fourteen-year-old to face on top of everything else.

'Any more questions?' Isa asked us both.

'I was wondering if Tilly might want to talk to someone at CAMHS,' I said.

Isa nodded. 'What do you think, Tilly? Would it help if I made a referral so you can talk to a counsellor?'

'Not fussed,' she returned absently.

'There's a waiting list, so I'll make the referral and then you can see how you feel when the appointment comes through.' Isa wrote and then said, 'If there's nothing else, I'll leave you to it. I'll phone once I have the time and date for the video interview. I'll also speak to your gran and mother about contact.'

She stood and I saw her to the door.

After Isa left, Tilly went straight to her bedroom to phone Abby while I made dinner. We still had to eat, whatever else was happening. Once it was ready, I called everyone to the table. Tilly came promptly but then only picked at her food and was very quiet. Adrian talked a bit about work and Paula wasn't her usual self, having just received her first job application rejection, without even being called for interview. She'd completed the application form online and had uploaded her curriculum vitae, as they'd specified, but had then received an email saying she wouldn't be called for interview as they'd received 678 applications.

She had thought she would get an interview even if she wasn't offered the position, but Adrian pointed out how many applications he'd submitted before receiving his present job offer. I know it's very difficult for young people now to get a foothold on the career ladder, as there are so few vacancies for trainee positions, internships and apprenticeships. I added my words of encouragement, and Adrian offered to look through Paula's curriculum vitae to check it was as good as it could be. After dinner, they went off to do that while Tilly and I remained at the table, talking.

We talked for over an hour about Dave, her mother and the video interview she would have to do the following week at the police station. On this matter, at least, I was able to reassure her, as I'd taken other children I'd fostered there before to give video statements. But I couldn't reassure her about much else. Tilly was obviously shocked to the core and upset, especially about her mother's possible involvement. It was this that was causing her the greatest distress, but I was very careful in what I said, for we didn't know enough to judge her. Heather had been abused and controlled by Dave for years. It was possible she'd suspected him, but had been too scared to tell, or he'd threatened her into silence.

There was also another, far worse possibility: that Heather had been complicit in taking the indecent images, having found some perverse pleasure in doing so. Horrendous though it sounds, sometimes it is the mother who has sexually abused her child, and it's even more emotionally damaging for the victim. We, and society, expect mothers to love, nurture and protect their children, even lay down their own lives for the sake of their child if necessary. The vast majority of mothers would do, but there are a few who don't.

At this point we simply didn't know into which group Heather fell.

My first responsibility and concern was for Tilly, but I was also worried about Nancy, who was now aware of the allegations against her daughter. What a dreadful position to be in, I thought. Little wonder Tilly had picked up on the atmosphere and said her gran wasn't herself.

'I'm not looking forward to going on Saturday,' Tilly admitted as we finally moved away from the table.

'It will be awkward,' I agreed. 'You don't have to go if you don't want to. I can telephone your gran and explain.'

'I'll see how I feel on Saturday,' she said. Then she went to her bedroom to try to do some of her schoolwork.

I'd just finished clearing up the dinner things when Nancy telephoned the landline. 'Has Isa been to see you?' she asked, her voice flat.

'Yes, this afternoon.'

'So you know?'

'Yes.'

'Heather is innocent. You need to tell Tilly Dave is lying,' she said passionately.

'Nancy, I can't tell Tilly that. Isa has explained the situation to her and that the police are still investigating.'

'Whose side are you on?' she snapped, then immediately apologized. 'I'm sorry. This is all getting on top of me. I don't think I can cope with much more.'

'I know,' I said. 'It's horrendous. I feel for you. I'm doing all I can to support Tilly.'

'Is she coming to see us at the weekend?' she asked. I guessed Isa hadn't yet had a chance to talk to her and Heather about the contact arrangements, as it had been after working hours when she'd left us.

'I think so,' I said. 'Isa is going to have a chat with you.'

'Tilly doesn't want to see us, does she?' Nancy said plaintively. I felt so sorry for her.

'I think Tilly wants to see you, but she can't face seeing her mother at present,' I said as gently as I could.

'But Heather hasn't done anything wrong. It's sick to think she could have.' But of course most mothers would say that of their daughter.

'I'm sorry,' I said. 'Wait until Isa has spoken to you. I know it's difficult.'

Nancy went quiet and then said, 'Give Tilly my love.' And the line went dead.

I returned the phone to its cradle with a very heavy heart. Nancy was elderly and not in good health. She'd led a straightforward, decent life, doing what she could to help her daughter when she'd got into trouble in the past. I worried this might set back her recovery. She'd been doing well until now. She loved Heather and couldn't believe ill of her, but she also loved her granddaughter. At some point, if it turned out Heather was involved, Nancy might have to choose between them. What an agonizingly painful decision to have to make.

Later that evening Lucy telephoned my mobile and asked if I could go into her bedroom and check if her passport was there.

'Are you going away?' I asked, surprised. She was eight months pregnant.

'No, Mum!' she laughed. 'I need it for ID.'

'Oh, I see.'

She stayed on the phone while I went upstairs to her bedroom.

'I think it's in the top drawer of my bedside cabinet,' she told me.

I crossed her room and opened the drawer. 'What are all these crisp packets doing in here?' I exclaimed with a smile.

'Oh yes. Midnight snack when I was feeling sick,' she laughed.

I found her passport. 'Yes, it's here,' I said. 'So is your Post Office savings account booklet.

'I'd forgotten about that. How much is in it?'

I sat on the bed and opened the booklet. All my children had savings accounts from when they were young, in which they'd saved some of their pocket money and also money they'd been given for birthdays. It was surprising how it had mounted up over the years.

'Seven hundred and forty-eight pounds, fifty-six pence,' I said. 'And there'll be some interest to be added on as well.'

'Fantastic!' she exclaimed. 'I'll call in over the weekend and collect it and my passport.'

We chatted for a few minutes longer and then Lucy suddenly said, 'I have to go, Mum, I need a wee.'

'OK, bye, love.' For many women in late pregnancy the need to pass urine is frequent and urgent as the baby presses on their bladder.

I remained sitting on Lucy's bed, gazing around what had been, and still was, her room. Some of her pictures and posters were still on the walls, and her Disney Winnie the Pooh rug was by her bed. A hand mirror she didn't need stood on top of the chest of drawers. Her bookshelves, like her bedside cabinet and wardrobe, were about three-quarters empty. She'd taken what she needed and had left what she didn't need to sort out later. The wardrobe contained some clothes and shoes she'd either outgrown, no longer wore or couldn't fit into now. The shelves contained children's books and CDs, ornaments and some soft toys. I wondered where Mr Bunny was. He was the soft toy Lucy had arrived with all those years ago, her other possessions having been lost in the frequent moves she'd had to make before coming into care. Mr Bunny had been her loyal companion and confidant, seeing her through some very difficult times. He'd been able to tell me of Lucy's suffering, her mouthpiece when she'd been too traumatized to tell me directly. He was treasured and had slept on her pillow for many years. I knew he'd be somewhere safe – possibly she already had him with her.

As I sat there remembering times gone by, a wave of sadness washed over me. Stupidly, my eyes filled. All those years when Lucy's childhood, like Adrian's and Paula's, had seemed it would stretch forever. The fun, games, laughter, outings, Christmases, birthdays – and of course the upsets, which had quickly faded. Then suddenly it's all over. They've grown up, and all that remains are a few belongings in a half-empty bedroom, some photos and heaps of memories. Thank goodness my memories were good ones. I'd done my best for my children and had few regrets.

Wiping my eyes, I came out and closed Lucy's bedroom door. Time to see how Tilly was doing.

CHAPTER TWENTY-THREE

A FAMILY SPLIT

sa telephoned late Friday morning, having spoken to Nancy. She said Nancy had been upset that Tilly wasn't going to see them for the whole weekend and felt that Heather was being unjustly blamed. Isa advised her not to discuss the police investigation with Tilly, but to keep their time together light and easy.

'You think I don't know how to talk to my granddaughter?' Nancy had said, annoyed. But she'd agreed to do as Isa asked. She also said Heather would keep out of Tilly's way, while adding that she didn't see why it was necessary, as she'd done nothing wrong.

'We'll see how it goes tomorrow,' Isa said to me with a sigh. 'If this arrangement doesn't work, I'll offer contact at the Family Centre, although I appreciate it's not what Tilly wants.'

Isa also told me that Dave was out on bail, pending further police investigation, which I'd half expected. His bail conditions included that he mustn't contact Tilly or Heather, so he couldn't approach them in person or phone or text. 'If he does then he's in breach of his bail conditions, so contact me straight away,' Isa said. 'If he's seen near your house or Tilly's school then call the police.'

She also told me that Tilly's video interview at the police station was set for 10 a.m. the following Thursday. 'I'll collect Tilly from you at nine-thirty, and then take her to school after,' she said. 'Unless she's too upset to go to school, then I'll bring her back to you. Will you let Tilly know, please?'

'Yes.'

She finished by wishing me a good weekend.

When Tilly returned home from school that afternoon she looked glum.

'What's the matter?' I asked as I went into the hall to greet her.

'Abby's a dick,' she said, pulling off her shoes.

'You've fallen out with her? Over what?'

'Me going to my gran's.'

I frowned, puzzled. I knew Tilly confided most things to Abby, but I couldn't imagine what had led to this.

'She thinks I shouldn't go if there's a chance Mum's guilty because Gran is sticking up for her,' Tilly said. 'She knows jack shit about it. I wish I hadn't told her.'

I understood slightly more now. 'Abby is a good friend,' I said. 'But she will struggle to understand how you are feeling. She lives with her parents and hasn't had to deal with anything like this. It's your decision if you want to go to your gran's tomorrow. Isa telephoned and said if it doesn't work out, she'll look into arranging contact at the Family Centre.'

'I've already told her I don't want that!' Tilly snapped.

'OK, but just bear it in mind. It's an option. She also said the video interview is next Thursday.'

'Great! That's all I need!' Tilly said angrily, and stormed upstairs to her bedroom.

Five minutes later Paula came down, also looking glum. By now I was in the kitchen, talking to the cat.

'I've had another rejection without getting an interview!' Paula declared.

'Oh dear. I am sorry, love.'

'Adrian checked my CV and said it's fine.'

'I'm sure it is. It's not you. Businesses receive hundreds of applications, especially at this time of year. How many applications have you sent off so far?'

'Twelve,' she said. 'I'm looking for jobs in a thirty-mile radius. I don't want to have to move.'

'Don't lose heart, love. Something will come up before long. In the meantime, you could register for some temporary work?'

'I have, just now,' she said.

I smiled. 'Well done. You're doing all you can then.'

'I hope so,' she said, and returned upstairs.

By the time dinner was ready, Tilly had made up with Abby, and Paula had completed another application online. She was feeling more positive, having had a chat with a friend who was going through similar. They had arranged to meet later for an evening out with some other friends. There was just the three of us for dinner as Adrian was going straight to Kirsty's from work.

As we ate, I mentioned the summer holidays, which were fast approaching. Tilly said again that she didn't want to sign up for any activities at the leisure centre, but now thought she might come with Paula and me to the holiday village I'd booked for August. Previously when I'd mentioned it – when Tilly had been happily spending the whole weekend at her gran's – she hadn't been keen, but now the idea seemed appealing.

'I don't want to go to Gran's for all that time you're away if Mum's there,' she said.

'No, you wouldn't,' I replied. 'If you're not coming with us then you'll have to go to another foster carer for the time we're away.'

'Who?'

'I don't know. It would depend on who was available.'

She pulled a face, so I thought the holiday was appealing to her even more.

After dinner, when Paula had gone upstairs to get ready, I told Tilly that Dave was out on bail and the conditions of his bail. 'So if he tries to contact you or you see him, call me, Isa or the police. If you spot him outside your school then tell a member of staff.'

'I will. And I've decided I would like to go on holiday with you.'

'Excellent. You'll have a great time. We all will.'

The following morning, Saturday, Tilly was in two minds again about going to her gran's. It was 8 a.m. and I was in the living room having a quiet coffee when she came down in her pyjamas.

'I want to see Gran, but I can't bear the thought of seeing Mum,' she said, coming into the living room. 'I've got nothing to say to her.'

'Tilly, it's your decision whether you go or not, but your mother has agreed to keep away from you. Also, remember, she hasn't been found guilty of anything yet.'

'Neither has Dave, but he's guilty,' she said forcefully, and left the room.

She went into the kitchen and poured herself a glass of juice, which she took up to her room. An hour later she came down again and had a little breakfast, then showered and dressed. I heard her on the phone to Abby and then at around 11.30 a.m. she appeared downstairs again and said she was going to her gran's for the afternoon.

'All right, love. Take care. If you want a lift home, give me a ring. I'm not going to see my mother until tomorrow, as she's out today.'

Tilly left subdued, despondent and ambivalent about going to her gran's. How different this was compared to a couple of weeks before, when she couldn't wait to go, stayed for the whole weekend and was looking forward to a time when she would live there permanently. Thank goodness Isa had put the brakes on that, or Tilly would very likely have been faced with another move back into care, and possibly not to me if I already had another child.

An hour later Lucy and Darren arrived to collect Lucy's passport and savings account booklet. They stayed for lunch. Paula was in and joined us, but Adrian was still with Kirsty. Lucy was feeling the heat, so we stayed indoors. The temperature was set to rise to 30°C in some areas. She'd finished work the day before and was now on maternity leave. She said they'd made a fuss of her on her last day. The manager had given a little speech and then presented her with a card signed by all the staff, a bouquet of flowers and a voucher for £50.

'I was chocked up and didn't know what to say,' Lucy said. 'I've promised to take the baby in for them to see as soon as she is born.'

'Lovely. Have you decided on a name yet?'

'Not yet.'

Later Lucy quietly told me that Bonnie had texted and asked if she'd had the baby yet.

'She can't even remember when it's due!' Lucy said indignantly.

'Did you reply?' I asked.

'Yes, I told her it was due end of July, but she didn't get back to me.' Which, I am sorry to say, was typical of Bonnie's contact with Lucy.

Lucy and Darren left around four o'clock. I went with them to the car. As I was standing on the pavement seeing them off, Tilly appeared coming down the street, earlier than expected. I knew this didn't bode well. She could only have been at her gran's for a few hours.

'Hello, Tilly,' Lucy called through her open car window.

'Hi,' she replied in a flat voice, and continued into the house.

'Oh dear,' Lucy said. 'What's the matter?'

'A few problems at home,' I replied, not wanting to burden her with all that was going on.

'I hope she's OK,' Lucy said, genuinely concerned. 'Give her my love and tell her if she wants to talk anytime to call me.'

'Thanks, love, that's kind of you.'

I leaned in through the car window to kiss Lucy goodbye and then waved as Darren drove them home.

It was still a warm, sunny day so I thought I might spend some time in the back garden once I'd spoken to Tilly. From the hall I could see through the patio doors in the living room to the garden beyond. Paula was out there now, reading a book. I went upstairs and knocked on Tilly's bedroom door. 'Can I come in?'

'If you want,' she replied sombrely.

I did want, so I went in. She was propped up on her bed, texting.

'How did it go at your gran's?' I asked.

'Dreadful. Gran kept trying to stick up for Mum. She said I was being unfair and Mum had suffered too, and me not wanting to see her was making it worse.'

Nancy had promised Isa not to discuss this with Tilly, but I could see why she felt the need to. She loved her daughter and granddaughter and just wanted everything to be all right. Unfortunately, sometimes things happen in life which mean it can never be the same again.

'I'm sorry,' I said, perching on the edge of the bed. 'That must have been very difficult for you.'

Tilly stopped texting and looked at me. 'Do you think I should go to the police station on Thursday for that taped interview?'

'Yes, of course. Why not?'

'I've been thinking that if I didn't go then perhaps the police wouldn't have enough evidence to prosecute Dave and Mum, and Gran would be happy and like me again.'

'Oh, love,' I said, taking her hand in mine. 'Your gran does like you. She loves you, but it's very difficult for her. I doubt your evidence is going to make much difference to the outcome. From what we've been told, the police already have plenty of evidence. They found a lot of indecent photographs and videos when they searched Dave's house. There was sufficient evidence to arrest him. Did your gran ask you not to go?'

She shook her head. 'No, I was thinking about it on the bus.'

'No one is going to force you to go, but I think you should. You can only say what you know. Answer the questions, and if you don't know, say so. Don't try to guess or make it up.'

'You think I should go then?' she asked, still doubtful.

'Yes, of course.'

'I'm not going to see Gran on Monday and Wednesday then. I'll wait until it's all over.'

'If that's what you've decided, I'll tell Isa.'

She gave a small nod but looked very sad. I put my arms around her and gave her a hug. 'The next few weeks will be difficult,' I said. 'But I think you will feel a bit better after Thursday. If you want to talk or have any questions, I'm here, and you can always phone your social worker. Lucy said to give you her love and you can phone her if you want to talk.'

'Does she know what's happened?' Tilly asked.

'No. She just saw you were looking down and offered to help. Is there anything else you want to share or ask me now?'

'I don't think Gran wants me to live with her any more,' Tilly said. 'Can I stay here with you?'

'Yes, I'm sure that's the plan Isa has too. We'll get through this and your relationship with your gran should start to improve.'

'I hope so,' she said with a sniff, and wiped a tear from her eye.

'Try not to worry, love. Now, it's a nice day outside. Paula is in the garden reading and I'm going to do some gardening. I'd like you to come outside and join us.'

'I've still got some homework to do,' Tilly admitted.

'Bring it outside.' I didn't want her sitting alone in her bedroom and worrying.

'I need the Internet.'

'The Wi-Fi reaches to the patio, so bring your laptop.'

Finally she agreed and, getting off the bed, picked up her laptop and came with me downstairs and into the garden. Paula helped us move the bench into the shade so Tilly had somewhere to work. For the next hour or so I did some gardening, Paula read and texted, and Tilly did her home-work and texted. While Sammy sat in the shade, watching us.

Later, when the sun had lost some of its strength, I suggested a game of badminton. The air was perfectly still so ideal for the game. The girls agreed and we fixed up the badminton net. As there was just the three of us, we took it in turns with the winner playing the other one. Sammy seemed to think the shuttlecock was something alive that needed to be caught and eaten. He jumped high into the air with an acrobatic twist every time it came near him. It was funny and finally Tilly began to laugh. That night I emailed Isa an update about contact, explaining Tilly wasn't going on Monday or Wednesday and the reasons why.

On Sunday Tilly and Paula came with me to visit my mother. Tilly hadn't seen her in a while as she'd been going to her gran's for the whole weekend. I hadn't told Mum about the indecent images Dave had taken or the police investiga-tion, as she didn't need to know. Tilly didn't mention it either and thankfully seemed able to put aside her worries while we were at my mother's. I think sometimes a change of scenery can help us forget, at least temporarily. Tilly was eager to help Mum and kept offering to do little jobs; for example, making a cup of tea or sweeping the kitchen floor. I guessed she did similar for her own grandmother and felt comfortable around Mum. My mother noticed and commented to me how kind and thoughtful Tilly was.

'She's a really nice girl,' Mum said. 'Will she be able to stay with you?'

'Yes, for as long as is necessary, which I think could be long term.'

'Good. I'm pleased.' Although Mum knew the decision on

where Tilly lived permanently wasn't mine and that plans could change in fostering – sometimes at very short notice.

We all had a lovely day at Mum's and returned home feeling buoyed up from having spent time with her.

Isa couldn't have spoken to Nancy on Monday about Tilly not going to see her, because when Tilly arrived home she said her gran had telephoned her while she'd been on the bus, asking where she'd got to.

'She was annoyed and upset with me,' Tilly said as she came in. 'I feel dreadful. Perhaps I should go on Wednesday, but I really don't feel up to it. Not before the police interview.'

'Would you like me to talk to your gran and explain?' I asked.

'Yes. Tell her I love her, but I just need some time out right now.'

'I will.'

While Tilly went up to her bedroom, I went into the living room and telephoned Nancy's landline.

'It's Cathy,' I said. 'How are you?'

'Not happy,' she replied a little tartly. 'And you can probably guess why.'

'Yes, Tilly has just come in. She's concerned she's upset you. I know it's difficult for you all, but she's worried about the police interview on Thursday and –'

'If she's that worried, she doesn't have to go,' Nancy interrupted.

'She does really,' I replied. 'Aside from giving her evidence, it will form part of the healing process. I've looked after other abused children, and being able to tell the police what happened to them does help, even if the case doesn't go to court.'

'Not in my book, it doesn't,' Nancy said tightly. 'It will keep the wound open. Tilly needs to forget about all this so we can get on with our lives. Her mother is having to hide in her bedroom when Tilly visits. It's ridiculous. I mean, it's not like he actually assaulted her.'

'Taking all those photographs and videos was an assault, and it's also illegal,' I pointed out. 'Hopefully after Thursday you will be able to start to move on.'

'Not if her mother's in prison,' Nancy replied sharply.

I could see I wasn't getting anywhere, so I said, 'I'm sorry, Nancy. My first priority is Tilly. Isa was aware Tilly wouldn't be coming today and it's a pity she didn't have the chance to tell you.'

'Is Tilly coming to see us this Saturday?' she asked.

'As far as I know. It's probably best if I phone Isa and ask her to call you. She can explain better than me.'

'Fine,' she said, and with a curt goodbye ended the call.

CHAPTER TWENTY-FOUR

POLICE INTERVIEWS

I immediately telephoned Isa and she said she'd call Nancy. I didn't hear anything further from her, and Tilly didn't go to her gran's on Wednesday. I let the school secretary know that she wouldn't be in until around lunchtime on Thursday as she had an appointment. If Tilly didn't feel up to going to school after the police interview then I'd ring again and let them know.

Tilly didn't sleep well on Wednesday night. I heard her moving around her bedroom a few times and then go to the bathroom. Around 3 a.m., when I heard her again, I went to her room and lightly knocked on her door. 'It's Cathy,' I whispered, and went in.

She was sitting up in bed with her bedside lamp on. 'Are you all right?'

'I keep thinking about tomorrow. Is it OK if I watch a film on my laptop?'

'Yes, just for tonight.' She picked up her laptop from where it lay on the floor by her bed. 'Don't have the volume up too high.'

'I'll use my earbuds,' she said.

'Then try to get some sleep.'

I came out, leaving her watching a film, and returned to my room. I didn't hear her again and the following morning she slept through Adrian getting up and leaving for work. At eight o'clock I woke her.

'What shall I wear?' she asked, immediately anxious.

'Your school uniform, in case you go into school after.'

I left her to get washed and dressed and half an hour later she came downstairs. She didn't want any breakfast, just a drink of juice. I also gave her a bottle of water to take with her, as it was destined to be another hot day. Isa arrived just before 9.30 and waited at the door while Tilly put on her shoes and threw her school bag over her shoulder. 'Don't worry, you'll be fine,' Isa told her.

I gave Tilly a reassuring hug and watched them go. Now all I could do was wait. I knew something of the procedure from having taking children for video interviews before. The interviewing suite is more like a small living room than a standard interviewing room at a police station, with a sofa and armchairs and toys for younger children. The police officers are specially trained to interview children and young people, and handle their questioning very sensitively, stopping for regular breaks when necessary. Nevertheless, it is daunting for the child, as they are having to talk about the abuse they've suffered and know that what they say is important.

It was 1 p.m. before I heard anything. Isa telephoned to say she'd dropped Tilly off at school. 'She did well,' Isa said. 'And is very relieved it's all over.'

'So am I.'

'Yes, indeed. Tilly's not sure if she's going to see her gran on Saturday. If she decides not to go, can you give Nancy a ring and tell her, please? Otherwise she'll be expecting her.'

'OK.' Although I thought I was going to be even less popular with Nancy than I was already.

Isa didn't give any details about Tilly's interview and wound up, saying goodbye. But five minutes later Tilly telephoned. It was still her lunchbreak.

'Have you had something to eat?' was my first question.

'Yes. The canteen was still open when I got back. I was starving.' She sounded much brighter.

'So everything went well?'

'Yes. I answered all their questions. The police officers were really nice. I'm pleased I went. I'll tell you about it tonight, but thanks for making me go. It felt good being able to tell them about Dave and his nasty ways.'

'Well done you,' I said.

When Tilly arrived home that afternoon her relief was obvious as soon as she came in. 'It wasn't nearly as bad as I thought it was going to be,' she admitted. 'I might still have to go to court, but I won't see him.'

'No. And we'll cross that bridge if and when we come to it.'

I made her a cold drink and we sat on the patio. Adrian wasn't home from work yet and Paula had gone out with a friend.

'Mum went to the police station yesterday for her interview,' Tilly told me. 'I don't know what she said, but I heard the police officer telling Isa she'd been.'

I nodded.

'During the interview they asked me questions about Dave's relationship with Mum and me,' Tilly said, sipping her drink. 'They showed me some photographs that he'd taken and asked me to confirm it was me in the picture and where they'd been taken. Also, they found a pair of my knickers in his bedroom and I had to confirm they were mine. I didn't even know they were missing. There were traces of his semen on them. I wasn't sure what that term meant.' She gave an embarrassed laugh. 'The police officer had to explain. Then they asked me if he'd ever molested me or tried to force himself on me sexually. I said he hadn't.'

I nodded.

'How do you think his semen got on my underwear?' she asked. 'I was talking about it with Isa in the car.'

'What did she say?'

'That he probably ejaculated onto them.'

'Yes.' The other possibility was that he'd raped Tilly, but thankfully that didn't appear to be so.

'The police officer said they'd also found his semen on my pillowcase,' Tilly said, grimacing. 'He must have gone into my bedroom when I wasn't there. They asked me if I thought Mum knew what he was doing. I said I didn't know, but she was shit-scared of him. Then I apologized for swearing and the police officer said it didn't matter, as she'd heard a lot worse. I don't know what Mum told them at her interview. They wouldn't tell me.'

'They couldn't because it could have influenced what you said.'

'Anyway, I've done it. It's over with now,' Tilly said with a sigh, and finished the last of her drink. 'I'd better go and do some homework. I've hardly done any this week.'

'OK, love. Let me know if you need help.'

'I will.'

Paula was the next to arrive home, from seeing her friend, and she was in good spirits. One of the temping agencies she'd applied to had telephoned and asked her to go into their office tomorrow for an interview.

'Fantastic,' I said. 'Well done.'

'What questions do you think they will ask me?'

'Probably around your skills and your hopes for a career. You told them it was just temporary work until you found a permanent post?'

'Yes, they said that was fine. They have a lot of students and those who have just left college looking for temporary work.'

When Adrian arrived home he too had good news. 'I had an interview with the big boss today,' he said. 'I've passed my probationary period so they're confirming my position within the firm.'

'Wonderful. I didn't even know it was today. You should have told me.'

'There was a lot going on for you with Tilly's interview at the police station.'

'Adrian, I've always got time for you and Paula,' I said, feeling guilty. 'You should know that.'

He smiled and kissed the top of my head. Yet one of the problems with fostering is that there is often so much going on with the looked-after child that the carer's own children, whatever their age, can fall into second place.

'Well done,' I said again. 'I'm very proud of you.'

'I'm proud of you too, Mum,' he said, which immediately choked me up. 'I'll phone Nana and tell her.'

'Yes, do. She'll be pleased.'

The following morning Paula went for her interview at the temping agency in the high street and was put on their books. They said they would phone her as soon as they had any work for her.

On Saturday Tilly went to see her gran just for the afternoon. I made an arrangement to see my mother on Sunday, as

I wanted to be in when Tilly returned. She arrived home shortly after five o'clock, subdued.

'How did it go?' I asked.

'All right,' she said with a shrug. 'Gran and I did some gardening, but she was very quiet.'

'Did she talk about your mother or the police investigation?' I asked.

'A couple of times. She said she'd gone with Mum to the police station, and it wasn't fair Mum had to stay in her room on a nice day like this.'

'OK.' It could have been worse, I thought.

Tilly went to visit her gran after school on Monday and Wednesday the following week for an hour and came back each time saying there'd been an atmosphere. On Wednesday her gran had asked her what she'd told the police and Tilly had said she didn't want to talk about it, which had put Nancy in a mood. I therefore began wondering if it would be better if contact was reduced, perhaps to a day a week for the time being, but that was for Isa to discuss with Tilly. I emailed Isa regular updates, copying in Joy Philips.

Paula hadn't received any work from the agency and was growing despondent. I told her not to worry and to concentrate on applying for permanent positions, and I could give her any money she needed. 'But I want to work,' she said. 'I've done all this studying and I want it to pay off.' Which I completely understood. On Thursday her spirits rose as she learnt she'd passed her exams and now had a degree in business studies. We were all delighted and that night we ordered her favourite Chinese takeaway to celebrate.

'You're so lucky,' Tilly said.

'She's worked hard,' I pointed out. 'You can achieve similar if you want to.'

'I just wish I was there already.'

'I can remember thinking that about Adrian,' Paula said. 'But the years have flown by.'

We were now in the first week of July and there were only three weeks before the schools broke up for the long summer holidays and Lucy's baby was due. Now she was on maternity leave, I visited her most days during the week, when she would sit with her feet up on the sofa and the windows wide open to let in what air there was. It was a gloriously hot summer, but it was proving too much for Lucy.

'I feel like a beached whale,' she said, hands cupped around her baby bulge.

I passed her a cool flannel for her forehead, did some housework and also some shopping. Sometimes I cooked their evening meal for them before I left so Darren didn't have to do it when he came home from work. He always texted me to say thank you and that they'd enjoyed it.

The second week in July, Tilly and I received notice of her next review – to be held in the last week of term. We filled in the forms and returned them in the envelope provided and Isa arranged to visit us. She was due for a visit anyway and social workers usually like to see the child just before a review. However, this time her visit wasn't just routine; she had something important to tell us and asked me to stay to begin with. I poured her the glass of water she wanted and we sat in the living room. She took out a notepad and pen and placed them on her lap. I had my fostering folder within reach in case I needed it.

'Yesterday I spoke to the police officer in charge of the investigation,' Isa began, looking at Tilly as she spoke. 'Your stepfather has been charged, but your mother hasn't been. However, Dave is pleading not guilty.'

There was silence as Tilly and I both digested what we'd been told.

'So Mum is innocent?' Tilly asked.

'She won't be charged. There is insufficient evidence,' Isa replied carefully. 'Dave tried to implicate her, but the police found no evidence to support his allegations.'

There was another silence. Being innocent and the police having insufficient evidence to bring a case weren't exactly the same thing, although I knew this was a standard phrase the police used.

'It's good news that Dave has been charged,' I said, breaking the silence. 'Do you know when the court case will be?'

'Thirtieth of November,' Isa replied.

'So the police don't think Mum knew what Dave was doing?' Tilly asked.

'That's correct,' Isa said. 'The police informed your mother and gran yesterday, and your gran telephoned me this morning. She is very pleased that Dave has been charged and Heather has been cleared. She said to tell you that when you go there in future your mother won't be hiding in her bedroom. She also said your mother wants to talk to you to clear the air. How do you feel about that?'

Tilly hesitated and then asked, 'Why did Dave say Mum knew what he was doing if she didn't?'

'I don't know,' Isa replied. 'Possibly revenge for her leaving, or there might be other reasons. I think that's what your mother wants to talk to you about. Your gran suggested tomorrow, but if you want me there it will have to be next week.'

'What does she want to tell me?' Tilly asked.

'About what happened at home between her and your stepfather. She wants to explain. Would you prefer it if I was present?'

'No. It's OK. I'll go to Gran's tomorrow and see Mum.'

'Sure?' Isa asked.

'Yes.' Then Tilly glanced at me and asked, 'Can Cathy come? She knows Mum and Gran.'

Isa looked at me for my reaction.

'Do you know exactly what Heather wants to tell Tilly?' I asked.

'Yes. I spoke to her on the phone this morning.'

'All right.' That was good enough for me. 'What time should we go?'

'Nancy suggested midday on Saturday, the same time Tilly has been going recently.'

I made a note. 'Will Tilly stay for the afternoon?'

'If she wishes. See how you feel,' she told Tilly.

Isa continued with the business of a normal visit and asked Tilly about school, her routine, pocket money, the summer holidays and so forth. Isa then asked me if she could have some time alone with Tilly, so I left them. They were in the living room for about ten minutes and then Isa completed her visit with a quick look around the house. As she left she said she'd telephone us on Monday to see how our meeting with Heather had gone, and she'd see us at the review.

After she'd left Tilly said, 'Isa thinks I'll probably have to go to court and answer Dave's barrister's questions. But I won't have to see him. Do you think Mum knew something? Is that why she wants to see me?'

'I really don't know,' I replied honestly.

'How could Mum not know what he was doing?' Tilly

asked anxiously. 'She was there the whole time. She wasn't allowed out without him.'

That was troubling me too. Was it possible to live with someone who had planted spy cameras in two rooms in your home and been secretly filming your daughter without you knowing, or at least having some suspicion? I doubted it, but I didn't say so.

'Let's hear what your mother has to say,' I replied, and left it at that.

CHAPTER TWENTY-FIVE

DIFFICULT MEETINGS

On Saturday morning Tilly appeared downstairs before Adrian and Paula were up and told me she was nervous about meeting her mother. I knew what she meant. Although the 'meeting' was informal and at Nancy's home, Isa had given us the impression Heather had something important to say and had even offered to go with Tilly. I couldn't really add anything, as I didn't know any more than she did, so I reassured her I would be by her side and we could leave whenever she wanted to. I was reminded of how flexible a foster carer has to be, as the role is rarely just looking after the child, but often extends to in-depth and emotional involvement with the child's family. This wasn't the first time I'd been present at a critical meeting between a young person and their parent, although not in these exact circumstances. Each child I looked after arrived with their own unique but very sad story.

As Adrian and Paula got up, I told them where I was going. At 11.30 I changed into smarter clothes and knocked on Tilly's bedroom door. 'Time to go, love.'

She came out with her earbuds in, listening to music on her phone. I threw her a reassuring smile and, calling goodbye to Adrian and Paula, we left the house. Tilly kept her earpieces in for the whole of the journey, I guessed as a distraction from worrying. Only when I parked outside her grandmother's bungalow did she take them out, and with an anxious sigh opened her car door. I joined her on the pavement and we went up the front garden path where Tilly nervously pressed the doorbell.

It was a few moments before Nancy answered. She looked well, her cheeks had some colour, but she also looked strained and anxious.

'Come in, the pair of you,' she said stoically. 'Not such a nice day out there.'

'No,' I agreed, although I'd barely noticed the weather. After days of sunshine there was now thick cloud cover with rain forecast.

We followed Nancy into her living room where Heather was already sitting in an armchair. Dressed in a light grey summer skirt and blouse, she too looked very tense.

'Hello, Heather,' I said with a smile.

'Hello,' she returned, her voice flat.

Nancy took her usual chair by the hearth and Tilly and I sat on the sofa so we were all facing each other. Tilly hadn't said hello to her mother as we'd come in, but she was now looking at her intently, although Heather was keeping her gaze away. Whatever she was about to tell us was clearly a big ordeal for her.

'How are you both?' I asked, breaking the awkward silence.

'A lot better now the police have seen sense,' Nancy said brusquely. 'But we won't beat about the bush. Heather has something to say. Isa told me you were staying, although I'm not sure why that's necessary.'

'Just to give Tilly a bit of support,' I said.

Nancy clicked her tongue disapprovingly but looked at Heather. 'Say what you have to and then we can all get on with our lives,' she told her, although I doubted it was going to be that straightforward.

Heather shifted self-consciously and cleared her throat. She looked at me, not Tilly, as she spoke.

'I didn't have anything to do with Dave taking those photographs and videos,' she began, her voice unsteady. 'The police showed me some of them. They're disgusting and I was shocked anyone could think I was involved. I wasn't, not in any way, although I knew something wasn't right with Dave and that's what I told the police.' She swallowed hard before continuing.

'Dave always preferred Tilly to me. I thought he was just spoiling her to get at me and try to make me jealous. I now realize he was flirting with her and not behaving as a stepfather should.'

'So why didn't you leave him?' Tilly interrupted angrily.

'Listen to what your mother has to say,' Nancy said firmly.

Tilly huffed but fell silent.

'I couldn't leave him,' Heather said, now looking at Tilly. 'I was too scared. You should know that. It was impossible, until that morning when I finally found the courage to leave. I didn't know he'd hidden cameras and taken photos and videos of you. Honestly, I didn't. But I had a suspicion he was doing something he didn't want me to see. I told the police that. He used to spend a long time on his computer upstairs in the bedroom he used as study. I wondered if he was watching porn, but I didn't for one moment think he was looking at indecent pictures of you. Not until ...' She stopped.

'Not until what?' Tilly asked.

'Not until he sent that photo of you in your underwear to my phone. I realized then it had been taken in our house. That's when I knew.'

'And you didn't say anything?' Tilly exclaimed in disbelief.

Heather shook her head. 'I should have done. I know that now. The police asked me why I didn't say something at the time, and I told them I was still scared of him.'

'Come off it, Mum!' Tilly snapped. 'You were living here with Gran by then. He couldn't have harmed you. How could you still be scared of him? You should have told us you knew he was the one who'd sent the photograph.'

'I know,' Heather admitted quietly, and despite everything I felt sorry for her. I remembered thinking at the time Tilly had discovered the photo on her mother's phone, that Heather could be hiding something when she'd claimed she didn't know who had sent it. However, I believed her when she said she'd been too scared of Dave to tell. She was probably still scared of him. But whether that was sufficient grounds for failing to protect her daughter, I didn't know. She'd only told the police now because Dave had implicated her and she'd had to defend herself.

'How did Dave claim you were involved?' I asked.

Nancy winced as if she knew what Heather was going to say.

'He told the police I'd known all along and I didn't mind. He said in his statement I used to enjoy looking at photos like this.' She shuddered. 'It's sick. I would never have done that. You're my daughter.' Heather looked at Tilly imploringly.

'Of course you wouldn't,' Nancy said. 'The police shouldn't have taken him seriously. How ridiculous that they could think that of any mother.'

Such things do happen, I thought but didn't say.

'Heather, the photograph of Tilly that Dave sent to you was the same one he sent to Tilly,' I said. 'But what I don't understand is how he obtained Tilly's phone number. She had a new SIM by then with a new number.'

'The police asked me that when they thought I was involved and working with him,' Heather said. 'They accused me of giving it to him, but I didn't, not intentionally. I couldn't remember Tilly's number, so I wrote it on a piece of paper and put it in my bedside cabinet. I assume Dave must have got it from there.'

It was feasible, I thought. Mobile numbers can be difficult to remember. But Tilly was less forgiving.

'You told me ages ago that you knew Dave went through your things,' she said. 'So why did you leave my number where he could find it? I thought it was one of my friends sending the photos.'

'It was stupid of me,' Heather admitted. 'But I've done a lot of stupid things in my life. I've made plenty of mistakes and bad choices.'

'You're right there,' Nancy said. 'Especially when it comes to men.' I glanced at Tilly, but there was no sign of compassion on her face yet.

'Was I a mistake?' Tilly asked her mother.

'No. Of course not. I wanted you.'

'So why didn't you look after me better and put me first?' Tilly said angrily.

Heather didn't reply. Her bottom lip trembled and she looked close to tears.

'I think that's enough,' Nancy said. 'Your mother has been honest with you and admitted what she's done wrong. There's no need for a post-mortem. We should put the past behind us now and look to the future.'

As far as Nancy was concerned the matter was closed, but my priority was Tilly and she was looking lost, confused and agitated as though she still had unanswered questions.

'Is there anything you want to say or ask your mother while I'm here?' I asked her gently.

'I don't know,' she said with a sigh.

'Good. That's the end of it then,' Nancy said. 'Cathy, I'm not being rude but you can go now and the three of us will have some lunch together and start to rebuild our lives.'

Tilly looked up sharply. 'I'm sorry, Gran, I don't feel like having lunch or playing happy families. I think I'll go with Cathy.'

Nancy was completely thrown and shocked by this, while Heather looked as she often did: sad, rejected and close to tears.

'Why are you going?' Nancy asked Tilly. 'This is your home. You need to stay, at least for the afternoon, and tell your mother you forgive her.'

'I can't, not yet,' Tilly said, and stood.

I stood too.

'I'm sorry, Gran. I love you,' Tilly said. She quickly crossed the room, kissed her cheek and fled.

I went after her. She was in the hall pulling open the front door. 'Tilly.'

She disappeared outside and I followed, closing the door behind me. I felt sorry for Nancy, but I needed to look after Tilly. I opened the car and she jumped in as I went round to the driving seat. She sat beside me, crying quietly.

'It's OK,' I said, and passed her a tissue. I waited while she dried her eyes. I didn't immediately start the car as I wondered if she'd want to go back inside and see her gran and mum once she was feeling a bit better.

But after a moment she said, 'Can we go home now?'

'Yes. If that's what you want.'

'I do.'

As I started the car Babs came out of her bungalow, but she didn't see us. Tilly sat quietly looking out of her side window as I drove. I sensed she needed some time to think, so I didn't say anything. After a few minutes she said, 'I couldn't stay there. I can't face Mum, not now. I know Gran has forgiven her, but I can't. There's been too many secrets and lies.'

'I understand,' I said. 'It will take time.'

She sniffed and twisted the tissue between her fingers. 'I've been doing a lot of thinking since all this started. It's not just about the photos and Mum knowing Dave was up to something and not saying. There's other stuff. I mean, she's never, ever put me first. All the decisions she made in her life were about her. Gran knows that. The first time Dave hit her she should have left him, not put up with his crap for all those years. It's completely messed up my head. There were lots of times when he was nice to me, so I came to believe he was right and it was Mum who was wrong. Then other times he was so horrible to Mum I had to step in and protect her. Between the two of them they've completely screwed me up and I can't help blaming Mum. She's my mother. She should have protected me and left him.'

I nodded. It was no use telling Tilly her mother was a victim too and probably wasn't in any position to protect her. I could imagine the mind games played in that house, resulting in Tilly feeling confused, alone and frightened. It would take time and probably counselling before she began to come to terms with everything that had happened. Some people never do and their adult years are blighted with the memories of their unhappy or abusive childhood.

'I hear what Gran says,' Tilly added quietly. 'But she wasn't there. She didn't have to live with all that shit for all those years.'

'I know, love.'

Once home, Tilly and I sat in the living room talking some more. I reassured her that what she was feeling was normal and she needed to give herself time and must never blame herself, which can happen. She was adamant she didn't want to see her mother or gran on either Monday or Wednesday of the following week, so later, when I emailed Isa an update on today's meeting, I included this. I also wrote it in my log notes.

Tilly was quiet for the rest of Saturday, and on Sunday she didn't want to come with me to see my mother. She said she was going to spend the day with Abby, which I agreed to. When she returned at six o'clock she was still subdued but said she'd had a nice day. They'd been to the cinema and had pizza afterwards, when they'd talked about her decision not to see her mother or gran. Abby had said it was the right decision.

'It's good to talk these things over,' I said. 'But remember, Abby has never been in your position, so whether you see your family or not has to be what you feel comfortable with.' I'd said similar before, but it is very easy to be influenced by a well-meaning friend when we're feeling down or fragile; a friend who, while having our best interests at heart, may not have the experience or expertise to offer sound advice.

On Monday morning before Tilly left for school, I checked with her that she was still planning on coming straight home. She confirmed she was.

'All right, love. I'll expect you around four o'clock,' I said, seeing her off at the door. 'Have a good day and give me a ring if you want to talk.' She nodded and I watched her go.

At 8.45, while I was making myself a slice of toast and a second mug of coffee, Paula came flying down the stairs in her pyjamas. 'I've got some temping work!' she cried, very excited. 'I've got to get there by ten.'

'Today?'

'Yes, they've only just phoned. Can you give me a lift, just for today?' she asked, grabbing the carton of juice. 'It's that big Smith's garage at the other end of town. You know it. They sell those fancy cars. Their receptionist has called in sick. I've got to wear something smart.'

'Calm down. I'll get you there on time.'

I was pleased for Paula but hoped that next time she was offered some temping work we got a bit more notice. While she dressed, I quickly made up a sandwich for her to have as a late breakfast or lunch or whenever she got the opportunity to eat. I then drove to the Smith's garage. She was nervous but looked very smart in a skirt and short-sleeved top. As I dropped her off, I wished her luck and told her to let me know if she needed a lift back.

I returned home and checked my emails. Isa had replied, thanking me for the information and saying she would tele-phone Nancy and Heather to let them know Tilly wouldn't be going today or Wednesday. She said we could discuss contact at the review on Thursday. Joy then phoned – I'd been copying her into the emails so she was up to date. 'Poor Tilly,' she said. 'Has she received an appointment for CAMHS yet?'

'No. Not yet. She's on the waiting list.'

'We'll raise it at the review on Thursday. I'd like to see you both tomorrow if possible at four o'clock.'

'Yes, that's fine.'

As with the child's social worker, the carer's supervising social worker usually liked to see the child just before a review so they had the most recent information. Once I'd read and responded to my emails, I texted Lucy to say I was planning on visiting her if that was OK and did she need any shopping? I never just turned up; I always asked first.

Great. See you soon. Milk and cream cakes, please, was her reply.

I stopped off at the supermarket on the way, bought what she'd asked for and also some fruit and an orchid in a ceramic pot with bright pink flowers. She was eating enough sweet things without me adding to it by buying her a gift of chocolates. She was delighted with the plant, especially when I said it didn't need much watering. The previous plant I'd given to her when she'd moved into the flat had been rather forgotten and had wilted.

I stayed for most of the afternoon and did what I could to help her. With only ten days before her due date, she was very uncomfortable and experiencing Braxton Hicks contractions, which made her wince. She also had lower-back pain and indigestion, and was going to the toilet every hour. She was worried her stomach would never recover from being stretched so far and that she would have stretch marks, despite rubbing in cream. 'I'm not doing this ever again!' she declared. 'I mean it.'

That afternoon, when Tilly arrived home from school, she had her end-of-year report, a copy of which would be sent to her social worker and mother.

'It's not good,' she said, taking it from its envelope and handing it to me. She stood beside me as I read. To precis what it said, she was making an effort to catch up and some progress had been made in some subjects, but her predicated grades for the exams she would be taking next year were low, some not even a pass.

'You've done your best,' I said. 'There's been a lot going on. You're gradually catching up. If you don't get the grades you need next year, you can always take the exams again.' She visibly relaxed.

'Miss Jenkins spoke to me – I could tell she was disappointed.'

'It's her job to be disappointed,' I said. 'As far as I'm concerned, you're doing the best you can in difficult circumstances.'

She smiled weakly and I gave her a hug.

I always encourage the children I look after – as I do my own – to do their best in whatever they approach, but I never put them under pressure. I feel young people today have enough pressures just growing up in our society without a pushy parent or carer imposing their expectations on them, which creates even more pressure. It wasn't the end of the world if Tilly didn't achieve the grades she needed next year; she could retake them until she did.

'Abby has done better than me,' Tilly confided. 'But she's worried about showing her dad her report.'

'Why?'

'He's expecting her to get grade As, but she's predicted mainly Bs with some As.'

'It's a pity he feels like that,' I said. I thought he was setting her up for failure before she'd even begun. 'What does her mother say?'

'She's more like you and just wants her to be happy.'

Paula arrived home at 6.30, elated but tired from a day at work. She told us over dinner what she'd had to do: answer the phone, reply to general-enquiry emails and greet clients who were considering spending huge sums of money on a car. The cheapest car in the showroom, she said, was £60,000 and many were £100,000 plus. It was a different world to the one we inhabited, but she'd been offered work for the whole of the week, which was good.

'Well done,' I said.

'Perhaps they'll give you a car at the end of the week as a thank-you present,' Adrian joked.

'I wish!' she laughed.

The following afternoon Joy visited us as planned and stayed for about an hour. She covered the usual business as well as talking to Tilly to see how she was, and then left saying she would see us at the review. After she'd gone, Tilly asked me, 'Do you think Mum and Gran will go to the review?'

'I don't know, love. Isa hasn't said. They will have been invited.'

'It could be difficult. I haven't spoken to them since Saturday.'

'Do you want to call them now? I'm sure they would be pleased to hear from you.'

'No.'

'If they go, it will be difficult for them too,' I pointed out. 'But the Independent Reviewing Officer will be there to keep the meeting on track.'

'Do you think I should go?'

'Yes. The review is about you.'

CHAPTER TWENTY-SIX

WORRYING NEWS

'I could have done without this today,' Miss Jenkins said as she showed me to the room we were going to use for Tilly's review. 'We break up next Tuesday and the end of term is always busy.'

I nodded sympathetically. Unlike the previous two reviews, this one was being held at Tilly's school.

'How many are we expecting?' she asked, lifting a chair from a stack.

'I'm not sure, eight to ten I would guess.' I was the first to arrive and I began helping her to arrange the chairs around the table. We set out ten. Just as we'd finished the door opened and the IRO, Joanna Hargreaves, came in with a bright, 'Good afternoon. I've got the right room then.'

'Yes. Do you want Tilly here for all of the review?' Miss Jenkins asked crisply. 'If so, I'll fetch her.'

'It's usual at her age, so yes, please,' the IRO replied. She sat at the top end of the table and took out her laptop. 'Cathy Glass, isn't it?'

'Yes. Tilly's carer.'

'I remember.'

I sat at the opposite end of the table. The door opened again and Joy Philips, my supervising social worker, appeared, followed by Isa, without her manager who'd accompanied her to previous reviews. Joy sat next to me and Isa to my right. Miss Jenkins returned with Tilly and I smiled at her. They sat opposite.

'Are we all here?' the IRO asked. It was now two o'clock, the time the review was due to start.

'Mrs Watkins, Tilly's grandmother, might be coming,' Isa said. 'So can we wait another five minutes?'

'Yes, of course,' the IRO replied.

'Is Mum coming?' Tilly asked Isa.

'I don't think so. I spoke to her yesterday and she wasn't feeling up to it.'

There were a few moments of silence and then Joy said to Tilly, making conversation, 'Not long until the end of term.'

'No,' Tilly agreed. I could see she was nervous. Whether this was from having to face her gran again or the review, or a bit of both, I wasn't sure. Each time she looked at me I threw her a reassuring smile.

'Are you going away?' Miss Jenkins asked Tilly.

'Yes, with Cathy and Paula to a holiday village in the country,' Tilly replied.

'Lovely, you'll have a wonderful time, I'm sure.'

There was a little more light conversation about the forthcoming summer holidays and then the door opened and the school secretary showed Nancy in.

'Welcome,' the IRO said to her.

'Sorry to keep you waiting. The cab was late,' Nancy said, and took one of the empty seats beside Isa.

The IRO waited a moment while Nancy settled herself, then opened the review and asked us all to introduce ourselves. Once we'd gone round the table stating our names and roles, she said to Tilly, 'This review is about you so perhaps you would like to go first? How have things been for you since your last review?'

'OK,' Tilly said in a flat voice. 'Mixed really. A lot has happened.'

'Yes, indeed.' The IRO would have been given the most up-to-date information before the review. 'What has gone well for you?' the IRO prompted.

'Dave being charged,' Tilly replied.

The IRO nodded as she typed. 'And school? How is that going?'

'I try to concentrate and do my best.'

'Good,' the IRO said, with an encouraging smile. 'I read on your review form that you are still happy living with Cathy.'

Tilly nodded, keeping her gaze away from her grandmother.

'And contact?' the IRO asked. 'I understand it was increased and then reduced.'

Tilly looked awkward and didn't reply.

'There hasn't been any since Saturday,' Isa said.

'No, and there should be,' Nancy put in.

'I understand,' the IRO said in a conciliatory manner. 'It is difficult at present.'

'But it shouldn't be that difficult,' Nancy said. 'Now we know her mother is innocent.'

'I'd like to let Tilly finish first,' the IRO said diplomatically. 'Then we'll hear from Cathy and you next. If that's all right.' This was the usual order at reviews and Nancy gave a curt nod.

'And you're healthy?' the IRO asked Tilly. It was a standard question.

'Yes,' Tilly replied.

'Excellent.'

'We'll discuss contact later after I've heard from Cathy and your grandmother, but is there anything else you would like to tell this review now?' she asked Tilly.

Tilly shook her head.

'If you think of anything just say.' The IRO then asked me to speak.

I began with the positives and said Tilly was a pleasant, friendly girl who was making good progress in all aspects of her life. I said her health checks were up to date and she'd had no accidents or injuries, that she arrived home on time, had a good circle of friends and her best friend was still Abby, who she often saw.

'Good,' the IRO said as she typed.

I continued with a brief description of Tilly's routine and what she liked to do in her spare time, as the review would expect to hear. I said, 'I know Tilly is worried about the court case in November.' But I didn't go into the details of the charges, as the IRO would have been given this information. 'Tilly thinks that talking to a counsellor might help her and she is on the CAMHS waiting list.'

'Any news on this?' the IRO asked Isa.

'Not yet, I'll chase it up,' she said, and made a note.

'Tilly is struggling with contact at present,' I said, choosing my words carefully. 'Isa is aware of this.' I then finished by saying that while Tilly hadn't wanted to attend any summer schemes, she would have the opportunity to try various sports activities while we were away. I gave the dates of our holiday, which the IRO noted.

She thanked me and asked Nancy to speak.

'My daughter has got herself in a right state because of all this,' she began, looking at the IRO. 'She's had to go back on antidepressants and couldn't face coming here today. It's dreadful. Tilly was supposed to be home by now, living with us. We got the room ready. You saw it,' she said to Isa. 'My cancer has gone and I'm recovering my strength from all the treatment. There is no reason why Tilly shouldn't be at home with us. We can't undo the past, but we can forgive. Goodness knows I've had to forgive Heather enough times. Tilly needs to do the same. We won't ever be able to move forward as a family unless Tilly forgives and starts to see her mother.'

It was heartfelt and I was deeply touched, but it was simplistic.

'What do you feel about seeing your mother?' the IRO gently asked Tilly.

'I can't face her right now,' Tilly said quietly. 'I need time to think and work things out.'

'You'll have plenty of time to think once you're home with us,' Nancy said. 'You've got a bedroom all to yourself.'

Tilly was looking uncomfortable and Nancy emotional, desperately wanting Tilly to make it up with her mother and go home.

'Would it help if you saw your mother and grandmother away from their home?' the IRO asked Tilly, something Isa had also previously suggested.

'Not really,' Tilly said.

The IRO made a note. I glanced at Nancy and felt so sorry for her.

'What about phone contact?' the IRO asked.

'There hasn't been any recently,' Isa said.

'Would you like to start phoning your gran and mother again?' she asked Tilly.

'OK,' Tilly agreed.

'That won't do any good,' Nancy put in. 'Tilly needs to make it up with her mother so we can move on.'

'I think Tilly is saying she doesn't feel up to doing that just yet,' the IRO said sensitively to Nancy.

'But Heather hasn't done anything wrong,' Nancy cried. 'She's not being prosecuted.' Her eyes glistened with tears and my heart went out to her.

'I'm sorry, Gran,' Tilly said, finally looking at her. 'I'll phone you. I promise.'

'And speak to your mother too?' Nancy said.

Tilly didn't reply.

Nancy took out a tissue and wiped her eyes. 'I thought that if I came here, I could make a difference,' she said. 'But I can see that isn't so. The longer all this goes on, the worse it will get. Unless you and your mother resolve your differences, we'll never be a family again.'

'You're trying to make me feel guilty,' Tilly said. 'But none of this is my fault.'

'No one is blaming you,' the IRO said. 'I appreciate it's difficult for everyone involved. Would you feel comfortable phoning your gran maybe once or twice a week?'

'Yes,' Tilly said.

'Is that all right?' she asked Nancy.

She shrugged. 'You know my feelings. She should be living with us, but I suppose it's better than nothing.'

The IRO typed and then asked Nancy if there was anything else she wanted to add, but there wasn't. She wiped her eyes again and I think we were all moved. What she wanted seemed so simple to her – for Tilly to forgive her mother, just as she'd had to forgive her in the past. But forgiving a child is part of being a parent and is often easier than a child forgiving a parent, who is adult and bears a responsibility to love, protect and nurture their child. I didn't think Nancy could see that.

The IRO moved the meeting on and asked Isa to give her report. She gave a brief résumé of what had happened since the last review and confirmed the care plan was for Tilly to stay in care with me for the foreseeable future. I glanced at Nancy, who looked close to tears again, although I felt sure Isa would have already explained this to her.

The atmosphere remained subdued as the IRO asked Miss Jenkins to give her report. She said what we already knew: that while Tilly had made some progress in her schoolwork, her predicted grades were disappointing, and she would have to make a big effort next term to catch up. She added that her subject teachers were on hand to help.

The IRO thanked her and then Joy Philips said she thought Tilly was doing very well at home and that she hoped the CAMHS appointment would come through before long. She finished by saying I was very professional in my fostering and Tilly was receiving a good standard of care, so she had no concerns. The IRO thanked her, set a date for the next review, which wasn't for six months, and then closed the meeting. Once a child is settled in care the reviews usually occur less frequently.

Miss Jenkins rushed off first. Then Nancy said, 'I need to call a cab.'

I'd given her a lift home before, but it wasn't really appropriate now.

'I'll phone for a cab for you,' Isa said, taking out her mobile.

Joy and I said goodbye, and then Tilly said, 'Bye, Gran.'

'Bye,' Nancy returned stiffly, without looking at her.

What a difference to their parting after the last review, I thought. Then, the warmth of their relationship had been palpable and they'd been looking forward to living together as a family.

It was nearly the end of school so I told Tilly I would wait in the car and give her a lift home. She returned to her class for the last twenty minutes of the lesson, and Joy and I left the building together, then went our separate ways. My phone had been on silent during the meeting and once in my car I checked it. My heart nearly stopped as I saw two missed calls from Lucy. I quickly played the voicemail messages. 'Mum, I've lost some blood. Can you take me to the hospital?' I could hear the anxiety in her voice.

The call had been made half an hour ago. I listened to the second voicemail message, left a few minutes after the first.

'Mum, I don't need a lift. Darren is leaving work now and is going to take me to the hospital.'

Angry with myself for not being available to help and worried about the blood loss, I called her mobile. It went through to voicemail so I left a message, 'It's Mum, love. Are you all right? Sorry, I've only just got your messages. I was in a meeting. I'll try Darren's mobile.'

I called his mobile but that too went through to voicemail. I left a similar message and asked him to phone me as soon as he had the chance. Should I drive to the hospital now? I could text Tilly and ask her to catch the bus. She'd understand it was an emergency. Or was I overreacting? Darren must be with Lucy now. Had she been alone I would have gone straight there. I didn't start the car but sent both Lucy and Darren a text message, asking one of them to call me as soon as they could.

A few seconds later Lucy phoned.

'Are you all right?' I asked worried.

'Yes. I'm at the hospital, waiting to see the doctor. But the nurse is almost certain it's "the show" and nothing to worry about.' I breathed a sigh of relief. 'The show', or 'bloody show' as it's also known, is when the mucus plug lodged in the cervix during pregnancy comes away. The blood is a result of small blood vessels in the cervix rupturing as it begins to dilate. This usually happens any time from a few days to two weeks before full labour starts and it is the body's way of getting ready.

'Is Darren looking after you?'

'Yes. I might have panicked a bit, but the nurse said I'd done right to come and get checked. Once I've seen the doctor, if everything is OK, I can go home.'

'Good. Text me, please, as soon as you know. I am so sorry I wasn't there for you. I was in Tilly's review.'

'It's fine, Mum, don't worry. Love you.'

'I love you too.'

But it's a parent's lot to worry and feel guilty. Sometimes I tortured myself for not being there for one of my children or saying or doing the wrong thing. I always apologized if I got it wrong and reminded them that parents also made mistakes. Thankfully my children were forgiving, and I hoped that in time Tilly would find it within herself to forgive her mother.

An hour later, after I'd arrived home with Tilly, Lucy telephoned. She was now in the car on her way home. The doctor had confirmed the bloody discharge was 'the show' and everything was fine with the baby.

'Fantastic. That is a relief,' I said.

'If all goes to plan my next trip to the hospital will be when I'm in labour,' she said.

'Yes.'

'I asked the nurse how I'd know for certain I was in labour, and she said when the contractions become too painful to talk through. I don't like the sound of that.'

'No,' I agreed. But it summed up the pain of labour perfectly!

CHAPTER TWENTY-SEVEN

EMMA

Tilly telephoned her grandmother on Sunday but didn't speak to her mother. She made the call from her bedroom using her mobile.

'Gran's OK,' was all she said when I asked her how it had gone.

'Good,' I said. I didn't push her for any more details, but I felt the phone call was a promising start to building bridges.

School broke up on Tuesday and Tilly was delighted, except for the homework some of her subject teachers had set for the holiday. 'I won't get a bloody holiday at this rate!' she groaned.

'Have a target of doing an hour a day,' I suggested. 'If you concentrate, it's surprising what you can achieve in an hour.' I'd studied for my degree in my spare time while my children had been little, so I knew something of this.

Tilly agreed that an hour was manageable but then subsequently fell into the routine of having a lie-in each morning and, once up, going out to see Abby.

'I'll start next week,' she promised me. 'We've only just broken up from school, so plenty of time.' But I knew from experience how the summer holiday could quickly disappear.

It seemed endless at the start and then suddenly it was all over and the new term was about to begin.

Paula was still sending off job applications for permanent work but hadn't been called for interview yet. However, she was given another two days' temping work, this time waitressing in an Italian restaurant where she had to wear a white top and black trousers or skirt. I continued to see Lucy most days, taking shopping when necessary. Sometimes I left Tilly in the house by herself. I wouldn't have done this with all the young people I'd looked after, but I trusted her, as she'd given me no reason to distrust her. Having been with us for seven months, she was one of the family now.

Lucy's due date came and went and the air of expectation in my house grew. Adrian, Paula and I regularly texted our WhatsApp group, asking Lucy how she was and if there was any news. Her replies were often grumbles about being the size of an elephant, house or whale, accompanied by emojis emphasizing her discomfort. There was no sign of the baby yet and she said the policy now was to let expectant mothers go a week overdue and then offer induction. More horrified emoji faces followed!

Then, on 2 August, as I was getting ready for bed that night, I received a text message from Darren saying they were at the hospital.

Is Lucy in labour? I texted back straight away, my heart missing a beat.

Yes. Happened quickly. Contractions every 15 mins then every 3 mins. Waters broke. Will let you know when there is any news.

Thanks. Love to you both. Good luck, I texted back.

I wondered if Adrian, Paula and Tilly were still awake so I could tell them. Before I could check, another message came through, this time from Lucy to our Glass WhatsApp group. *Hi guys. I'm in labour but can only message between contractions! F***ing painful.* 😖

I replied: *Thinking of you, Love Mum xx*

Adrian also replied: *Good luck, Lucy. Look forward to being an uncle. Is Darren with you?*

Yes. Too right he is! He's not getting out of this! 😃

There was nothing from Paula so I assumed she was asleep. I would tell her and Tilly in the morning. All of a dither, and with a mixture of concern and elation, I finished getting ready for bed. I was looking forward to the birth of my first grandchild, but poor Lucy was having to go through what would probably be the most physically painful experience of her life. I would have done anything to have taken that pain away from her. As it was, all I could do was hope for the best and wait for news.

I climbed into bed and then lay with my lamp on and my phone beside me, hoping, willing that everything would be all right. Most births do go to plan, but it's still a trauma for the mother (and baby). I wouldn't rest until I knew they were both safe and well.

It wasn't long before another message arrived, this time from Darren: *Midwife just examined Lucy. Baby's head engaged, but cervix not yet dilated to 3cm. Lucy on gas n air but in a lot of pain.*

Is she having the water birth? I texted back.

No. She's in too much pain. Might have an epidural later. Too soon yet.

Give her my love, I replied. And I worried some more.

Needless to say, I didn't sleep. Eventually I switched off the lamp and lay in the dark, thinking of Lucy and grabbing my phone every time it buzzed with an incoming message. Nothing more from Lucy, but plenty from Darren. I might not have been there, but it was as though I was feeling every contraction! I prayed it would be all right.

By 2 a.m. Lucy was 3cm dilated, so she was entering what's known as the 'active stage' of labour. Darren texted that her contractions were still coming every three minutes. I knew this stage could last hours, hence the term labour. It's not only painful, but also very hard work as the baby makes its journey down the birth canal.

I tried to close my eyes, but it was impossible to sleep.

Around four o'clock Darren texted: *Lucy is 5cm dilated.*

Has she had an epidural? I replied.

Yes. Just now.

Good. Give her my love. How are you?

OK.

Then it went quiet – no more messages – and my anxiety level soared. I switched on my bedside lamp and stared at my phone, willing it to buzz with good news. The sun rose. I could see the sky lighten through the gap in my bedroom curtains. At 5.30, desperate for news, I texted Darren: *Any news yet?*

There was no reply. I got dressed and, exhausted from lack of sleep, sat on the edge of my bed, my phone in my hand, wondering what to do for the best. Go to the hospital? Continue to wait for news? Phone Darren? I was about to text him again when a message came through from him.

She is here at last! Our darling daughter, Emma, born at 6.05, weighing 7lb 3oz. Mother and baby well. 😍

My eyes filled. I was so happy and relieved. I could barely see the keypad to text a reply. *Wonderful. Congratulations. I'm overjoyed. Don't forget to tell your parents*, I reminded him.

I have, came Darren's reply. *Been texting Mum all night too! Come to the hospital as soon as you can and meet Emma.*

I'm on my way! I replied.

Everyone else was still asleep so I quickly sent Adrian, Paula and Tilly the same text message, saying Lucy had had her baby, all was well and I was going to the hospital. I crept downstairs but before I left the house my phone buzzed again. Darren had sent a photograph, the first of baby Emma. Just born and with that slightly purple, scrunched-up look, but beautiful and perfect. I could see a likeness to both Lucy and Darren in her – or perhaps that was me being romantic. Another photo arrived as I got into the car. It must have been taken by the midwife as it was a group photo of Lucy and Darren, smiling proudly and cradling baby Emma between them. I wiped away another tear and started the car.

It was still very early, but as soon as my mother was up I'd telephone her and tell her the good news. She was now a great-grandmother. I could imagine her delight. But with this thought came a small stab of sadness that my dear father was no longer with us to share in our joy. He'd always been such a family man, doting on his children and grandchildren. He would have been overjoyed to be a great-grandpa and I could picture him with the baby. But as at other significant moments in my life since his passing, I still felt his presence close by, his warmth, kindness and protectiveness. I knew he was sending his blessing and watching over us now, just as he had in life.

I parked the car in the hospital car park and made my way to the maternity unit. The door was security-locked so I pressed the buzzer and waited. It was a few moments before a voice came through the intercom. I gave my name and proudly said that I'd come to see my granddaughter. The door opened and I followed the sign pointing to the rooms upstairs. A number of doors led off this main corridor and I wasn't sure which room they were in. I was about to phone Darren when the second door on my right suddenly opened and he appeared, grinning broadly. 'We're in here. The nurse said you'd arrived.'

'Congratulations, love,' I said, kissing his cheek. He was looking very pleased with himself. I followed him into the room.

Lucy, wearing a hospital gown, was on the bed, resting back on the pillows. She looked a bit dazed, but well, considering she'd been in labour all night and had just given birth. Baby Emma swaddled in white lay in her arms.

'Well done, love,' I said, giving her a hug. 'She's beautiful.' My eyes filled again.

'It was horrible, giving birth, Mum, and I've had to have stitches,' Lucy said, grimacing.

'But you didn't feel them?'

'No. I was still numb from the epidural.'

'It's all over now,' I said. I gave her another hug then gazed longingly at Emma.

'Would you like to hold her?' Darren asked, joining us.

'Yes, please.'

Lucy carefully placed little Emma, still asleep, into my arms and I moved to a chair and sat down. Darren took a photo of Emma and me and sent it to my phone. I continued to gaze quietly at Emma, completely mesmerized and besotted, as nurses came and went. They were clearing up the room after the birth and also checked Lucy's blood pressure as it was a bit low, which apparently can happen after an epidural. They also brought her toast and tea, as she hadn't eaten since yesterday lunchtime. Then the last of the numbing effect of the epidural began to wear off and Lucy asked a nurse for pain relief. Darren, clearly still shell-shocked from the whole experience, told me step by step what had happened since yesterday afternoon – when Lucy had telephoned him at work, panic-stricken, and shouted that he had to come home as she was experiencing regular painful contractions – right through to Emma's birth.

After a while I laid Emma in her crib. As I did, Lucy asked Darren to open her zip bag and take out Mr Bunny.

'So he is here,' I said. 'I've haven't seen him in a long time.'

Lucy smiled, and it was obvious that Darren knew the significance of Mr Bunny. Taking him carefully from Lucy's bag, he placed the much-loved soft toy beside his sleeping daughter.

'You'll be safe now,' Lucy told her. My heart clenched. For many years before Lucy had come to live with me, Mr Bunny had been her one true companion and protector.

I waited until eight o'clock before telephoning my mother and told her the good news. She, of course, was elated and spoke to Lucy and Darren, congratulating them. The midwife returned and spent some time showing Lucy how to breast-feed, which, although natural, isn't always easy to establish. Then shortly before nine o'clock Darren's parents, Tod and Tina, arrived, very excited but looking as though they hadn't had much sleep either. We greeted each other warmly with a hug and kiss.

'I understand you had an all-night running commentary too,' Tod joked to me.

'Yes, and I wouldn't have missed it for the world,' I smiled.

'Me neither,' Tina replied.

We chatted for a while as they admired Emma and then I felt they would probably like to spend time alone with their new granddaughter. I said goodbye and told Lucy I'd come back later and to let me know if there was anything they needed.

Once home, I made myself a coffee and some breakfast. Adrian had left for work. Tilly was still in bed. Paula was up and dressed. She didn't have any work that day so she said she'd come with me later when I returned to the hospital, and that Adrian and Kirsty were planning on visiting Lucy straight after work. When Tilly got up around mid-morning I told her and she was pleased for Lucy and said she'd celebrate by doing an hour's homework.

'Joker,' I said. 'You need to do more than an hour to catch up.' But I felt I'd said as much as I could about the importance of doing well at school, so it was up to Tilly now.

'OK, I'll do two hours as I'm not seeing Abby until later today,' she offered.

'Excellent,' I said.

That afternoon, on our way to the hospital, Paula and I stopped off in the high street and bought two helium-filled balloons to go with the presents and cards we'd already bought. One announced 'Baby Girl' in sparkling letters and the other 'Congratulations'. When we arrived at the hospital, just Lucy, Darren and baby Emma were in the room and Lucy was dressed. She looked a bit fresher now. She and Darren loved the balloons, and Paula was instantly besotted with Emma. She sat in a chair, cradling Emma in her arms as I had done while we took photographs. Lucy said that there was a good chance they would be able to go home later, once the doctor had done her rounds and was satisfied she and Emma were well enough. Lucy unwrapped our cards and gifts as Darren watched. My main gifts had been a pram and cot, but the one I'd gift-wrapped and brought with me now was for Emma – a soft toy identical to Mr Bunny, only smaller.

'Where on earth did you get that?' Lucy exclaimed, delighted.

'I ordered it online from a store in America,' I said. I then explained how I'd hunted around to try to find an exact replica of Mr Bunny, and this was the closest.

'His younger brother,' Darren said with a smile. 'He is cute.' He sat him at the end of the cot next to Mr Bunny senior.

'That was very thoughtful of you, Mum,' Lucy said. 'Thank you.' I was glad she liked it.

Paula had given them baby clothes as a gift, as Lucy had asked, and she thanked her. When Emma woke, Lucy dressed her in one of the outfits – a lemon-coloured romper suit – and we took more photos. I could tell Paula was pleased.

A couple of hours passed, Lucy fed Emma, but there was no sign of the doctor who needed to discharge them. Then, at five o'clock, a nurse came in and said there'd been a medical emergency and the doctor who needed to discharge Lucy and Emma was in the operating theatre, so it was likely to be a few more hours yet. Lucy said she was tired and would try to get some sleep, so Paula and I said goodbye and left.

As I drove home Paula texted Adrian, telling him that Lucy was still in hospital waiting to be discharged. He texted back that he was planning on arriving around six but would phone her first to make sure it was OK and she was still there.

Tilly arrived home from seeing Abby shortly after us and she and Paula made dinner while I sat on the sofa and closed my eyes. Having been awake and on tenterhooks all night, I was now exhausted. Adrian texted at 6.30 to say he and Kirsty were at the hospital as Lucy hadn't been discharged yet, and not to save him any dinner as they would get something after they'd left the hospital. Lucy then texted to say the nurse had said that if it got too late, they wouldn't be discharged until the following morning so would spend the night there. I replied asking her if she had everything she needed, and she said she did. Paula, Tilly and I had dinner together and Adrian arrived home around eight-thirty, clearly besotted with his little niece. Shortly before nine o'clock, as I was getting ready for an early night, Lucy telephoned.

'We've finally been discharged,' she said. 'The doctor has checked Emma and me and we can go home.'

'Great.'

'Darren has just gone to bring the car from the car park to the maternity entrance, so it's not far to walk.'

'All right, love. How are you?'

'Not too bad. They've given me some painkillers to take home.' Then she answered a question that I had wondered about since the birth of Emma. 'Mum, I texted Bonnie and told her. She wants to see Emma.'

'That's OK, isn't it?'

'Yes, but will you come too? Otherwise it will be awkward with just Darren and me. You know how Bonnie can be sometimes.'

'Yes. I can. When is she coming?'

'Tomorrow. She wants to see Emma while she's tiny.'

'What time?'

'She thinks around four o'clock but is going to text.'

'Don't worry. I'll be there.'

CHAPTER TWENTY-EIGHT

BONNIE

Lucy usually met Bonnie, her birth mother, by herself, but I could understand why she now wanted me present. She'd be feeling fragile and emotional after the birth and very protective of her daughter. Bonnie could be highly excitable, erratic and volatile at times. She'd had substance misuse problems in the past, and it was impossible to know for certain if she was still using or what sort of mood she'd be in. If she arrived under the influence, I was more experienced and in a better position to gently but firmly deal with her than Lucy or Darren. Also, she would be meeting Darren for the first time and, as far as I knew, he would be the first of any of Lucy's friends or boyfriends that she had ever met. Lucy kept that part of her life separate and usually met Bonnie in a coffee shop or snack bar away from town, settling the bill herself, as Bonnie never had any money.

As I lay in bed thinking about all of this, it occurred to me it would probably be better if Lucy met Bonnie as she had been doing, in a public place on neutral territory, once she felt up to it. It wasn't too late, so I texted her: *Have you given Bonnie your address yet?*

Yes. Why? I wondered after if I shouldn't have done.

No worries. I am sure it will be fine. I'll be there. See you tomorrow. Love Mum.

I thought about it some more and then finally dropped off to sleep.

But in typical Bonnie style, she cancelled. When I switched on my phone the following morning I found a text message from Lucy sent late the night before after I'd fallen asleep. *Bonnie messaged. She can't make today. She said she'll be in touch next week.*

I texted back: *OK. Let me know when and I'll be there if you still want me to, but remember we're on holiday 12–16 August. How was your night?*

Up every hour feeding and changing. 😖

Will I still see you later?

Yes, if that's all right with both of you, I replied as I didn't want to intrude.

Of course! Lucy texted back. *But not too early. We're going back to bed.* 😴

I went to see Lucy, Darren and Emma in the afternoon and every afternoon of that week. Tilly came with me one afternoon and Paula another, and then she was offered some more temporary work, so she went in the evening instead. As well as gazing adoringly at my grandchild, I did what I could to help. As any new parent knows, when you return home with your bundle of joy chaos reigns, for the first few weeks at least. Your previous calm and well-ordered routine is smashed to pieces as you try to establish a new routine centring around the demands of the baby, who sometimes isn't sure what they want.

Darren's parents went most evenings after work and Adrian and Kirsty visited the following weekend. I was concerned that Darren's paternity leave would be coming to an end at the same time I was going away on holiday, so Lucy would be by herself all day during the week. Darren reassured me he would be in regular contact with her during the day, and also that his parents would look in most evenings as they had been doing. I didn't doubt that Lucy was a capable mother – Emma was thriving – but Lucy (and Darren) were exhausted from all the sleepless nights and I knew they appreciated help. Lucy was persisting with breastfeeding but also giving Emma some 'top-up' bottles of formula in the evening when she was refusing to settle. Lucy commented she felt a failure for having to do this. I quickly reassured her she certainly wasn't a failure and lots of mothers bottle-fed their babies and she shouldn't stress about it.

Bonnie hadn't been in touch again and Lucy thought, as I did, that her moment of wanting to see a tiny newborn baby had passed and she probably wouldn't be in touch again for many months. Paula, Tilly and I packed for our holiday and left early on 12 August, arriving at the holiday lodge at 11 a.m. It was only when I'd parked the car that I checked my phone and saw two missed calls from Lucy, five and ten minutes before, but no voicemail message. Concerned, I quickly got out of the car and pressed her number. She answered straight away, upset and angry. I could hear Emma crying in the background. 'Oh Mum, you won't believe what's happened!'

'What?' I asked, my heart pounding with fear. I thought something was wrong with Emma.

'Bonnie has been here. She's just left.'

'She came to see you today?'

'Yes, she turned up half an hour ago. No text or phone call. I was still in my pyjamas. I'd only just got Emma off to sleep in her crib. Bonnie wanted to pick her up, but I told her not to. She began criticizing me, saying the flat looked a mess. I lost my temper and shouted at her. I know I shouldn't have, but I told her she was a waste of space and never to come near me or Emma again.' Her voice broke. This was what I'd feared might happen, and of course I wasn't there to comfort Lucy.

'Calm down, love,' I said. 'Bonnie had no right to just turn up and then criticize you, but she'll get over it.'

'She said some horrible things, like I was going to struggle being a mother just like she did.'

I could see why Lucy was so upset. This was her Achilles heel, her vulnerable spot: that she might take after her birth mother and not be able to look after Emma. We'd already spent some time talking about this.

'That's utter rubbish!' I said forcefully. 'Bonnie knows nothing about you or your skills.' I moved slightly away from the car as Paula and Tilly got out. I could still hear Emma crying in the background. 'See to Emma first and then we can talk,' I told Lucy.

'I've fed and changed her. I don't know what else to do. Perhaps the shouting has upset her.'

'Yes, it would have done. Pick her up and give her a cuddle. I'll wait on the phone.'

'What's the matter?' Paula asked me, realizing something was wrong.

'Lucy is a bit upset,' I said. 'Can you and Tilly unload the car?' I threw her the key to the lodge. 'I'll be with you when I've finished.'

Emma stopped crying and Lucy came back on the phone. 'I've got her on my lap now. She's OK.'

'Good. She probably just wanted to be held.'

'What am I going to do about Bonnie?' Lucy asked. 'I feel bad now, but she really wound me up. She's got no right coming into my home and slagging me off.'

'I know. She speaks before she thinks. You know that. What else did she say?' I glanced at Paula and Tilly, who were carrying our bags from the car into the lodge, and mouthed 'thank you'.

'Lots of stuff,' Lucy said. 'Some of it I could ignore, but her comments about me being a shit mother really hurt.'

'I know and it's so untrue. You are your own person. Trust me, you're doing a fantastic job looking after Emma. I know a good mother when I see one, and it's you.'

'Thank you. I needed to hear that. I feel bad I shouted at her.' As she always did after she'd argued with Bonnie.

'If you still want her to see Emma, I suggest you do it one weekend when Darren can be with you, and meet in a coffee shop or café as you have been doing.'

'Yes, I regret giving her my address. I don't want her coming here again and upsetting me and Emma.'

'Would you like me to speak to her?' I offered.

'Please. I can't take a lot of stress at the moment. Tell her she can see Emma in a few weeks when I'm feeling up to it.'

'All right. Have you told Darren what's happened?'

'I texted him but he's working. He said he'd phone at lunchtime.'

'Don't worry him. I'll call you when I've spoken to Bonnie.'

Tilly and Paula had just finished unloading the car and were on their way into the lodge. 'I'll join you in a minute,' I called after them. 'I've got to make another call.'

I moved to under a canopy of oak trees. The lodge, like the others here, was detached and set in beautiful parkland with an abundance of flowers and local wildlife. There were activity centres for guests offering a wide range of sports, including swimming, horse riding, canoeing, abseiling and many others. It promised to be a good holiday, but for now I found Bonnie's mobile number in my contact list and pressed it. I hadn't used her phone number for many years, so I hoped it was still current.

It was. She answered straight away with a curt, 'Hello.'

'It's Cathy.'

'Yes, your number came up,' she said with an edge to her voice.

'Congratulations on the birth of our grandchild,' I said, hoping this would defuse the situation.

She seemed taken aback. There was a short silence, then she said more easily, 'Thanks. I guess Lucy phoned you?'

'She did and she's upset your visit didn't go as planned. She asked me to call you. She'd like you to see Emma properly, but in a few weeks, when she is more on top of things. You could meet up for a coffee or lunch as you usually do.'

'Suits me,' she said.

'Good. I'll let her know. And probably best not to just turn up at their flat without phoning or texting first.'

'Why?'

'Lucy wanted to create a good impression and was disappointed when you caught her off-guard. I always phone or text first.'

'I was in the area and thought I'd pop in, but I won't again.'

'Thank you. And you're keeping well?'

'Not so bad.'

'Good, well, take care,' I said, and was about to end the call.

'Cathy,' she said, 'does Emma look like me?' There was a vulnerable, childlike edge to her voice that touched me.

'I am sure she does, although I can see a lot of Lucy and Darren in her,' I said diplomatically.

'I think she does. I only saw her for a moment, and she was asleep, but I think she's got my eyes.'

It was highly unlikely she could have seen this given Emma was asleep, but Bonnie wanted to believe there was a likeness, as it meant something to her.

'Yes, she's a lovely-looking baby,' I said. 'I'll let Lucy know we've spoken and everything between you is OK.'

'Can you ask her to send a photo of Emma to my phone? I didn't have a chance to take one.'

'Yes, I will.' We said goodbye. Despite the fact that she'd upset Lucy, I couldn't help but feel sorry for her.

I stayed outside the lodge to phone Lucy. I told her of my conversation with Bonnie and her request for a photograph. She was relieved I'd smoothed things over and said she'd send her a photo. Although Bonnie played virtually no part in her life, Lucy didn't like being on bad terms with her.

I told Lucy I'd phone her again later and went into the lodge, where a chilled drink was waiting for me. The three of us then sat outside and planned the rest of our day, taking in a couple of activities and a country walk. That afternoon, as we were having a late lunch at one of the restaurants in the village, Paula received an email on her phone inviting her to attend an interview the following Thursday. It was for a permanent position with a company a short bus ride away from our house. She was delighted and replied immediately, confirming she would attend. Tilly and I congratulated her.

Our days were filled and between activities we relaxed outside the lodge or by the lake on sun loungers provided by the centre. Tilly telephoned her gran at least twice to my knowledge but didn't speak to her mother. She still didn't want to visit her gran because her mother would be there and she remained very angry with her. However, I felt the now-regular phone calls were a good sign. Tilly mentioned a few times during our holiday that she was worried about the court case looming in November because she would be cross-examined by her stepfather's barrister. I reassured her as best I could, but I appreciated how daunting it must be for her.

I phoned or texted Lucy each day. She sounded fine and was over her upset with Bonnie. Our five-day break flew by and, once home, Tilly found a letter from CAMHS waiting for her. She could start therapy the following Wednesday. I was pleased and hoped it would help her come to terms with what had happened.

'I've still got to go to court and face that barrister,' she said.

'I know, love. Try not to worry.'

However, two days later a police officer telephoned Tilly's mobile while she was out with Abby. Tilly phoned me straight away with the good news. She wouldn't have to go to court as Dave had changed his plea to guilty. Not from any sense of altruism, regret or contrition, but to reduce his sentence. His barrister had advised him that there was so much video evidence against him he was certain to be convicted, so it made sense to plead guilty and receive a reduced sentence. Tilly wasn't pleased about that, but she was relieved she wouldn't have to go to court and be cross-examined by his barrister.

She attended her first therapy session on Wednesday, going by bus to the hospital. I offered to take her in the car and wait but she said she'd be fine, which I accepted. When she returned I asked her how it had gone.

'Yes, OK,' she said. 'We talked about a lot of things.'

'Good.'

That was all she said and I didn't press her for more. She would share what she wanted to, if anything, and was happy to keep going once a week.

Paula attended her interview on Thursday but unfortunately wasn't offered the position. One of the interviewers called to tell her the outcome and of course she was disappointed. It helped a little that he'd said the competition had been fierce and she'd come a close second. Putting aside her disappointment, she set about sending off more applications and was also offered some more temping work.

The last week of the school holiday disappeared, as I knew it would. Tilly spent many hours in her bedroom completing her homework. Abby had some to finish too, and they texted constantly. Isa came to see us for one of her routine visits, as did Joy Philips. However, as it turned out, Joy's visit wasn't just routine. It was about to change the course of my life.

She saw Tilly and then went through her usual business, ending by checking my log notes and taking a look around the house. We returned to the living room, where I was expecting Joy to take out her diary to arrange her next visit, which would be in about a month's time. But she sat upright in her chair, hands in her lap, and looked at me in earnest.

'You've done a good job with Tilly,' she said.

'Thank you.' It was always nice to hear.

'She's obviously very settled with you and is likely to remain here for some time.'

'Yes. I'd just like to get her talking to her mother again,' I replied.

Joy nodded. 'But Tilly isn't causing you any problems with her behaviour.'

'No. She's coping very well.'

'That's down to you being a highly experienced carer.'

'I suppose so,' I said, thinking I'd never had so many compliments all in one go.

'You're used to managing challenging behaviour, aren't you?'

'Yes, I've had to in the past.'

'Good. Because we've got a ten-year-old boy coming into care shortly who is exhibiting very challenging behaviour. His mother is so desperate she's putting him into care voluntarily. We think you would be ideal for him.'

'I'm sorry,' I said, puzzled. 'But I can't take him while Tilly is here.'

Joy paused. 'I think you can. You have a spare room now, don't you?'

I frowned questioningly.

'Your daughter Lucy has moved out and is now living with her partner. They have a baby. You told me yourself.'

I met her gaze. 'You mean, I would use Lucy's room?' I said, the penny finally dropping. 'You want me to clear out the rest of Lucy's belongings so I can foster this boy?'

'That's what I'm hoping for, yes.'

'Oh,' I said. 'I'm not sure. I hadn't really thought about that. It's Lucy's room. I'll need to talk to her first.'

'Yes, of course, and Adrian, Tilly and Paula. Have a chat with your family and I'll phone you tomorrow for your decision. I'm afraid I can't give you any longer as we need to move him quickly.'

I nodded dumbly as Joy took out her diary and arranged her next visit, then I saw her out.

CHAPTER TWENTY-NINE

A DIFFICULT DECISION

I closed the front door and stood in the hall, deep in thought. Clear out Lucy's room? The words were ringing in my head. It had always been Lucy's room. It still was, although I realized she wasn't living with us any more. But supposing she wanted or needed to use her room again, even for a few nights? How would she feel if it was no longer hers? Hurt? Rejected? Shut out?

I turned from the front door and went slowly upstairs, where I opened the door to Lucy's bedroom. It was as she'd left it. Her duvet and matching pillowcase still on her bed. The shelves, drawers and wardrobe containing those items she didn't need at present. Lucy had said a few times she'd come over and sort out her room, but I'd told her there was no rush. And there hadn't been before. Now I was being asked to foster another child whose family would be in crisis. The social services needed to move him quickly, but there was always a shortage of foster carers. Joy was phoning me tomorrow for our decision.

With a final glance around the room and the decision unmade, I came out, closed Lucy's bedroom door and then went to my bedroom. Tilly was downstairs, and I needed to have this conversation with Lucy first in private. I sat on the edge of the bed and picked up the phone. It was the middle of the afternoon so Darren would be at work. If Lucy was busy with Emma, I'd call her back. She answered straight away but in a whisper. 'Mum, I'm going into the kitchen to talk. Emma is asleep in her crib.'

'OK, love.'

I waited as she moved silently out of hearing range of Emma and then came back on the phone, now speaking in a normal tone. 'We can talk now without disturbing Emma. How are you? Is everything OK?' she asked.

'Yes, and no,' I said. 'There's something I need to discuss with you that has taken me by surprise.'

'What? Surely not someone else in my family is pregnant?' she joked.

I smiled weakly. 'No, not as far as I know.' I paused and chose my words very carefully. 'Joy Philips, my new supervising social worker, was here this afternoon and she's asked me to foster a ten-year-old boy, but Tilly will also be staying for the time being. Joy asked if I can use your bedroom for him. My first reaction was to say no, it's yours, but I wanted to know what you think. Tell me, please, honestly. I don't know what to do for the best. They're obviously desperate to place him, but it is your room.'

Lucy gave a small, affectionate laugh. 'Mum, if you need the room, use it. I'm living with Darren now. I'm not about to leave him and come back to live with you, even if we argue, which we do sometimes.'

'But I was going to keep it as it is. It's still your room.'

'The ten-year-old needs a home. I'm fine with him having it. Honestly.'

'Are you sure? What about if the three of you want to stay the night – for example, at Christmas?' I asked. Then I answered my own question. 'I suppose you'd use my room or the sofa bed downstairs in the front room.'

'Yes, of course. Mum, it's got to be your decision, but I'm fine with him having my room.'

'Thank you, love. I'll need to discuss it with Adrian, Paula and Tilly. But if they agree, you think I should go ahead?'

'Yes. I'd offer to clear out my belongings, but I have my hands full at present, so bag up the rest of my stuff and I'll sort it out when I have more time.'

'OK, love. Thank you.'

We talked for a while longer, mainly about Emma, and then said goodbye.

I still wasn't wholly convinced. All it needed was for Adrian, Paula or Tilly to object and I'd phone Joy and tell her no.

I waited until we were all seated at dinner before I broached the subject, although my appetite had largely gone.

'There is something important I need to ask you all and I want honest opinions, please,' I began. They looked up from eating, intrigued. 'Joy, my supervising social worker, was here today and she has asked if we can foster a ten-year-old boy who has behavioural issues. He'll have Lucy's room. I've spoken to Lucy and she is all right with it, but I want to hear what you all think about him living with us. Honestly.'

'Behavioural issues – deep joy,' Paula sighed, having experienced similar before with children we'd fostered. 'Why is he playing up?'

'I don't know. I haven't been given any more details yet. I'll be told if we decide to go ahead.'

'Are you sure you're not taking on too much?' Adrian asked, concerned.

'Probably, and it will affect us all, as you know.'

'I can help you with him,' Tilly offered kindly. Although I wasn't sure she fully appreciated what living in a house with a child who was constantly challenging you and kicking off really meant.

'We'll all help as much as we can,' Adrian said. 'But the burden will fall on Mum.'

'What about Lucy's belongings?' Paula asked. 'There's still a lot of her things in her room.'

'Yes. She's asked me to bag them up and then she'll sort them out when she has time. That's not a problem.' I looked at them, waiting for firm replies. I wasn't making this decision without them. 'Well, what do you think? I would like yes or no answers, please. I have to tell Joy our decision tomorrow.'

'Yes, I'm happy to have him,' Tilly said.

'If Lucy is OK with it then that's fine with me,' Paula agreed.

I looked at Adrian. 'Well? Yes or no?'

'The kid needs a home and Lucy's room is free, so yes, if you're sure.'

'I am now. Thank you.'

So that was how Jackson arrived and Tilly stayed. I continue their stories in my next book, where I hope you will join me again. Thank you.

For an update on Tilly and the other children in my fostering memoirs, please visit www.cathyglass.co.uk

SUGGESTED TOPICS FOR
READING-GROUP DISCUSSION

————————

Is Tilly right to be so angry with her mother?

Heather is unable to protect her daughter because she is a victim. Discuss.

How does Dave control Heather?

What is the catalyst for Heather finally being able to leave Dave? Why does she continue to live in fear of him?

To what extent might a student's homelife impact on their ability to concentrate and study? How can schools better support these children?

Abby is a good friend of Tilly's, so why does Cathy warn her not to accept all her advice?

Discuss the role of the review for looked-after children. Is it necessary? How effective is it? How might it be improved?

Describe Nancy's relationship with Heather and Tilly.

Modern technology allows us to track/spy on our children and loved ones. In what circumstances, if any, can this be justified?

Discuss Cathy's love for her daughter, Lucy. How does she support her?

Cathy raises the question of whether it is possible to live with someone who has been secretly filming your child and not know. What do you think and why?

At the end of the book Tilly is staying with Cathy. How do you see her story developing?

Cathy is hoping that eventually Tilly will forgive her mother. Why do you think that is important and how do you see it happening, if it does?

Cathy Glass

————

One remarkable woman, more than **150** foster children cared for.

Cathy Glass has been a foster carer for twenty-five years, during which time she has looked after more than 150 children, as well as raising three children of her own. She was awarded a degree in education and psychology as a mature student, and writes under a pseudonym. To find out more about Cathy and her story visit **www.cathyglass.co.uk**.

Too Scared to Tell

Oskar has been arriving at school hungry, unkempt and bruised. His mother has gone abroad and left him in the care of 'friends'

Cathy is asked to look after him, but as the weeks pass her concerns deepen. Oskar is clearly frightened of someone – but who? And why?

Innocent

Siblings Molly and Kit arrive at Cathy's frightened, injured and ill

The parents say they are not to blame. Could the social services have got it wrong?

Finding Stevie

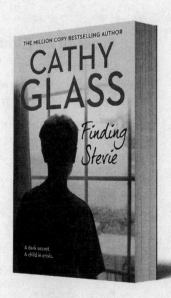

Fourteen-year-old Stevie is exploring his gender identity

Like many young people, he spends time online, but Cathy is shocked when she learns his terrible secret.

Where Has Mummy Gone?

When Melody is taken into care, she fears her mother won't cope alone

It is only when Melody's mother vanishes that what has really been going on at home comes to light.

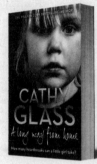

A Long Way from Home

Abandoned in an orphanage, Anna's future looks bleak until she is adopted

Anna's new parents love her, so why does she end up in foster care?

Cruel to be Kind

Max is shockingly overweight and struggles to make friends

Cathy faces a challenge to help this unhappy boy.

Nobody's Son

Born in prison and brought up in care, Alex has only ever known rejection

He is longing for a family of his own, but again the system fails him.

Can I Let You Go?

Faye is 24, pregnant and has learning difficulties as a result of her mother's alcoholism

Can Cathy help Faye learn enough to parent her child?

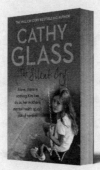

The Silent Cry

A mother battling depression. A family in denial

Cathy is desperate to help before something terrible happens.

Girl Alone

An angry, traumatized young girl on a path to self-destruction

Can Cathy discover the truth behind Joss's dangerous behaviour before it's too late?

Saving Danny

Danny's parents can no longer cope with his challenging behaviour

Calling on all her expertise, Cathy discovers a frightened little boy who just wants to be loved.

The Child Bride

A girl blamed and abused for dishonouring her community

Cathy discovers the devastating truth.

Daddy's Little Princess

A sweet-natured girl with a complicated past

Cathy picks up the pieces after events take a dramatic turn.

Will You Love Me?

A broken child desperate for a loving home

The true story of Cathy's adopted daughter Lucy.

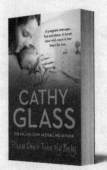

Please Don't Take My Baby

Seventeen-year-old Jade is pregnant, homeless and alone

Cathy has room in her heart for two.

Another Forgotten Child

Eight-year-old Aimee was on the child-protection register at birth

Cathy is determined to give her the happy home she deserves.

A Baby's Cry

A newborn, only hours old, taken into care

Cathy protects tiny Harrison from the potentially fatal secrets that surround his existence.

The Night the Angels Came

A little boy on the brink of bereavement

Cathy and her family make sure Michael is never alone.

Mummy Told Me Not to Tell

A troubled boy sworn to secrecy

After his dark past has been revealed, Cathy helps Reece to rebuild his life.

I Miss Mummy

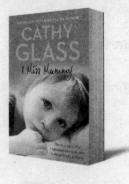

Four-year-old Alice doesn't understand why she's in care

Cathy fights for her to have the happy home she deserves.

The Saddest Girl in the World

A haunted child who refuses to speak

Do Donna's scars run too deep for Cathy to help?

Cut

Dawn is desperate to be loved

Abused and abandoned, this vulnerable child pushes Cathy and her family to their limits.

Hidden

The boy with no past

Can Cathy help Tayo to feel like he belongs again?

Damaged

A forgotten child

Cathy is Jodie's last hope. For the first time, this abused young girl has found someone she can trust.

Run, Mummy, Run

The gripping story of a woman caught in a horrific cycle of abuse, and the desperate measures she must take to escape.

My Dad's a Policeman

The dramatic short story about a young boy's desperate bid to keep his family together.

The Girl in the Mirror

Trying to piece together her past, Mandy uncovers a dreadful family secret that has been blanked from her memory for years.

About Writing
and How to Publish

A clear, concise practical
guide on writing and the best
ways to get published.

Happy Mealtimes
for Kids

A guide to healthy eating
with simple recipes that
children love.

Happy Adults

A practical guide to achieving lasting
happiness, contentment and success.
The essential manual for getting
the best out of life.

Happy Kids

A clear and concise guide to
raising confident, well-behaved
and happy children.

CATHY GLASS WRITING AS

LISA STONE

www.lisastonebooks.co.uk

The new crime thrillers that will chill you to the bone ...

THE DOCTOR

How much do you know about
the couple next door?

STALKER

Security cameras are there to
keep us safe. Aren't they?

THE DARKNESS
WITHIN

You know your son better than
anyone. Don't you?

Be amazed
Be moved
Be inspired

Follow Cathy:

 /cathy.glass.180

 @CathyGlassUK

www.cathyglass.co.uk

Cathy loves to hear from readers and reads
and replies to posts, but she asks that no plot
spoilers are posted, please. We're sure
you appreciate why.